The Psychology Major's Companion

Everything You Need to Know to Get You Where You Want to Go

SECOND EDITION

Dana S. Dunn
Moravian College

Jane S. Halonen
University of West Florida

worth publishers
Macmillan Learning
New York

Senior Vice President, Content Strategy: Charles Linsmeier
Program Director: Shani Fisher
Executive Program Manager: Christine Cardone
Assistant Editor: Dorothy Tomasini
Associate Media Editor: Stephanie Matamoros
Marketing Manager: Katherine Nurre
Director, Content Management Enhancement: Tracey Kuehn
Senior Managing Editor: Lisa Kinne
Senior Workflow Project Manager: Susan Wein
Senior Project Manager: Aravinda Doss, Lumina Datamatics, Inc.
Production Supervisor: Lawrence Guerra
Director of Design, Content Management: Diana Blume
Design Services Manager: Natasha Wolfe
Cover Designer: John Callahan
Art Manager: Matthew McAdams
Photo Editor: Sheena Goldstein
Permissions Editor: Michael McCarty
Composition: Lumina Datamatics, Inc.
Printing and Binding: LSC Communications
Cover Image: Peter Cade/The Image Bank/Getty Images

Library of Congress Control Number: 2019936420

ISBN-13: 978-1-319-19147-4
ISBN-10: 1-319-19147-9

Printed in the United States of America

Worth Publishers
One New York Plaza
Suite 4600
New York, NY 10004-1562
www.macmillanlearning.com

IN MEMORY OF

J. William Hepler and Margaret A. Emelson

Dana S. Dunn is Professor of Psychology and Director of Academic Assessment at Moravian College in Bethlehem, PA. He earned his PhD in experimental social psychology from the University of Virginia and his BA in psychology from Carnegie Mellon University. A fellow of the American Psychological Association (APA Divisions 1, 2, 8, and 22) and the Association for Psychological Science, Dunn is active in the Society for the Teaching of Psychology (STP–APA Division 2) where he served as president in 2010. In 2013, Dunn received the Charles L. Brewer Distinguished Teaching of Psychology Award from the American Psychological Foundation and in 2015 he was the APA's Harry Kirke Wolfe lecturer. He is a member of the editorial boards of several journals and is a frequent speaker at national and regional psychology conferences. Dunn is past president of the Eastern Psychological Association (EPA) and president-elect of APA Division 22 (Rehabilitation Psychology). He is the author or editor of 30 books and writes a blog on the teaching of psychology called "Head of the Class" for *Psychology Today*. He is currently editor-in-chief of the *Oxford Bibliographies in Psychology*.

Jane S. Halonen has been a professor of psychology at the University of West Florida for more than 15 years. She has been fortunate also to have great professional families at James Madison University and Alverno College. Jane's most recent research has focused on strategies for turning good psychology departments into great ones as well as on ways to help legislators understand the true nature of psychology in tough economic times. Jane has been involved over the course of her career with helping the American Psychological Association develop standards of academic performance from high school through graduate levels of education. In 2000, the American Psychological Foundation honored her with the Distinguished Teaching Award and the American Psychological Association named her an Eminent Woman in Psychology in 2003. In 2019 she was named Distinguished Psi Chi member. She served as the Chief Reader for the Psychology Advanced Placement Reading from 2004 to 2009. A self-identified teaching conference junkie, Jane has been a member of the National Institute on the Teaching of Psychology board and has presented at nearly every regional teaching conference in psychology. With Peter Seldin, she also codirected the International Conference on Improving University Teaching from 2001 to 2008.

BRIEF CONTENTS

CONTENTS

One of our favorite childhood books is *Oh, the Places You'll Go!* by Dr. Seuss. We have always been impressed by the open-ended prospects that the phrase invokes; we always smile when we hear it. We both experience that same sense of optimism when we hear students identify psychology as their chosen major.

Selecting a major is one of the most significant decisions one can make in young adulthood. Selecting the wrong major is an expensive and inefficient means of getting through the undergraduate years. In contrast, selecting the right major can make those years rich in present experiences and prepare you for your future.

Although psychology is a popular major, it is also hugely misunderstood. That misunderstanding is held not just by loved ones who worry about career opportunities but also by some who major in psychology. With good advising, hard work, and focused energy, a degree in psychology can open a wide range of amazing possibilities for any student. However, poor advising and lackluster performance in psychology can reinforce some people's perceptions that it is a weak major. Therefore, the objective of this book is to help students to declare the psychology major if it is in their best interest to do so, to successfully leverage what they learn in the major, and to prepare for a psychology-related future.

Note to Students

We wrote this book for you, whether you are a traditional-aged college student or a more seasoned adult learner interested in exploring the options associated with being a psychology major. You might be a college-bound student fresh out of high school who is curious about psychology. Or perhaps you are already enrolled in college and about to decide on an academic major area of study and you want to know if majoring in psychology is right for you. Some readers may have already taken the plunge and want some guidance about what careers are available to psychology majors or advice on how to pursue graduate study in psychology.

Whatever your background, *The Psychology Major's Companion: Everything You Need to Know to Get You Where You Want to Go* is designed to satisfy your needs. We address a variety of key questions, including:

- What do psychologists do? Where do they work?
- Is majoring in psychology the right choice for you?
- What skills and benefits does an undergraduate degree in psychology provide?
- How can I get the most out of my psychology major while becoming a focused, high-performing student?

- ■ How can I leverage my major by pursuing the right organizational memberships, summer jobs, and internships?
- ■ What can I do with a major in psychology after graduation?
- ■ What jobs are available to bachelor's–level psychology majors who decide not to pursue a master's or a doctoral degree?
- ■ How do I begin a job search right out of college?
- ■ If I decide to go to graduate school in psychology, what's involved in the application process?
- ■ What area of psychology should I pursue after college?
- ■ How can I make my application a compelling one?
- ■ Of what benefit will psychology be to my life beyond my education and my career?

We strongly believe that both prospective and current psychology majors should know what to expect from the undergraduate major, the larger discipline, and the marketplace beyond campus. This book will give you a good start in planning your future once psychology piques your interest.

Note to Instructors and Advisors

We wrote this book to serve multiple purposes for the psychology instructor. First, we think the text can serve well in psychology courses that introduce students to the major. Such courses are often titled *Introduction to the Psychology Major* or *Careers in Psychology*. Our book could be the main text or a supplemental text in these courses. The book provides a solid foundation for students interested in the discipline. We also hope that students will find the *Companion* valuable enough that they will use it to help them make the decisions that will follow their entry into the major.

Some instructors may wish to use the *Companion* as a supplemental text in introductory psychology courses exclusively aimed at psychology majors, research methods in psychology courses, and in psychology seminars. We purposefully designed the book to allow teacher-instructors to discuss and delve into academic as well as practical issues with students.

Instructors may also find the *Companion* useful as a supplemental text in capstone courses. A very strong trend in psychology curricula over the past few years is to require a course that encourages students to integrate what they have learned across their psychology courses. Because the *Companion* focuses on preparation for the steps after graduation—whether those might involve entering the workforce or pursuing graduate or professional school—we think it can provide appropriate guidance about the important decisions that lie ahead.

In this new edition, we have updated and revised some special features that should help students engage in and personalize their learning. Each chapter has a feature called "A Major Success Story" that profiles former students who have successfully navigated life after graduation. In later chapters we include multiple examples to illustrate just how broad the occupational options can be. We hope these will be inspirational and provide some good exemplars to cite when students discuss their choice of the psychology major.

The *Companion*'s "Reality Check" features help students assess their progress in each chapter. The Reality Checks provide an opportunity to apply the principles of the chapter to their own course and career planning.

A new feature, "Measuring Up," gives students a chance to do some self-assessment and to reflect on how the material in each chapter applies to their lives and educational experiences in the psychology major. Relating what they learn and think about to their own experiences will help students retain valuable information that can guide them in the future.

We are proud that the *Companion* uses emerging best practices from the collaborative national efforts on the undergraduate psychology curriculum from the American Psychological Association (APA). Our discussions of curriculum design and assessment strategies reflect recent work from the APA's Puget Sound Conference and the *Guidelines for the Undergraduate Psychology Major, Version 2.0*. As participants in those efforts, we wanted to ensure that our work here represents the most current and helpful content.

Supplements

To support instructors in student assessment and in teaching, we have prepared an Instructor's Manual and written a test bank comprised of multiple-choice and essay questions as well as lecture slides that summarize the content of each chapter. These materials are password protected and are available from the book's website (www.macmillanlearning.com).

Academic/major advisors in psychology departments (primarily faculty members) should welcome the text and its supplements as resources to assign or to recommend to students. Advisors often find that they must answer the same set of questions over and over again. We hope that by providing a comprehensive treatment of curricular and career issues, we present a resource that students can use to find the answers to some of these questions.

Note to Student Advocates

We know that students who choose psychology sometimes encounter well-intentioned concern from friends and family members who suspect the choice isn't a good idea. Most of the objections rest with the belief that the degree won't adequately prepare students for employment after graduation. Concerned allies should find this book helpful in allaying fears and in helping students come up with the best plan for their future.

Acknowledgments

We are delighted to be a part of the Worth/Macmillan family and are grateful to our executive editor and good friend, Christine Cardone, for suggesting we work on this book together. Her enthusiasm for the project, coupled with her perceptive suggestions, helped us to refine our vision for the book. During the publication process, we appreciated the precision and professionalism of the production and editorial teams, including that of Aravinda Doss, Lisa Kinne, Dorothy Tomasini, Stephanie Matamoros, and Anna Paganelli. We thank the peer reviewers who have provided us with feedback over the years: Karen Baker (University of Memphis Lambuth), Suzanne C. Baker (James Madison University), Rachelle Cohen (Georgia State University), Deborah Danzis (High Point University), Kathryn England-Aytes (California State University, Monterey Bay), Nicole Fleischer (Temple University), Timothy Franz (St. John Fisher College), Madeleine Fugère (Eastern Connecticut University), Brian Johnson (University of Tennessee, Martin), Stephen Lewis (University of Guelph), Jana McCurdy (College of Western Idaho), Michael Poulakis (University of Indianapolis), and Russell Walsh (Duquesne University).

Dana is grateful to his children, Jake and Hannah, and his daughter-in-law, Stefana, for their interest in and support of his work. He is also grateful to—and thankful for—Jane, whose friendship has taken him many places he never expected. His colleagues in the Department of Psychology at Moravian College and in APA Division 2 continue to inspire his teaching efforts and he appreciates their dedication to good pedagogy.

Jane marvels at how great married life can be when your husband is your best friend. Her husband Brian makes uncomplaining sacrifices so she can craft a satisfying professional life. She is distinctly grateful for the APA Psychology Partnerships Project that brought Dana and her together, little realizing how intertwined their professional lives would become. It has been a fulfilling collaboration that just keeps elevating the bar. She also wants to acknowledge the support she has had from her colleagues at three different institutions—Alverno College, James Madison University, and the University of West Florida—who have fingerprints all over the ideas presented in this text.

A Final Note

This is by no means our first writing project together but it was certainly the most fun to do. Why? Simply because we got to swap stories and perspectives on the wonderful students we have taught over the years. We also had ample opportunity to rely on the wisdom of our many colleagues in psychology, including perhaps especially those who are so active in the Society for the Teaching of Psychology (Division 2 of the APA).

We welcome comments and suggestions from instructors regarding our second edition of the *Companion*. We hope you have as much fun reading the *Companion* as we did in writing and revising it.

Dana S. Dunn
Bethlehem, Pennsylvania

Jane S. Halonen
Pensacola, Florida

Charting Your Course in College and Psychology

If you don't know where you are going,
you might wind up someplace else.

~Yogi Berra

The most important and influential decision you will make in college is about what will be the best fit between your talents and the array of possibilities that colleges and universities have to offer. We wrote this book primarily to appeal to several types of college students:

Students enrolled in introductory or general psychology. You may be taking this popular first psychology class and wondering whether psychology would be a good choice of a major.

Brand new majors in psychology. You have decided that psychology is the major for you but don't yet understand what that choice may mean for your future.

Transfer students. Perhaps you began your educational journey at a community college and transferred to a 4-year institution to finish your degree in psychology.

Those who want a job immediately after college. Perhaps you declared a psychology major but are wondering what you can do with an undergraduate degree in psychology after you graduate.

Students who want to attend graduate school in psychology or another field. You are already a psychology major and you are thinking about attending graduate school in psychology or a related field.

Adult learners. As a nontraditional-age student, you want to learn how psychology can help you in your future, whether that includes postgraduate employment or another degree.

Throughout this book, we offer important advice and information for students who fall into each of these groups. We have a sneaking suspicion that another group who will benefit from reading the book are parents and loved ones who want to understand and support your selection of the psychology major.

■ ■ ■

Regardless of the reader group you belong to, we trust you'll find substantial help within these pages to reinforce your confidence in choosing psychology as a major, to make the most of the opportunities ahead, and to prepare wisely and well for the various pathways that lie beyond graduation. We intend our comprehensive guide to the psychology major to provide friendly support (hence, to serve as your "companion") throughout your journey. This text will help you not just to survive the work involved in completing an undergraduate degree in psychology, but to thrive as the result of the wise choices you make along the way. You may just be starting your story. It is our fondest hope that the *Companion* will help you create a memorable one. If you are almost done with your major, we hope that you have gathered wonderful memories and few regrets.

We'll define just what psychology is and is not in Chapter 2; for now, we want to share some facts about the college experience and the attitudes of those heading to or already enrolled in a college or university.

The Nature of the College Experience

College is not just about what happens in the classroom but what happens outside of it, too: making new friends, trying new things, working in groups, learning to be responsible for oneself, possibly holding down a part or full-time job in addition to studying, as well as perhaps living away from home for the first time.

What's the difference between a college and a university? Generally, community colleges offer a 2-year associate's degree and 4-year colleges and universities grant bachelor's degrees. A university is a large institution comprised of various colleges and schools, including those dedicated to educating graduate students (students who already hold a 4-year degree and are working toward the next level of education or training). Universities grant undergraduate and graduate degrees in many different courses of study. Whether you go to a college or a university, you will have the company of many other students from diverse backgrounds and with interesting stories.

Heading to College: Today's Students

Is college the right solution for you? Answer the questions in *Reality Check: Is College the Right Path for You?* to assess whether college is a good fit for your future.

Who goes to college? More than 1.5 million high school graduates became first-time, full-time students in the fall of 2016, enrolling in a 4-year college or university (Eagan et al., 2017). Why do students go to college? The following eight reasons were rated as "very important" among those fall 2016 freshmen:

- to be able to get a better job,
- to gain a general education and appreciation of ideas,
- to make me a more cultured person,
- to be able to make more money,
- to learn more about things that interest me,
- to get training for a specific career,
- to prepare myself for graduate or professional school, and
- to please my family.

✅ Reality Check

Is College the Right Path for You?

Consider the following self-assessment questions:

- ☐ Do I have a clear understanding of my motives for seeking a degree?
- ☐ Do I know which kind of higher education context has the greatest appeal to me?
- ☐ Does my academic record predict a successful transition to college?
- ☐ Do I have a reasonable idea about the kind of major I want to pursue?
- ☐ Can I set aside the time it will take to earn a diploma?
- ☐ Have I taken steps to determine whether I would qualify for financial aid?
- ☐ Have I considered what kind of living arrangements I'll be able to afford?
- ☐ Will I be able to cope with the debt load that may result from my degree?
- ☐ Am I excited about the prospect of learning with a wide variety of people?
- ☐ Will I be able to function independently from my family?
- ☐ Will I be able to balance family and friends with school demands?
- ☐ Am I prepared to seek academic advising to clarify my direction?
- ☐ Have I developed reasonable time-management strategies to keep up with multiple courses?

Review your answers. Obviously the more items to which you can respond "yes," the better prepared you will be for making the commitment to a college education.

Our feature *Measuring Up: What Are My Drivers?* encourages you to think about your personal priorities during your college experience. The "Measuring Up" sections give you an opportunity to self-assess, that is, to speculate about how the material in the chapter applies to you, and to review important concepts and personalize the content of the chapter.

Today's college-bound students also expressed definite opinions about how they see themselves. They rated the following qualities as being a "somewhat strong" or "major strength" of theirs compared with the average person their age:

- the ability to see the world from someone else's perspective,
- tolerance of others with different beliefs,
- openness to having their own views challenged,
- the ability to discuss and negotiate controversial issues,
- the ability to work cooperatively with diverse people,
- critical thinking skills, and
- the ability to manage time effectively.

How do you view yourself in terms of each of these qualities?

↑ Measuring Up

What Are My Drivers?

What factors drive you toward seeking a degree? Although all of the motives listed below might be relevant to your decision, some will carry more weight than others.

Step 1: Rank order each of the following motives, using "1" to designate your most important driver, "2" as the next most important, and so on, until you have assessed all eight of these items.

_____ get a better job
_____ gain a general education and appreciation of ideas
_____ expand my cultural horizons
_____ make more money
_____ learn more about things that interest me
_____ train for a specific career
_____ prepare for graduate or professional school
_____ please my family

Step 2: Find a partner in your class and spend some time talking about your responses. Explain your priorities.

Step 3: Following the discussion, reflect on whether your priorities are likely to help you stay motivated to complete your degree or if your motivation might need some adjustment.

Just over 60% of these students considered it either "essential" or "very important" to become an authority in their career field, while more than 57% wanted their contributions to be recognized by peers in that field. Regarding their objectives in going to college, more than 82% of the freshmen ranked "being very well off financially" as either "very important" or "essential," and over 77% ranked "helping others who are in difficulty" as very important or essential. Surprisingly, only 47% viewed developing "a meaningful philosophy of life" as "essential" or "very important."

College turns out to be a very positive experience for most students. After a year of college, the majority of students — 75% — report that they are satisfied or very satisfied with their experience (HERI, 2013). And 81% of students are satisfied or very satisfied with their overall academic experience.

Where does psychology fit into the mix? In fall 2016, a little under 4.5% of new freshmen indicated that they saw psychology as their likely major (interestingly, 2% of all freshmen that year reported that becoming a clinical psychologist was their intended occupation; Eagan et al., 2016). In fact, as a possible major, freshmen tend to prefer psychology over all other social science majors, including political science, sociology, and economics.

What about 4 years later? How many students graduate with a bachelor of arts (BA) or bachelor of science (BS) degree in psychology? According to the National Center for Education Statistics (2018), in the 2014–2015 academic year, for example, 118,000 students graduated from a college or university in the United States with a degree in psychology (compare that number to the estimated 1.7 to 2 million undergraduates who enroll in an introductory psychology class each year; Curing, 2013; Steuer & Ham, 2008). Only a small percentage of those psychology majors will go on to graduate school to continue their studies in the discipline. Most will enter the job market right away. Others will end up furthering their education by pursuing a graduate degree in some other educational area that isn't related to psychology. However, the skills the students acquired through the psychology major serve them well, whatever professional paths they follow.

Common Concern: The Cost of College

A college degree can be expensive. Nearly 56% of the students who enrolled in fall 2016 expressed concerns about their ability to finance their degree (13.3% reported major concerns; Eagan et al., 2016). As a result, many students and their families wonder whether college is worth the cost. The short answer is that a college education remains an excellent investment — and using the word *investment* rather than *cost* is probably a good way to frame the issue. Working toward an undergraduate degree is an investment in your future.

Nearly all students who are considering college, are in college, or are fresh out of college worry about finding a job, launching a career, and managing debt, especially student loans. It's no wonder people question whether a college degree is worth the money. An expert on college costs (Leonhardt, 2014) recently claimed that "For all the struggles that many young college graduates face, a four-year degree has probably never been more valuable" (p. A3). How so?

The evidence is actually quite clear: In 2013, Americans who were graduates of 4-year colleges and universities earned on average 98% more per hour than those without a degree. Other findings make the case this way: Skipping college and instead heading right into the workforce will cost you about half a million dollars across your working life — unrealized earnings that having a college degree would have provided. That's something to consider when weighing the costs of attending or not attending college.

What about the issue of incurring debt by taking out student loans? College graduates in the class of 2017 carry an average debt of $37,172 (Mitchell, 2016). That's not a small amount of money unless you compare it to that half-million dollars having a degree provides. In that light, borrowing money to attend college seems worth it, as the risk seems to be a modest one. Of course, it is extremely important to understand how much you are borrowing over the long term and to be certain you understand what any loan entails.

Making the Most of College

We wrote this book primarily to help you make the most of psychology as a major, but we also want to point out that college provides students with many opportunities. Studying and going to class are important parts of being a student, but so is participating in what colleges and universities refer to as "cocurricular activities," educational experiences that take place outside of formal classes. In fact, it's a very good idea to learn to establish some balance in your life during your college years. You should make time to study, eat as healthily as you can, and get regular exercise, of course, but also make sure to have some downtime. In other words, you might play on an athletic team, join a club or one of the numerous organizations found on your campus, pledge a fraternity or a sorority, or do volunteer work in the community. A recent survey of first-year students revealed that more than 79% found a balance between their academic subjects and extracurricular activities (HERI, 2015). Having some constructive outlet renews your energy and outlook so that you can approach your studies with a positive attitude. After all, a balanced life will help you to retain what you learn in class.

Becoming Psychologically Literate

There is very good news for psychology majors and would-be psychology majors: An undergraduate education in psychology provides students with a multitude of skills, values, and outlooks that enable them to pursue and succeed in a variety of endeavors — that is, it makes students *literate* in psychology. To be literate is to be an educated person who knows a great deal about some subject area, in this case psychology. Being **psychologically literate** turns out to be both personally and professionally valuable (Cranney & Dunn, 2011a). **Table 1.1** lists some traits exhibited by psychologically literate students. The students used their time as psychology majors wisely and well. They also tended to avoid being perfectionists; they were better able than their peers to get whatever task they faced done, practically and quickly.

TABLE 1.1

Characteristics of Psychologically Literate Students

Solve problems in creative, amiable, and skeptical ways

Possess a well-defined vocabulary of psychological terms and concepts

Appreciate and respect diversity and diverse groups and individuals

Reflective about their own thinking processes and those of others

Good at evaluating information and using technology

Able to apply psychology principles to understanding and improving personal relationships, work issues, and things happening in the community

Act ethically, not out of self-interest

Communicate well and in different ways (writing, speaking, public presentations) to different types of people and audiences

Information from: Cranney & Dunn (2011b, p. 4). Oxford University Press.

Making valid or truthful judgments about our own behavior is really hard to do. We tend to have built-in biases that make it hard for us to see ourselves as others see us. A particular distortion called the **Dunning–Kruger effect** — sometimes called the *overconfidence effect* — is the tendency to overestimate the quality of one's own performances (e.g., Kruger & Dunning, 1999). Students regularly show the Dunning–Kruger effect when they become overconfident about how well they have studied and end up failing an exam. Ironically, even faculty members are prone to overconfidence. For example, 90% of all college professors report that they are above average in teaching quality — a statistical impossibility. You can counter the effects of such overconfidence by examining evidence to determine whether there is sufficient support for the conclusions you draw.

How psychologically literate are you? Review the characteristics of psychologically literate people in Table 1.1. Pick the three or four that you believe either already fit you or are qualities you would like to develop. What behavioral evidence would you need to demonstrate each of the characteristics you chose? Of the characteristics you have selected, do you think your perception about your skill level might be overblown? How would you verify whether your assessments are accurate? What are the risks of overestimating your skills? Of course, you could also be underestimating your true ability levels.

One other vehicle we use throughout the *Companion* is success profiles (*A Major Success Story*) that we hope will inspire you. We chose people from diverse backgrounds who majored in psychology and created satisfying stories that illustrate the range of possibilities that a psychology major can provide. We asked the people we interviewed to share their best advice about how to have a story with a happy ending. We also thought it would be useful to share our own stories to explain how we became fascinated with psychology.

Dana S. Dunn, PhD, Social Psychologist and Professor of Psychology

Dana began his college career knowing he wanted to major in psychology. In fact, he decided that psychology was his calling during high school, when he took a psychology class that was taught by a beloved teacher. He knew his choice was the correct one during his undergraduate years at Carnegie Mellon University. There, Dana had the good fortune to serve as a research assistant to a graduate student and later to a faculty member and, during his senior year, he conducted an experiment for his honors thesis in psychology. At the University of Virginia, he refined his focus onto the then-burgeoning area of social cognition, earning his PhD in experimental social psychology.

Because Dana loved college and university life, he decided to build a career in academia. He knew that being a good teacher and researcher was an important part of that, and he has continued to hone his teaching and research skills over his now 30-year career in psychology. In his experience, the process of designing and conducting research feeds his teaching, and vice versa. During his academic career he has held a variety of roles:

■ Applied researcher for a medical school and a nursing school

■ Professor of psychology

■ Researcher, author, and editor (researcher and author of articles, chapters, book reviews, textbooks, and editor of psychology books and journals)

■ Visiting professor at other colleges

■ Administrator (department chair, dean for special projects, director of academic assessment)

■ Consultant (academic program reviewer, assessment, faculty development)

Best Advice: Always assume there is something new to learn, on your own and from others, each and every day. Work steadily and always submit what you do early or on time, never, ever late.

Jane S. Halonen, PhD, Clinical Psychologist and Professor of Psychology

Like so many psychology majors, Jane didn't start out as one. She thought being a playwright or a journalist would be a good possible future. However, taking introductory psychology felt like coming home, and she began to pursue a new goal to become a clinical psychologist. Her earliest research interests involved attachment theory, which helped her as she prepared for an internship and later a career in working with children and families.

Although she never aspired to be a teacher, Jane was surprised at how satisfying her graduate teaching assistantship was, particularly because she suffered long-standing anxieties about public speaking. Being involved in some aspect of education and training has dominated her professional life. Over the course of an almost 40-year career, she has enacted diverse roles for which her major in psychology prepared her, including:

- Director of a school for children with severe emotional and physical disabilities
- Professor of psychology
- Administrator (program coordinator, behavioral science division head, department head, dean of college of arts and sciences)
- Researcher and author (textbooks, articles, podcasts)
- Private practitioner (child and family therapist)
- Mental health practice (co-owner and manager)
- Consultant (academic program reviewer, faculty developer)
- Chief reader for the Advanced Placement (AP) Psychology Exam
- Leadership trainer

Best Advice? Don't make promises you can't keep and keep all the promises you make. Your diligence will make you stand out when others may lose their way.

Jane and Dana's Shared Story

Both of us have had deep interest in what makes psychology students learn more effectively and efficiently. In service of that, we both applied to be participants in a conference by the American Psychological Association called the *Psychology Partnerships Project*, which was held at James Madison University in 1998. Happily, the organizers assigned us both to the same interest group on assessment, which looks at how we measure changes that take place in learning. Compatible in work ethic, sensibilities, and sense of humor, we gravitated toward other projects that would launch our writing partnership; we've never looked back.

Our shared projects have included working on the APA *Guidelines for Undergraduate Psychology Major 2.0*; multiple articles on faculty development and student learning; participation in APA Summits on High School Psychology and the Summit on National Assessment in Psychology. We also collaborate on faculty development interest pieces for the *Chronicle of Higher Education*.

We have both served as president of the Society for the Teaching of Psychology (Division 2 of the American Psychological Association) and we are proud that we both won national recognition as distinguished teachers with top honors from the American Psychological Foundation.

FIGURE 1.1 Dana S. Dunn & Jane Halonen share a moment at a teaching conference.

Jane Halonen

Why We Wrote This Book for You

As psychology professors, each of us has taught thousands of students, both psychology majors and nonmajors, about the discipline we love. One of the things we've noticed across our careers in higher education is that some students struggle to see how knowledge gained in the classroom can be applied to everyday work and life. We want students to be mindful and intentional as they pursue the psychology major. If they do so, they will be more satisfied with their choices both before and after graduation.

We wrote this book so that students like you can use their college days well, as a launching pad for whatever comes next — career, internship, graduate school, or something altogether different. We discuss key topics, including:

- ▓ Why do students major in psychology? (Chapter 2)
- ▓ Should *you* major in psychology? Is it right for you? (Chapter 3)
- ▓ Developing psychology-related skills to enhance your career options and opportunities (Chapter 4)
- ▓ How to hit your stride as a student (Chapter 5)
- ▓ Charting your course in the major (Chapter 6)

- Tackling psychological research from start to finish (Chapter 7)
- Using psychology to improve leadership skills (Chapter 8)
- What career options are out there for students with a BA or BS in psychology? (Chapter 9)
- How do you land a great psychology workforce job? (Chapter 10)
- What about graduate school in psychology — what does it take and where might it take you? (Chapter 11)
- How do you apply to and get in to quality graduate programs? (Chapter 12)
- Keeping connected to psychology after college (Chapter 13)
- Learning to write and format an APA-style paper (Appendix A)

As you read each chapter, don't forget this important fact: Among all the things that college is, it is a privilege. Census data show that as recently as 2013, only about 32% of adults in the United States had a 4-year college degree. Despite the popular hype that "college is now a necessity," most of our fellow citizens have not had the good fortune to complete a college degree. Having the opportunity to go to college is still a singular event and one that can be life changing. When coupled with the right major, your college education should prove to be satisfying and fulfilling. We hope you feel this way, just as we hope that the insights we share with you about psychology will help you to make the most of your education.

Thought Questions

1. What do you hope to get from a college education? Why?
2. At this point in time, what interests you about psychology? Why?
3. Do you know anyone who is already majoring in psychology? What do they like about their studies?
4. What kinds of extracurricular activities do you think you might like to pursue during college?
5. If you had decided not to attend college, what would you have done instead? Why?

2

The Nature of Psychology and the Psychology Major

Psychology, unlike chemistry, unlike algebra, unlike literature,
is an owner's manual for your own mind.
It's a guide to life.

~Daniel Goldstein, Cognitive Psychologist

Jane remembers what a struggle it was to try to help her grandmother understand what she planned to do in college. Jane described how excited she was to be learning about human behavior in her psychology classes and that she might be able later to do research on unsolved questions about human behavior. She told her grandmother that she hoped to someday be a clinical psychologist so that she would be able to use what she learned to help people with their problems. Grandma nodded appreciatively. Later, Jane overheard her bragging to a neighbor that her granddaughter was studying to be "a brain surgeon."

■ ■ ■

It isn't surprising that the discipline of psychology can be a hard one to grasp. When Jane and her grandmother had that conversation in the late 1960s, we didn't have many visible representatives who could help the unschooled come to terms with what it meant to study psychology. Although we now have abundant examples of psychology in the media, many exemplars involve narrow or misleading stereotypes that don't do much to reveal the true nature of the discipline. Despite the fact that psychology has produced some Nobel Prize winners, most people tend to think of "Dr. Phil" (McGraw) as the quintessential psychologist.

Most depictions in the entertainment media involve the noble (and sometimes flawed) clinical psychologist who strives to make a difference in people's lives, often in a forensic or legal setting. These portrayals tend to be great at drawing students into the major but also unfortunately set them up to think that the sum total of the major is about the diagnosis and treatment of mental health problems, causing them disappointment when they learn that clinical matters actually represent a very small percentage of the undergraduate curriculum.

To set the stage for later personal explorations of fit with the psychology major (Chapter 3), in this chapter we will discuss two key topics: What exactly does the discipline of psychology entail, and what can you expect from a major in psychology?

What Is the Story of Psychology?

In this section, we take a look at how psychology has evolved from its origins to its complex contemporary character, where both research and practice are important. We explore the difficulty the discipline has had in trying to establish a clear-cut identity for itself. We conclude this section by equipping you to dispel the myths that persist about the nature of psychology, myths that you may encounter as you navigate your way through the major.

How Do We Define Psychology?

Compared to most other sciences, psychology is the new kid on the block. Most historians trace the formal beginnings of the science of psychology to 1879, when Wilhelm Wundt founded an experimental laboratory in Leipzig, Germany. This development marked a departure from the related but nonscientific discipline of philosophy. Psychology is less than 140 or so years old (by comparison, physics in some form has been around since ancient Greece, if not before). Although the discipline of psychology is fairly young, it has already undergone an evolution in character and definition.

During the earliest days of exploring psychology as a scientific endeavor, psychologists were interested in mapping the most basic functions of the human body. This version, or *orientation*, of psychology is referred to as **structuralism**. The label makes sense because the questions were **empirical** (that is, based on direct observation and experimentation) attempts to map human capacity. For example, the structuralists were curious about how much weight would need to be added to a standard stimulus before we could perceive it as heavier. They spent significant amounts of time testing and reporting individual perceptual experience about weights, sounds, tastes, and other dimensions of the senses through a scientific self-report process called *introspection*. Structuralists would be dazzled today if they could see what has happened to the discipline they helped to establish.

Many other psychology orientations have emerged over time, including functionalism, **behaviorism**, humanistic psychology, psychoanalysis, and cognitive psychology. It's beyond the scope of this book to have a systematic discussion of all of the trends and orientations in psychology. (If you are in the major, you may have the opportunity/obligation to study that evolution in a course on the history of psychology.) To be fair, psychologists have not yet arrived at a shared paradigm for studying behavior, which contributes to the confusion about what psychology truly represents.

Most contemporary psychologists would agree with the definition of **psychology** as *the scientific study of mind and behavior in human and nonhuman animals*. Thus, psychology majors scientifically study the way living organisms behave, learn, think, and feel. An undergraduate degree doesn't qualify psychology majors to claim the title of psychologist, but psychology majors learn to think as psychologists do by completing the major.

To help to explain why the major is so easily misunderstood and might not appeal to everyone, let's take the definition of psychology apart. First — and psychologists tend to be quite passionate about this point — psychology is a SCIENCE. We use scientific methods to draw conclusions about mind and behavior. Stanovich (2019) summarized that a science is not defined by any specific content area or technologies but by the general characteristics of the process used for validating conclusions. He suggested that the sciences concentrate on (a) reliance on systematic **empiricism** (direct observation); (b) commitment to making findings public to expand and build our understanding; and (c) application of key ideas in solving problems.

Psychologists like to describe behavior with a high degree of precision, carefully distinguishing descriptions of behavior from inferences drawn about behavior. We demonstrate the value of carefully defined behavior by relying on **operational definitions**, meaning we define behaviors through the use of observable processes. For example, if we are going to research playground aggression, we must carefully delineate what counts as an aggressive act. Do we count only punches thrown or can mean words count as aggressive acts? The rules of science obligate the psychologist to define key ideas in such a way that others could reproduce the same research protocols. We measure behavior and subject our measurements to statistical analyses to establish whether our experiments or research designs produce the outcomes we expect. Psychologists use a variety of research techniques, from self-report measures to behavioral observations to fMRI scans — that is, all of the approaches psychologists use adhere to the scientific method.

"Mind and behavior" is an expansive way to talk about the content of what psychologists study. Over time, some subgroups in psychology have concentrated on one area or another. For examples, behaviorists, who declared their founding principles in a historic manifesto (Watson, 1913), believed that the only valid focus of study was observable behavior. If you couldn't directly observe a phenomenon, then it had no place in their labs. In contrast, **cognitive psychology** broadened the focus to include studying covert activity, such as dreaming and thinking. This field uses 1956 — the year George Miller published a seminal article about the capacity of human information processing — as its official origin.

Psychologists don't restrict themselves to the study of humans. Contemporary psychology labs can feature primates, planaria, or pelicans, among others. Virtually any life form that engages in behavior can be the focus of a psychological investigation. Although enthusiasm has waned a bit for requiring students to work with animals as a standard practice, psychologists remain committed to conducting research on animals as long as they abide by strict rules to protect and care for those animals (Plous, 1996). Similarly, research with humans is also governed by a standard set of regulations.

Psychology's Struggle for Identity

Although the definition of psychology is fairly straightforward, the discipline has been plagued with identity problems from the outset. William James, arguably the founder of American psychology, described psychology as a "nasty little science" (Hunt, 1961). Frustrated by the constraints of structuralism, James (1892/1961, p. 335) concluded, "This is no science, it is only the hope of a science." James was guardedly optimistic that psychology could evolve into a respectable natural science and opened the first experimental lab in America, at Harvard. He later founded **functionalism**, shifting attention to the motives behind and the purpose of behavior and away from structuralism's focus on sensory capacity.

Although many other orientations have since been developed, no one orientation has led to a unified psychology. Contemporary critics (cf. Henriques, 2014) suggest that the proliferation of viewpoints and knowledge in the discipline reduces the coherence of psychology and may foster a deep sense of fragmentation within the discipline.

Psychology also operates in two distinct but related scientific spheres, as it has elements of both natural science and social science. As a natural science, psychology attempts to explain and predict natural phenomena that parallel the focus of chemistry and biology. For example, studies on the effectiveness of a new antidepressant medication clearly illustrate the natural science focus of psychology. As a social science, psychology strives to explain and predict social phenomena, using empirical methods that are similar to those used in economics, anthropology, and political science, among others. A social science study might explore why sports victories can sometimes result in mob violence, for instance. Any introductory course in psychology will ground students in both the natural and social dimensions of the discipline.

Another dichotomy complicates psychology's contemporary identity. Broadly speaking, professional psychology has been characterized as having two cultures (Kimble, 1984). The first culture represents the psychologists who create new knowledge through scientific research. The second culture includes those who apply psychological principles to solve problems. Popular culture tends to concentrate on the second culture — psychologists as helpers. Indeed, the vast majority of psychology majors initially start out in psychology in response to the impulse to help people. However, work in the first culture — research psychology — is also used to help people. *A Major Success Story: A Career That Blends Two Cultures* illustrates how one psychology major successfully combined these two orientations in her first job following her master's degree.

Kelly Toner,
MA, Project Manager

FIGURE 2.1 Kelly Toner manages research projects in genetic counseling, which allows her to blend her expertise in research with her well-developed counseling skills.

A Career That Blends Two Cultures

Kelly Toner discovered her career trajectory when she took a psychology class as a senior in high school. She always knew that helping others would be central to her life's work. Taking the class persuaded her that psychology provided the opportunity she was looking for. Kelly says that in addition to helping her prepare for her career, being a psychology major helped her become a kinder and more conscientious person.

Internships were instrumental in helping Kelly make meaningful decisions about her future. During her undergraduate years, she interned in an adolescent inpatient psychiatric unit, assisting in group therapy sessions, observing family sessions, and helping with group activities. This experience solidified her commitment to psychology and prompted her to pursue graduate training. Her internship in her master's program developed her clinical skills but also fine-tuned her professional skills of time management and improved her self-confidence and flexibility.

Her current position involves a blend of expertise in counseling and competence in research design. Kelly is a research assistant in a multidisciplinary neurodevelopmental clinic, working with children and young adults whose genetic profiles warrant additional support. The clients have an intellectual disability or autism. Kelly assists genetic counselors in helping families understand their options. She also coordinates interdisciplinary genetic research projects, such as exploring the relationship between specific genes and diseases.

Best Advice? "Take advantage of building strong relationships with your professors and seek liberal guidance from them throughout the major. Hands-on application experiences, such as internships or service-learning courses, help reveal what you can do and also what you may not like, which can be especially helpful when it is time to join the workforce."

❯❯❯

The existence of two cultures has had an impact on professional affiliations for psychologists. G. Stanley Hall founded the American Psychological Association (APA) in 1892 to create a professional community of psychologists. The APA currently has 77,550 members, including researchers, educators, consultants, and clinicians. Although critics suggest the APA's attention is dominated by clinical or applied matters, the APA's mission is broader than that, encompassing research, practice, education, and public advocacy.

In 1988, the **Association for Psychological Science (APS)** launched an alternative professional organization whose primary mission is to promote psychology as a science. According to the organization's website (2019), the APS has more than 30,000 members and is the leading international organization concentrating on advancing scientific psychology. Both the APA and the APS offer student affiliate memberships; application information is available on their respective websites.

Simply contrasting the psychology communities as "research" or "practice" doesn't quite capture the richness of the topics that can be studied in psychology. The APA publishes a list of the specialized areas of interest in psychology; this list can be very helpful in exploring the wide range of topics that psychologists explore (**Table 2.1**). These areas reflect both research concentrations and different types of

TABLE 2.1

Special Interest Areas Listed by the American Psychological Association (with APA Division Number)

Addiction Psychology (50)	Environmental, Population, and Conservation Psychology (34)	Pharmacotherapy (55)
Adult Development and Aging (20)	Experimental Psychology and Cognitive Science (3)	Psychoanalysis and Psychoanalytic Psychology (39)
American Psychology-Law (41)	General Psychology (1)	Psychological Hypnosis (30)
Applied Experimental and Engineering Psychology (21)	Group Psychology and Group Psychotherapy (49)	Psychological Study of Social Issues (9)
Aesthetics, Creativity, and the Arts (10)	Health Psychology (38)	Psychopharmacology and Substance Abuse (28)
Behavior Analysis (25)	History of Psychology (26)	Psychotherapy (29)
Child and Family Policy and Practice (37)	Humanistic Psychology (32)	Public Service (18)
Clinical Psychology (12)	Independent Psychology Practice (37)	Quantitative and Qualitative Methods (4)
Clinical Child and Adolescent Psychology (53)	Industrial and Organizational Psychology (14)	Rehabilitation Psychology (22)
Clinical Neuropsychology (40)	Intellectual and Developmental Disabilities/ Autism Spectrum (33)	Religion and Spirituality (36)
Community Research and Action (27)		School Psychology (16)
Consulting Psychology (13)	International Psychology (52)	Sexual Orientation and Gender Diversity (44)
Consumer Psychology (23)	Media Psychology and Technology (46)	Sport, Exercise, and Performance Psychology (47)
Counseling Psychology (17)	Men and Masculinities (51)	
Couple and Family Psychology (43)	Military Psychology (19)	Teaching (2)
Culture, Ethnicity, and Race (45)	Peace, Conflict, and Violence (48)	Theoretical and Philosophical Psychology (24)
Developmental Psychology (6)	Pediatric Psychology (54)	Trauma Psychology (56)
Educational Psychology (15)	Personality and Social Psychology (8)	Women (35)

Source: http://www.apa.org/about/division

jobs in professional psychology. As you can see in Table 2.1, only some topics deal explicitly with the clinically or counseling-oriented issues.

To foster communities of interest, APA built a divisional structure that allows people with shared interests to connect, collaborate on research, and move specialized interests forward. The divisional structure entails 54 subdisciplines, only a few of which are clinical in orientation. For example, both Dana and Jane belong to Division 2, the Teaching of Psychology. In addition, Dana is a member and recent president of Division 22 (Rehabilitation Psychology). See the APA website for a complete listing of divisions.

However, this wide range of specializations also entails some threat to the integrity of psychology as a unified discipline. For example, psychologists who strongly identify as neuroscientists or developmentalists may view their association with psychology as secondary to their core interests. The strengthening of subdisciplines ultimately may further aggravate identity problems for psychology as a whole.

Dispelling Myths About Psychology

There are many myths, or compelling but untrue beliefs, about the discipline of psychology (Lilienfeld, Lynn, Ruscio, & Beyerstein, 2010). Psychology's popularity is in part based on the ease with which all of us create on-the-spot theories about why people behave as they do. After all, most of us are steeped in our own and others' behavior (much of it ordinary, some of it downright wacky) from the moment we wake up until the moment we go to sleep. We can't help ourselves: Actions require explanation.

Part of the fault also lies with psychologists themselves. Collectively, we have not done a very good job of public relations in countering the falsehoods or half-truths about the discipline and the people who work in it.

If you are thinking about majoring in psychology, then you need to understand the most basic myths so that you not only don't fall prey to them yourself but so that you can gently but firmly counter those ideas when others offer them as truths. What follows are some of the myths that surface most frequently about the nature of psychology. You may recognize some of them from firsthand experience.

Myth 1: Psychology is nothing more than common sense. When people read about psychological research or hear about it (even in the classroom) they have a tendency to react as if the reported scientific findings are clear and obvious — how else could the findings have turned out? In reality, of course, the results only *seem* obvious. Psychologists refer to this as **hindsight bias**, or the "I-knew-it-all-along effect;" learning how things turned out makes good sense once you know the outcome but when people are asked about their expectations *before* they know the outcome, they often have a different response (Roese & Vohs, 2012). In a classic example from 1991, psychologists Martin Bolt and John Brink asked a group of college students to forecast the outcome of the U.S. Senate vote to confirm or not confirm nominee Clarence Thomas to the Supreme Court (Cherry, 2014). Before the vote, 58% of the students predicted that Thomas would be confirmed but when they were polled after his confirmation, 78% asserted that they had predicted before the vote that he would be confirmed. Even the most thoughtful and judicious people can fall prey to this everyday bias because once we know how something has turned out, we find it very hard to entertain alternatives.

In addition, psychology contains a plethora of research findings that challenge common sense or are counterintuitive. For example, if you are out driving and you suddenly need help with a car problem, are you better off on a low-traffic country road or on a busy city street? Intuition tells you that a higher traffic volume would produce more potential helpers, but as confirmed in the classic work of Darley and Latané (1964) on **diffusion of responsibility** ("the bystander effect"), your better bet is the country road; people are more likely to perform altruistic acts when they don't see others who can be counted on to intervene (see also Fischer et al., 2011).

Humans assume a lot of cause-and-effect relationships that just aren't accurate (Lilienfeld et al., 2010). For example, the right-brain (logic) versus left-brain (creative) distinction is overblown; adolescents don't necessarily demonstrate turmoil during their teen years; and students don't learn better when teachers teach in a manner that matches the students' preferred style. These are just a few of the commonsense conclusions that scientific psychology has challenged. Much of what we tacitly accept as true thrives as common sense but falters under scientific scrutiny.

Myth 2: Whatever it is, psychology is not a science. Psychology often doesn't get much respect as a science because many of its areas of inquiry are more familiar and accessible (love, depression) than those associated with older sciences, such as physics (black holes), biology (genetics), chemistry (covalent bonding), and some other scientific disciplines. Laypeople generally assume that science is defined by what is being studied rather than by how the study is being done.

In actuality, a science is defined by the research methods it uses to pose and answer questions. Like other sciences, psychology relies on the **scientific method** (hypothesis testing, careful observation and experimentation, manipulation and measurement of variables, rigorous analysis, **replication**) rather than subject matter (psychologists study the behavior of organisms — everything from mice to marsupials, not just people). Neuroscience and the study of the brain are highly technical parts of psychology; psychology, then, is very much a science.

Myth 3: Psychology is a pseudoscience. Nothing rankles a psychologist more than to have the false comparison of psychology with nonscientific behavioral explanations. Although horoscopes, numerology, and handwriting analysis can be fun and even compelling, psychologists protest the absence of scientific validation in the predictions that **pseudoscience** produces. In fact, the pseudosciences generally have no empirical data to support the claims they make about behavior (Lilienfeld, 2004).

Myth 4: Psychologists know how to read minds. As psychologists, it gives us pause when we hear the question, "What do you do for a living?" Answering "I'm a psychologist" is risky. Many people get nervous, begin to watch their words with care, and often inquire, "Are you going to read my mind?" On the other hand, others see the lucky encounter as a way of getting free expert input on some psychological problem. (Saying you are a professor is almost as bad — people begin to worry you will correct their grammar.)

As should be clear, psychologists are scientists who use careful theories and research methods to study how people think, feel, and act — they don't read people's minds. If a psychologist has any particular insight into the human condition, it is likely the result of years of study, careful observation and inference, and honest hard work, not demonstrating intuition or being a mentalist.

Myth 5: Psychologists = therapists. Only some — by no means all — psychologists do counseling or therapy with people. In the popular mind, psychologists are supposed to do some form of counseling with people who are struggling with mental illness, for example, or some other psychological issue (e.g., chronic shyness). Jane, for example, fits the stereotype. She was trained as a clinical psychologist; although she does not currently have a practice, she maintained a private practice part time as a therapist for a dozen years while she established her academic career. In contrast, Dana is a social psychologist, a researcher, and has no training in clinical or counseling skills. Both of us are interested in teaching, research, and educational issues, including clarifying the nature of psychology as a science.

Because the media overrepresents clinical psychologists when portraying the discipline, many students come into psychology with the wrong idea about what the major will entail. Perhaps from an overexposure to media depictions of psychologists, they eagerly anticipate courses that will be filled with case studies and fun speculations about what separates the normal from the abnormal. They are stressed when they learn how good they will have to be at mathematics to handle the demands of statistical analysis and conversely how limited their studies will be in the clinical realm. They can be horrified when confronted with the amount of biology they need to learn to understand the functioning of the brain.

Myth 6: To get a job in psychology, you have to go to graduate school. Let's be clear about this important point: The majority of students who major in psychology do *not* go to graduate school. Heading into the workforce is not just an acceptable alternative; it is an honorable one. To get a job as a psychologist, you do have to go to graduate school for a master's degree and possibly a doctorate. We refer to this pathway as preparing for *professional* psychology. However, nearly any workforce position that deals with people or data qualifies as a *psychology-related* position. The baccalaureate degree serves as a passport into workforce employment into psychology-related areas.

Myth 7: Psychology is personally defined. No, it's not. Although some orientations in psychology are distinctly friendly to personal experience (e.g., humanism, phenomenology), psychologists have carefully built the knowledge corpus of the science of psychology (i.e., empirical observations, controlled comparisons, ruling out alternative explanations). In addition, cognitive psychology has dramatically demonstrated how flawed personal reasoning and judgment can be. Consequently, personal experience as "proof" of a behavioral phenomenon is simply unacceptable to psychologists. A good example is the all-too-common belief that the full moon tends to induce higher levels of human craziness. No full moon effect has ever been verified (Arkowitz & Lilienfeld, 2009). A bad day as a barista during a full moon doesn't constitute solid proof of a psychological principle.

In *Measuring Up: Seize the Narrative*, we encourage you to think through the challenges that will lie ahead when you tell people that you have chosen psychology as a major. We think each critical encounter is a unique opportunity to help others not just understand your choice but to learn to think accurately about the nature of psychology.

↑ Measuring Up

Seize the Narrative

Nothing is more predictably frustrating than having a conversation that leads you to feel regret about not having been able to express yourself as well as you wanted to. "I should have said . . ." is a distinctive form of hindsight bias. If you are like most psychology majors, you are bound to have many exchanges in school in which you will be called on to explain or defend your choice of major. If you can predict these awkward moments, you can prepare your response in a way that will minimize your regrets.

Think about how you might take command of these situations — seize your narrative — to respond to questions such as those below with answers that demonstrate your commitment to, and perhaps even your pride in, choosing psychology as a major.

> *Isn't psychology just good common sense?*
> *Did you go into this major to work out your problems?*
> *So you must be planning on going to graduate school?*
> *Why don't you go into some science major?*
> *You do know you won't be able to get a job when you graduate…*
> *Aren't you picking a pretty unchallenging major?*
> *Are you going to read my mind?*
> *Can you tell me how to fix the problems I'm having with my roommate?*

Remember, every ill-informed question is an opportunity to teach those who don't know enough about the discipline you have chosen to call yours.

What Is the Nature of the Psychology Major?

According to the APA's Center for Workforce Studies, interest in the psychology major is robust (Clay, 2017). **Figure 2.2** illustrates that the psychology major continues to grow. Approximately 120,000 undergraduate degrees are awarded each year. Between 6 and 6.5% of all undergraduates major in psychology, which is the most popular STEM field (*STEM* refers to science, technology, engineering, and mathematics).

In this section we take a look at the process of becoming a psychology major, from the moment of decision on. We look at opportunities that can optimize the experience in the major. We also identify the misperceptions that abound regarding what it means to major in psychology.

FIGURE 2.2 Psychology Degrees Awarded, 2006–2016

Data from: APA Center for Workforce Studies

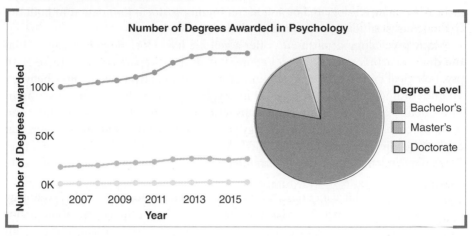

Declaring the Major

Students usually end up in the psychology major via one of two paths. Through personal experience with therapists or representations in media, a student may decide that being a psychologist looks fulfilling and pick the major when beginning college. Many high school students can take courses in psychology and so come to college with experience of a psychological worldview and have a reasonable idea of what they are getting into. Dana fits this pattern; he knew from the start that psychology would be his disciplinary home.

However, often psychology represents a "found" major. That is, students start out in a different major but move to psychology when they discover the fit of the original major wasn't satisfying and something about the content of psychology was. The dynamic can grow out of taking a class with a charismatic psychology teacher or the recognition that something about the concepts and frameworks in psychology feels right. Jane gravitated toward psychology when she found her original choice of journalism to be unsatisfying. Regardless of whether students commit from the beginning or switch during college, they can find a true comfort zone in psychological ways of thinking that will help them endure the rigors of the major.

The Typical Major Structure

Psychology departments across the country tend to offer majors that are fairly similar but not identical. Although all use a science-based curriculum, the philosophy or mission of the programs can differ. For example, some might concentrate more heavily on a humanistic orientation, while others may primarily use neuroscience or cognitive behavioral frameworks. Examining the research emphases of the faculty can sometimes reveal a program's overall orientation if it is not explicitly stated in the mission statement.

From a curriculum standpoint, most students begin with an introductory psychology course. Students sometimes have the option of getting college credit in psychology in a high school dual-degree or advanced placement (AP) program. The introductory class often includes descriptions of the professional careers that might grow out of a psychology major and at minimum provide a foundation in both the natural and social science elements of psychology.

Many psychology departments offer a generic bachelor's degree, meaning that the degree includes the skills and content areas that prepare students to be good psychological thinkers. The curriculum of such a degree typically involves between 30 and 40 hours of specialized work in psychology, including such classes as an introductory course, a research and statistics course, content courses with lab components, perhaps a history of psychology course, and electives and other classes that explore how psychology can be applied. A comprehensive study of undergraduate curricula (Stoloff et al., 2010) determined that there is no standard undergraduate program.

Many programs have incorporated the concept of a capstone course in psychology to help students pull together what they have learned over the course of the major (Dunn & McCarthy, 2010). A capstone course might be a seminar in history, an advanced introductory psychology course, a course on professional issues, or another course designed to facilitate students' integration of their learning across classes. Participation on research teams or in psychologically oriented workplace internships can also provide a fertile format for capstone-level work (see Chapters 7, 8, and 9).

Specializing Within the Major

Some schools offer a bachelor of arts instead of a bachelor of science in psychology. This distinction is not standard across colleges and universities, and individual departments can define the difference. Generally speaking, a bachelor of arts degree focuses on psychology's liberal arts side, frequently including an emphasis on foreign language and a slightly reduced emphasis on science. The bachelor of science degree has less humanities influence and more emphasis on the sciences, often including computer classes and additional math or statistics courses. Some departments have made their departments more STEM-oriented and changed the degree name from *psychology* to *psychological science*.

Another trend has emerged in psychology curriculum that reflects the growth of specializations and concentrations within the major. For example, students can pursue degrees in human development, neuroscience, or neurobiology, all of which use psychology as the academic base. Some undergraduate programs offer certificates that document concentrated time spent in human resources, addictions, child development, or other content clusters that can add an impressive line on a résumé and help set students apart from their competition.

One common error some undergraduate students make is saying that they are majoring in *clinical* psychology. It is unlikely that undergraduate programs offer a clinical psychology major, because preparation for this career direction requires much more than an undergraduate degree. Consequently, students who say they are majoring in clinical psychology communicate that they don't really understand the major they have chosen. (A better strategy for talking about this is to note that you are majoring in psychology and adding that you have a special interest in clinical issues or hope to pursue a clinical specialization in graduate school.)

Enriching Your Major With a Minor

Most graduation requirements leave room for students to go beyond requirements for the major and add areas of concentration. The choices you make in filling in your education reveal a great deal about your priorities. For example, some students choose a particular minor because of their intrinsic interest in that field. Others pick a minor that will make them more fit for a specific career path. See *Reality Check: Adding Value to the Major* to explore profitable minors, whether to enhance your career or to satisfy your soul.

 Reality Check

Adding Value to the Major With the Right Minor

Consider how the following minors might enrich your major and set you apart from your competition, either for getting in to graduate school or for the workforce. Which appeal the most to you when thinking about your career plans?

Minor	Graduate School Advantage	Workforce Advantage
Biology	Most graduate psychology programs have extensive requirements in biology.	A strong background in biology can qualify you for entry in health care and pharmaceuticals.
Business	Psychologists who plan to be private practitioners also need to be good at business.	Business courses enhance your value in many entry-level positions.
Communications	Graduate school and the professions entail substantial speaking and writing activities.	Psychology and communications produce a great background for public relations and marketing.
Computer science	Executing research can be enhanced by using technology.	Most jobs have a strong intersection with information technology.
English	Concentrated practice in clear writing helps with writing one's thesis and dissertation.	Being able to write capably about psychological phenomena can open interesting entry-level job prospects.
Mathematics	Even clinicians need to complete a variety of statistics classes.	Knowing how to collect and analyze data is helpful in both the profit and nonprofit sectors of business.
Philosophy	The writing and thinking practice involved in philosophy improves intellectual capacity.	Some entry-level jobs have a lot of opportunity for deep thinking and creative problem solving.
Sociology	Sociology assists in the advocacy and community-organizing components of graduate training.	Understanding both individual and group behavior can help in community organizing.
Theater	Graduate school showcases presentation skills and offers teaching opportunities.	Theater experience can build one's confidence in self-presentation.

What the Psychology Major Is Not

In our experience, people tend to harbor misconceptions about the nature of the major itself. We address some of the most popular misconceptions here.

Psychology is a very easy major. Psychology gets a bum rap as being easy for the simple reason that people are so familiar with human behavior (their own and others') that they assume they know all there is to know about it. Many students approach taking introductory psychology with the attitude that the course will be a breeze — because psychology is based on common sense — but often face a rude awakening when they get back their scores on the first exam. What sounded so plausible and obvious during class turns out to have many subtle and nuanced effects when it appears on a test.

By comparison, few students or parents will suggest that majoring in architecture, chemistry, mechanical engineering, or even German studies is easy. People don't have as many theories about what students, let alone professionals, do in these fields (just ask someone to explain what mechanical engineers or people in German studies do — then ask about people interested in psychology). Not to put too fine a point on it, but if psychology were the "academic gut" major it is often portrayed to be, then most majors would get straight A's (alas, they don't). The scientific, mathematical, and biological components of psychology quickly prompt new majors to recognize that a psychology degree won't be effortless. If psychology courses are taught properly, the major is far from easy (Halonen, 2012).

Psychology majors can function as therapists. Having a bachelor's degree in psychology does not mean you are a psychologist and can officially counsel people or do therapy. First, a bachelor's degree is an undergraduate degree, one signifying the completion of some breadth of study (what are usually called liberal arts or general education courses) coupled with study in one or more majors (like psychology). Undergraduate degrees are required before students can pursue graduate education — that is, intensive study in some area for a master's degree or a doctorate or some other advanced (also called *terminal*) degree. People who call themselves psychologists must usually have a doctorate (often a PhD, PsyD, or Master's) and must be licensed to practice. So, let's be crystal clear: Having an undergraduate degree does not entitle students to call themselves psychologists, nor can they perform professional-level therapy. As we shall see in Chapter 7, however, there is a variety of helping-oriented employment opportunities available for students who have an undergraduate degree in psychology.

To do any form of professional counseling, a person must have additional years of training — the average undergraduate completes a degree in 4 years, while a master's degree may require an additional 2 years and a doctorate can take 4 to 6 years or even longer. Advanced degrees in psychology and being admitted to graduate school in psychology are topics we discuss in detail in Chapters 10 and 11, so we will postpone going into further detail until then.

Psychology majors often relish having their friends come to them with their problems. Perhaps you've been told you are a good listener or someone who gives good advice. That's fine, so far as it goes. Just understand that in order to work as a professional psychologist offering guidance to people requires advanced training, a degree, and being licensed to practice, and involves processes that are much more nuanced than merely giving advice. If you want to become a clinician or a counselor, we encourage you to undertake the academic journey — just don't misrepresent yourself along the way.

Majors choose psychology so they can solve their own problems. Although students who have experienced emotional setbacks may be drawn to psychology as a major, there is little in the undergraduate curriculum that focuses on the development of insights into one's personal makeup. The degree concentrates on communicating concepts, principles, and theories about human behavior from the vantage point of science. The more direct route for deep insight into yourself and personal change is therapy, not baccalaureate study (Halonen, 2014).

The psychology major is a pathway to riches. The majority of psychology graduates do not go on into clinical psychology or graduate school, but instead use their degree to enter the workforce. Unfortunately, psychology majors who move into entry-level positions do tend to make relatively lower wages (Halonen, 2012). However, such salaries merely open the door to a career that may be rich in opportunities for promotion and substantial pay increases over time.

Table 2.2 lists the starting salaries of several college majors as of 2017. It is probably not surprising that students who major in traditional STEM fields have higher starting salaries than those who major in the other liberal arts. The starting salary for those with a social science degree was $46,707. The figures in the table are no

TABLE 2.2

Starting Salaries for Class of 2017 College Graduates

Computer science	$72,677
Engineering	$65,539
Mathematics and statistics	$60,631
Health science	$53,872
Business	$52,456
Social science	**$46,707**
History	$38,997
Communications	$38,897
Visual and performing arts	$37,887
English	$37,825

Information from: National Association of Colleges and Employers (2018)
https://www.naceweb.org/job-market/compensation/class-of-2017s-overall-starting
-salary-shows-little-gain/

guarantee that your friend who majored in communications is going to have a starting salary of $38,897 in her first job, of course, but they do indicate that students who
major in the liberal arts can hold their own in workforce competition.

A recent salary survey published by the APA shows that the median annual salary for employees (ages 25 to 59 years) who have a bachelor's degree in psychology
is $49,000. Degree recipients trained in some subfield of psychology earned more.
For example, people with training in industrial/organizational psychology earned a
median salary of $66,000, while those who specialized in social psychology made
a median salary of $51,000. For comparison, the median salary for people with a
bachelor's degree in any field, including psychology, was $61,000. Here is something
else to consider: Psychology majors who complete a graduate degree earn on average
33% more than those who only have a bachelor's degree (American Psychological
Association, 2016). **Figure 2.3** shows how median salaries differ according to type
of position. **Figure 2.4** compares the median salaries of different subspecialties in
psychology.

Of course, starting salaries aren't static; the potential to earn higher salaries,
depending on the context, improves over time with strong performance. Psychology
majors who pursue business positions, such as those in organizational psychology,
marketing, or consumer behavior, will likely earn on the higher end of the scale.
Those who go into social services will generally make less than the average. Regardless of major, starting salaries in the human service fields are going to be somewhat

FIGURE 2.3 Median Salaries by Position Type

Data from: APA Center for Workforce Studies

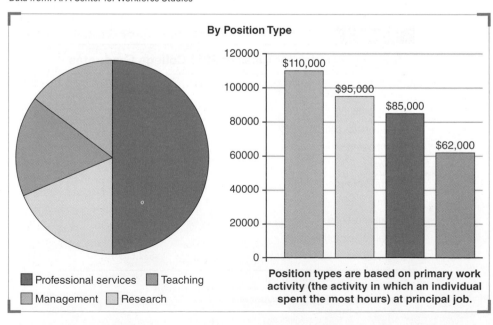

FIGURE 2.4 **Median Salaries by Field of Highest Degree**

Data from: 2015 National Survey of College Graduated, National Science Foundation

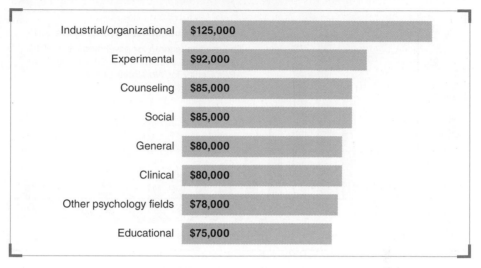

Industrial/organizational	$125,000
Experimental	$92,000
Counseling	$85,000
Social	$85,000
General	$80,000
Clinical	$80,000
Other psychology fields	$78,000
Educational	$75,000

lower than those in business, but people who opt to work in social services still can earn a respectable living.

Now, what about incomes for professional work? How much do psychologists earn? **Table 2.3** lists the average salaries for some groups of psychologists, and includes data on the average growth in salary that is related to the number of years of work experience. Note that these are averages — some psychologists earn less than shown here and others earn more.

According to the National Bureau of Labor Statistics (2013), the cost of living in a particular area also has an impact on how much you earn (California and metropolitan New York are more expensive than many places in the Midwest or the South, for example). Still, a cursory examination of the numbers in Table 2.3 indicates that

TABLE 2.3

Average Salaries for Psychologists

Experience	0–5 years	5–10 years	10–20 years	>20 years
Clinical psychologist	$69,000	$78,000	$90,000	$94,000
Counseling psychologist	$53.000	$64,000	$65,000	$72,000
Forensic psychologist	$60,000	$72,000	$82,000	$118,000
School psychologist	$54,000	$60,000	$66,000	$72,000
Industrial-organizational	$61,000	$94,000	$112,000	$131,000

Data from: Psychology Career Center (2018).

FIGURE 2.5 Can Psychology Make You Rich?

Data from: 2015 National Survey of College Graduated, National Science Foundation

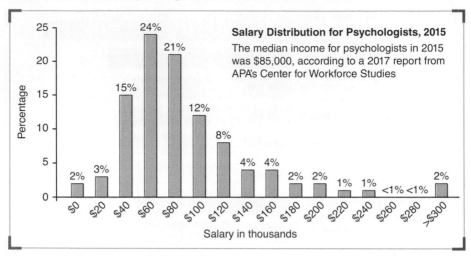

even though the typical psychologist makes a comfortable living, the vast majority would not be considered rich. **Figure 2.5** provides a frequency distribution that shows most psychologists in the comfortable range of annual incomes. So, while most psychologist do fine financially, they don't necessarily make "a considerable amount of money" (National Association of Colleges and Employers, 2014).

The belief that psychologists are wealthy tends to be fueled by extrapolating from how much people pay for therapy. Although a psychologist may charge as much as $200 per therapy hour, imagining that a psychologist earns that much every hour he or she works can make people overestimate income potential and develop fantasies of riches. At first blush, a 40-hour workweek should translate into a tidy haul of $8,000 a week. However, a full-time caseload realistically represents more like 20 than 40 hours of direct service, as psychologists need time for record writing, correspondence, marketing, consultation, and meetings. In addition, fees must cover the cost of office rental, support staff, an answering service, insurance, office supplies, and continuing education — and that is after taxes.

What the Psychology Major Is

In summary, the undergraduate psychology curriculum offers a splendid opportunity to learn about the behavior of living organisms from a scientific standpoint. As such, it proves to be very useful in the workplace in part because psychological principles can be applied to solve problems. And for high-performing and strongly motivated students, the undergraduate degree is a proving ground to demonstrate you can manage the challenge of a graduate program; from there, professional choices can be even more focused on the content and skills sets of psychology.

Thought Questions

1. Why is the discipline of psychology so frequently misunderstood?
2. In what way does psychology qualify as a science?
3. What myths complicate a layperson's understanding of psychology?
4. What misconceptions did I have about psychology before reading this chapter?
5. What are the key features of the undergraduate psychology curriculum?
6. What minors will provide the best support for my psychology major?
7. What are some inaccurate ideas about the nature of the psychology major?
8. Does my undergraduate program have a distinctive philosophy, orientation, or specialization?

Should You Major in Psychology?

Destiny is a name often given in retrospect
to choices that had dramatic consequences.

~J. K. Rowling, author of the Harry Potter series

Ever since he was a junior in high school, Dana knew that he wanted to be a psychologist and that majoring in psychology was more or less a foregone conclusion. Dana worked for his father the summer after his freshman year of college. He remembers sitting in the passenger seat of his father's car one summer afternoon, holding forth about why psychology interested him and how he was already hoping to attend graduate school. If graduate school turned out not to be in his future, he was sure that his psychology degree would provide him with lots of opportunities (though he was not sure what those might be). Dana remembers vividly how his father, a small-town businessperson, listened quietly and, never taking his eyes from the road, said pointedly, "Yes, but will you be able to support yourself?" In other words, would a degree in psychology pay the bills? Dana was speechless for a moment because he realized that he had never thought about the practical implications of majoring in psychology — he just *assumed* it would all work out, that he was following his passion, and so on. He remembers thinking, "Uh-oh."

■ ■ ■

Uh-oh, indeed. Although many people may applaud your choice of a psychology major, we suspect that you are likely to hear at least some concerns from friends and family about the wisdom of choosing psychology. Dana's father's concern about the economics underlying majoring in psychology is fairly typical and should encourage reflection: Should you — should anyone — major in psychology? We believe the answer can be a resounding "yes."

To that end, this chapter helps prepare you to become an effective psychology major. It makes sense to develop your rationale for choosing a psychology major from all the available options. It's inevitable. When you meet new people and they learn that you are in college, they will often ask what major you have chosen and why. You will be most impressive when you can explain your choice by describing your values and your professional goals with confidence. Basing your choice on your values and goals can also be important in helping you stay steady should the going get tough.

You may also need to address the other concerns that parents, friends, and loved ones often have about choosing the psychology major. We believe you can constructively respond to such concerns but you should have a solid understanding of their origins and the rationales behind them. It's a good idea for you to engage in some self-assessment: Is your personality a good fit for psychology? What are your current skills and interests?

In this chapter, we explore the familiar debate about whether to choose a career for meaning or for money, an important issue given the typical length of most people's work lives. We close the chapter by identifying and discussing the characteristics of students who don't make particularly good psychology majors.

Reflecting on Your Choice of Major

Pleasing the significant people in your life matters, but it can sometimes be challenging. They want what they believe is best for you and may have their own notions about what kind of major would be most suitable for you.

Many people will be enthusiastic about your choosing to major in psychology. From their own understanding of what the major entails (whether or not that understanding is accurate), they can envision psychology being a great match for your interests and talents. They will be receptive to the idea and excited that you have found an area of study that will sustain your interests over the course of your education. They may even ask exploratory questions about your experiences so they can share in your joy of discovery.

Nonetheless, it is not unreasonable for those who care about you to have some concern about your choice of major. Not surprisingly, the main concern often revolves around simple economics: Will a college major provide you with a reasonable salary following graduation? Will the salary also allow you to pay back any college loans, cover rent, and pay for all your other living expenses? These are real concerns that many people overlook or assume will take care of themselves once they find the "right" job. If you are a returning student majoring in psychology, you are already familiar with the challenges of the job market.

Many students pick majors that are practical (meaning those that ordinarily lead directly to employment) or that have a high payoff in the form of starting salary, job security, and so on. As a result, many students go to college and become business or economics majors because they assume that understanding accounting, marketing, finance, and related areas will assure them of a well-paying job right out of college. Or they look for majors that lead to jobs that are predictably in high demand, such as nursing or medical technology. Other students choose majors that have particular skills associated with them, including lab sciences like chemistry and biology as well as engineering or computer science. All of these majors are excellent choices for students who have both a genuine interest in them and are capable of learning the skills required to do well in their studies. In the case of most of the majors noted above, solid quantitative skills — that is, knowledge of math and statistics — are necessary.

Although psychology is a science (recall our discussion in Chapter 1), in higher education psychology is considered one of the traditional liberal arts majors. By **liberal arts**, we mean those areas of higher education that provide students with general knowledge (literature, mathematics, history, philosophy, as well as social sciences like sociology, political science, and anthropology) rather than specific technical knowledge (like that associated with the natural sciences or the applied sciences, including engineering) or specific training needed for a profession. Studying the liberal arts effectively teaches students how to learn because it emphasizes critical thinking, attentive reading, clear writing, and so on, all of which help people to develop general intellectual abilities that are transferable to a variety of situations, not to mention an array of jobs and careers.

Critics of the liberal arts tend to focus on the economics of such fields, but we must not overlook this important fact: Not everyone truly wants to commit to a particular academic path just because it can lead directly to a job; the pursuit of learning is sufficiently rewarding to justify their investment. Other students are unsure of what they want to do in the near future, let alone for the rest of their lives. Many students choose a major out of intrinsic interest in or even fascination with the topic (note that we are *not* claiming that professional or technical majors are not interesting or fascinating — just that students should pursue a discipline because they are truly drawn to it).

Following the recommendations or guidance of others without question is not a good idea, as you might simply settle for a major that isn't engaging or inspiring to you, thus making it hard to do your best work and stay in the major all the way through to graduation. Making a choice based on others' guidance can be problematic in other ways as well: Would you want to work in a field for 30 or 40 years if you really had no interest in it? If nothing else, the field of **positive psychology** demonstrates unequivocally that money does not guarantee happiness (Diener & Biswas-Diener, 2008). If you are not especially interested in the work demanded by some professional or technical majors, then your grades may end up reflecting that. Will employers want to hire people with high grade point averages (GPAs) or low ones? That answer is fairly obvious.

There are the real and personal costs that result from being persuaded to major in something that does not really speak to your heart and mind. Consider this cautionary tale: Several years ago a student — let's call her Maria — majored in education and psychology (in some states, people who major in education are required to have a second full major). At that time, teachers in elementary, middle, and high school were in great demand and the available jobs provided solid salaries and job security, not to mention the attractive 9-month cycle of teaching with summers off. Maria's parents pushed her to be a teacher because they believed it was a low-risk/high-payoff career. Maria performed well in her education and psychology classes. During the fall of her senior year, she did a stint of student teaching, which essentially involves being in a school classroom 5 days a week, learning from a supervising teacher and doing actual teaching. This was Maria's first and only teaching experience on the other side of the desk.

Halfway through the semester Maria went to see her academic advisor and reported that she was miserable. She never realized what went into being a teacher and she wanted no part of it. She spent the rest of her time in college — about five months — trying to figure out what she did like and what she might want to do in the future. Imagine spending more than three years of your life pursuing someone else's dream, one that turned out not to interest you in the least? We have had dozens of students who pursued a career in teaching and ultimately thrived in their occupational choice, but they made their choices on their own because they were interested in being teachers, not because it would satisfy their parents' (or someone else's) dreams.

What about economic and job security concerns — are they justified? Yes and no. Yes, it is reasonable for college graduates to become economically independent, buy their own homes, have good careers, start families, and so on. But no, as there is not much to be gained if students pursue majors that do not interest or motivate them, or to which they are not suited or, in some cases, for which they are not even qualified. What you need to do is to plan to work very hard to succeed in whatever major you eventually pick, whether it's psychology or something else.

If you do choose psychology, then you will want to develop skills that will help you do well in the job market or in whatever future you plan for yourself.

Knowing Yourself: Self-Assessment of Your Personality and Skills

Industrial and organizational (I/O) psychologists argue that people's *personalities* — their unique and consistent behavioral traits — can be linked to the type of work they do best. In fact, there are a variety of standardized occupation interest inventories that tie people's traits to vocational possibilities and enable them to do a **self-assessment** of their personality and skills. Your college or university's career services center may make these available to you; drop by and ask.

The same argument regarding personality can be made for choosing a college major — do your own traits, your likes and dislikes, fit the major or majors you are considering? Use *Measuring Up: Take Your Full Measure* to identify whether you possess some traits that might be a good fit for a psychology major.

↑
▭▭▭ **Measuring Up**

Taking Your Full Measure

- What are your best features or skills?
- Do you like interacting with people one-on-one? What about in groups?
- Do you like to work alone or do you prefer to be part of a team?
- Do people tend to seek you out for advice?
- What activities do you enjoy? Why?
- Do you have any particular hobbies or things you do when you aren't studying or working?
- What would your perfect work environment be like?
- Do you deal with interpersonal conflict well?
- What creates stress for you? Did part of any past job make you feel stressed?
- How do you manage stress?
- Do you like to work on small details or do you prefer the "big picture"?
- How do you define success?
- Does your life have a purpose? What is your destiny?
- What would you like to be known and remembered for in the long run?
- To make the world a better place, what would you change? Why?
- What is the one word you use to describe yourself?
- What is one word others might use to describe you?

If you are unsure about how to answer some of these questions, think back to any jobs (including part-time or summer jobs) you have had. What aspects of the job(s) did you like? What specifically appealed to you? Was there anything that you did not like about the work? If you currently have a job, you might start keeping a journal in which you write at the end of each workday about what you like and dislike about the job. Doing so may help you reach some conclusions about how much autonomy you like to have, if you like working alone or with others, if doing desk work is appealing to you, and so on. The fit between the person and the environment — the worker and the setting — matters.

Seeking a Fit Between You and a Working Environment

Psychologist John Holland (1996, 1997) developed what is known as a **trait model** of career choice, one designed to help people link their personality qualities (e.g., interests, needs, skills, values, learning styles, attitudes) to particular settings where work occurs. His model categorizes individuals into one of six personal orientations and organizes occupations into one of six work environments. All else being equal, a person with a particular personality orientation should prefer to be in the linked work environment. Holland's main point is that people express their personalities, particularly their interests and values, in the work they choose to do. People who end up in educational or work environments that fit or are relatively close fits to their personality are more likely than others to be fulfilled, successful, and determined in what they do in their major and career. In the long run, those with a good fit are apt to remain in their chosen careers longer than those who are less satisfied with their work.

Holland's (1996, 1997) six personal orientations are summarized in **Table 3.1.** Most people identify more than one orientation that could describe their personality.

TABLE 3.1

Holland's Six Personal Orientations

Realistic. The realistic personality orientation values concrete and physical tasks. Realistic people perceive themselves as possessing mechanical skills but they generally believe they lack social or interpersonal skills. They are drawn to manual and athletic activities and enjoy using tools and machines. They tend to be practical and focused on solving problems.

Investigative. Individuals with an investigative personal orientation love to solve scientific, intellectual, and mathematical puzzles and problems. They view themselves as being methodical, self-reflective, critical, curious, and highly analytical. They value their independence and enjoy taking courses in the physical and biological sciences, as well as in mathematics and chemistry.

Artistic. People with an artistic personal orientation are drawn to unstructured projects that provide freedom and breadth to explore and express feeling and emotion. Such projects include painting, sculpture, music, writing, and dramatic performance. People with this orientation see themselves as independent, free-spirited, expressive, and imaginative. They like to be innovative.

Social. People with a social personal orientation are drawn toward educational, helping, and religious careers. They like to work with others, especially on teams, and to work toward achieving group goals. Such people take pleasure in socially engaging settings, such as religious communities or schools, as well as groups that involve reading, music, and theater. They tend to be cooperative, friendly, conscientious, persuasive, and insightful. Social people are sensitive to others' needs and greatly value social and educational issues.

Enterprising. People with an enterprising personal orientation like to lead, motivate, inspire, and persuade others, especially where selling material goods or convincing people to adopt particular views are involved. They value economic and political achievement, relish the chance to supervise, and enjoy exerting control as well as being recognized for their verbal expressiveness. Being powerful, wealthy, and possessing status is appealing to them. They perceive themselves to be extroverted, sociable, happy, self-confident, and popular, and they have little trouble asserting themselves.

Conventional. People with a conventional personal orientation like order and prefer to engage in systematic, concrete tasks that are prescribed and use both verbal and quantitative data. They see themselves as conformists and tend to identify with their clerical and numerical abilities. They excel at following rules and orders and typically are very detail oriented. They are drawn to straightforward rather than open-ended problems.

Information from: Holland (1996, 1997).

To begin, try to select the one type from Holland's six orientations that is the best fit for you. Then choose a second and a third, but keep in mind that these are all idealized types — no one person will fit any type or types perfectly.

Now we turn to descriptions of the work environments that link to those personal orientations. **Table 3.2** has summaries of these work environments, along with a list of some representative college majors. As you review these six environments and their related majors, ask yourself whether each of the three personal orientations that most closely describe you are linked to work environments that sound pleasing to you and whether they would be plausible options for you.

TABLE 3.2

Holland's Six Work Environments Linked to Personal Orientations

Realistic settings. Realistic work environments are characterized by the presence of concrete, physical tasks that use mechanical skills, physical motion, and considerable persistence at tasks. Sample careers include draftsperson, automobile mechanic, law enforcement or corrections officer, electrician, engineer, cook or chef, pilot, and machine operator. Sample majors include electrical or aerospace engineering, architecture, criminal justice, and environmental studies.

Investigative settings. Work environments that are investigative include research laboratories, scientific groups or teams, and medical settings in which case conferences are held. Sample careers include computer programmer, clinical psychologist, veterinarian, dentist, marine biologist, physician, physician's assistant, and chemist. Sample majors include computer science, biology, biochemistry, astronomy, and anthropology.

Artistic settings. Artistic work environments include concert or performing halls; theaters; libraries; radio or television studios; and art, photography, design, or music studios. Sample careers include actor, painter, advertiser, sculptor, musician, author, editor, designer, photographer, interior designer, and architect. Sample majors include English, art, art history, interior design, graphic art, advertising, architecture, design, and interior design.

Social settings. Social settings include hospitals; colleges and universities; public and private schools; churches, temples, and synagogues; recreational centers; and mental health organizations, including psychiatrist's offices and social service agencies. Sample careers include counselor, teacher, professor, nurse, social worker, judge, minister, rabbi, sociologist, and psychologist. Sample majors include human development, psychology, philosophy, sociology, religious studies, education, special education, and social work.

Enterprising settings. Enterprising work settings include places like advertising companies, courtrooms, congressional offices, car sales offices, retail stores, and real estate firms. Sample careers include attorney, realtor, politician, salesperson, and manager. Sample majors include business administration, economics, broadcasting, hospitality and tourism, industrial relations, and finance.

Conventional settings. Conventional work settings are office settings generally, as well as banks, post offices, any business office, and filing rooms. Sample careers include receptionist, financial counselor, accountant, banker, bookkeeper, data processor, office clerk, and court reporter. Sample majors include accounting, finance, medical records, mathematics, and statistics.

Information from: Holland (1996, 1997).

The goal of reviewing these personal orientations, work settings, and majors is to get you to think about yourself by identifying — and ranking — your top three personal orientations. For example, in **Holland code**, you could be an RCE (realistic, conventional, enterprising) or an SEA (social, enterprising, artistic). Assessing your three-letter Holland code in detail is beyond the scope of this book. Instead, we want to get you thinking on your own about your orientations, possible work settings, and potential goals for the future. You may be wondering which three-letter Holland code psychologists tend to have. It's SIA (social, investigative, artistic). Psychologists — but not *all* psychologists, of course — tend to be sociable and inquisitive and to have an appreciation for the arts.

If you selected these three letters as your Holland code, then a psychology major might be a solid choice for you. On the other hand, if you are or want to be a psychology major but did not choose all three — or even any of the three — psychologists tend toward, don't despair. All the Holland code indicates is that at this point in time you may (or may not) have interests that are similar to those of psychologists who earned their doctorate. Your code may change over time or it might not; remember, it's meant to be a guide, not a definitive diagnostic tool. This is one piece of information that you can think about along with your responses to the preference and "like/dislike" questions that are at the start of this section. You can then add these bits of data to your other responses, including those in which you identify your reasons for choosing the psychology major.

If thinking about your traits and skills and how they might fit into various workplaces interests you, then consider taking advantage of some of the resources available on your own campus. If your college or university is like most, there is probably a career services or career development office that helps students find internships and later, jobs. (Our **Major Success** profile for this chapter features a psychology major who entered the psychology workforce and became a professional advisor.) Why not drop by or make an appointment to learn what services are available to help you plan your future career?

Know Your Motives (Meaning versus Money)

Being happy is a good motive for making some choices rather than others regarding education, work, and career. No one would complain about accepting a job that pays a very high salary but, as we already noted, pursuing well-paying work just for the sake of money is unlikely to lead to real happiness. Research demonstrates that once people exceed an income of about $75,000 per year, their happiness levels do not change much (Kahneman & Deaton, 2010); in effect, more money does not buy more happiness. Moreover, as people make more money, the time they need to devote to work increases substantially. Ironically, by putting in more hours to maintain or increase their income, they subsequently have less time to devote to leisure and recreation. More money generally means less fun outside of work and less time for relaxation, which tends to mean no increase in happiness (Kahneman, Krueger, Schkade, Schwarz, & Stone, 2006). Making a good living to cover existing expenses is important, but something is lost if happiness is sacrificed in the process. Making more money, then, is unlikely to be a worthy motive for you to pursue with abandon.

A **Major** Success Story ‹‹‹

Jane Halonen

Tim Moore,
BA, Academic Advisor

FIGURE 3.1 Professional advisor Tim Moore offers career advice to psychology major Gage Moyer.

How to Stay on Campus Without Homework

Tim was not sure what kind of psychology he wanted to pursue after graduation. He just knew that thinking about behavior and predicting what people will do under various circumstances was satisfying. Tim loved his college experience and was really appreciative of how much personal development he gained through campus life. He also knew he did not want to commit to graduate or professional school. Although he viewed his desire to help people as one of his most important values, he was tired of homework and deadlines and wanted to see what kind of career options he had with his undergraduate degree.

Tim's occupational solution was ideal. He became an academic advisor at the campus he loved and was able to pursue the satisfying professional goal of helping undergraduate students reap the most benefits from their own college experiences. Tim cites the extensive experience he had in developing his communication skills in his major as essential to his success. Tim honed his listening skills, demonstrating expertise in probing students' answers to his questions. He learned how to help groups make good decisions, an ability that comes in handy in his sponsorship of a campus fraternity. His strong problem-solving skills are put to the test every day, and Tim faces the challenge with confidence.

Best advice? "Although this is your decision to make, do not hesitate to seek advice; there are plenty of people willing and able to listen or help. To ensure the greatest fulfillment in your chosen career, consider what you value, enjoy doing, are passionate about and are good at. Realize that your college major or current work experience does not limit you to one specific occupation or direction."

›››

A better motive is to search for work that provides meaning and satisfaction in your life. By **meaning**, we refer to having a sense of direction in life, as well as possessing coherent values and a personal philosophy. If you see meaning in what you do — in why you are following one major and not another, one career path instead of another — then you will have a strong sense of purpose to guide you. Each day (or most days) you will approach your studies or your work with commitment, interest, and sometimes joy. In fact, doing work that is enjoyable provides a feeling of fulfillment — what we do improves us as people and makes the world we live in a much better place to be (Wrzesniewski, Rozin, & Bennett, 2003).

One way to approach the issue of meaning is to reflect on how you view your work. Professionals tend to see their work as falling into one of three categories: jobs, careers, and vocations. We've used the word "career" in a broad way in this chapter; now we will contrast it with these two other terms.

Jobs. A **job** is a source of income to support life outside of work. Jobs can provide financial security but the people who hold them often derive little satisfaction from the work they do — it's literally just a job. For example, people who work a job would not recommend others choose their line of work (and if they themselves could do it all over again, they would do something else). Jobholders continually anticipate weekends, holidays, and vacations; most cannot wait to retire.

Careers. Having a **career** means holding a position for long enough to succeed in it before receiving a promotion and moving on to the next (higher) position. The particular work in a career is sometimes challenging or interesting, sometimes not. However, to rise higher — to get the next pay raise, the more important title, the bigger office, and so on — people with careers have to do reasonably well in their positions. Promotions indicate that someone pursuing a career is working well and is successfully competing with (and perhaps advancing past) coworkers. Careers have a competitive element so that careerists are often looking for the next opportunity.

Vocations. Having a **vocation** is like following a calling, where work is an integral part of a person's life, providing satisfaction, pleasure, and identity. People who have a vocation love what they do, tell others about it, often socialize with peers who do the same or similar work, and belong to organizations that relate to it. People in a vocation routinely bring their work home and may take it with them on vacation (but are not usually workaholics). They do not long for retirement (many don't look forward to retiring; quite a few don't plan to stop working if they can help it). Work is more or less play, as well as a source of meaning and purpose.

Now, which would you prefer to have: a job, a career, or a vocation?

What we do know is that people who see their work as a vocation manage to blend the eagerness for what they do with the responsibilities inherent in the work (Wrzesniewski, McCauley, Rozin, & Schwartz, 1997). Quite simply, people who have a vocation are more satisfied with their work and their lives compared to those who have jobs or careers, and they devote more time to their work than those in the other groups. Very often people who have a vocation indicate that working is more satisfying than leisure, presumably because they are passionate about what they do.

We are not trying to push you to seek a vocation over a job or a career; however, there are clear advantages associated with enjoying what you do on a daily basis. People who have a vocation are dedicated to what they do, so much so that others take notice. Although money, status, promotions, influence, and the like do not particularly motivate them, many people who have a vocation acquire these things anyway because others recognize their sincere commitment to their work and to the ideals embodied within it. Bear in mind, of course, that while some callings (e.g., caring for children or older adults, running a not-for-profit organization) can lead to satisfaction and sometimes even civic accolades, they may not provide ample salaries.

Only you can decide what your vocation, if you are to have one, will be. Perhaps psychology — and being a psychology major — represents a good start. If not, perhaps our discussion has pointed you in another direction, toward a different major that captures your imagination and motivates passion and commitment on your part. We suggest that meaning may simply be a more important life commodity than money (assuming the latter is available to provide you with sufficient support).

Choosing Psychology and Sharing Your Choice

Let's imagine you do choose to be a psychology major. In this chapter and in Chapter 1, we explored perspectives that support your choice. You should be well prepared to explain, and perhaps even defend. your choice of major based on correcting misconceptions, clarifying issues of fit, and communicating how careful you have been in considering the consequences of your choice. We raise some other points that can help you explain why psychology makes sense as your major.

If you are a nontraditional-aged student, you might think that you will be in for less grief about your major choice. You may be right. Your friends and loved ones may expect that your life experience has helped you make an informed choice. But don't be surprised if you are on the receiving end of a lot of teasing or eye rolling. Being a nontraditional-aged student provides a lot of advantages (See **Reality Check:** **The Older Psychology Major**), but it doesn't prevent other people from offering their opinions about your choices.

 **Reality Check**

The Older Psychology Major

Some readers of this book may be *nontraditional* students, that is, some of you are older and more experienced than traditional 18- to 22-year-old college students. You are starting or returning to college after doing other things. For example, you may already have lived on your own, held one or more jobs, and even started a family. Your seasoned perspective will likely set you apart from your traditional-aged counterparts in the classroom (Weaver & Qi, 2005).

Because of life experiences, nontraditional students:

☐ tend to be highly motivated and want to get the most they can from their college major and their undergraduate education;
☐ are usually well-prepared for each class meeting;
☐ are very likely to participate actively in the classroom and usually don't worry about how their peers or instructors will react to their comments and ideas;
☐ are often confident and very likely to interact with their instructors;
☐ react favorably to the structured nature of college courses and enjoy learning about the course subject;
☐ tend to be less tolerant of classroom activity that strays from the course objectives.

If you are a nontraditional student, you have had more time to consider your options and you may be more certain about your intended career path, including your choice of psychology as a major.

Value-Added Benefits of Majoring in Psychology

Although a psychology major can ultimately provide meaningful career direction, there are significant secondary gains that arise from mastering psychological content and skill at the undergraduate level (Cherry, 2014). These include:

Strengthening your self-regulation abilities. Psychology majors often learn how to manage their home and work environments to keep things running well. In other words, they are adept at **self-regulation**. They believe they know the value of establishing goals and can implement reward strategies to improve the likelihood of meeting those goals. They are intentional in minimizing distractions and avoid multitasking because it nearly always produces poorer performance. They also learn strategies for unleashing their creativity.

Enhancing your ability to lead. Psychology majors tend to be effective at paying attention to both the outcomes of discussions and the process through which those outcomes develop. Their awareness of the quality of individual contributions and interactions tends to improve the caliber of the whole outcome. They conscientiously solicit opinions from all members and deal with conflict in a way that strengthens both the solutions and the relationships among group members.

Improving your communication skills. Because the psychology curriculum promotes well-developed observation and inference skills, psychology majors can become better at reading people than some nonmajors. They learn that good eye contact is an important part of building trust and they carefully interpret nonverbal communications to decode nuances. They can be more adaptable in dealing with people who don't share their heritage or experiences, treading carefully and sensitively when surprised in interpersonal interactions.

Deepening your empathy and understanding. Awareness of human emotion can lead to deeper self-understanding and also undergird perspective-taking skills (i.e., recognizing others' points of view as well as your own). Emotions are fleeting, and psychology majors recognize more readily than others that bad situations and unpleasant feelings are most likely temporary, not permanent.

Improving the quality of your decisions. Psychology majors learn about the array of cognitive errors that humans are inclined to make. They recognize when defense mechanisms may distort perceptions. They learn to look for disconfirming evidence to minimize confirmation biases (seeing what they expect to see) and to avoid holding onto discounted beliefs. They also learn systematic strategies for making sound decisions. Their reliance on objective evidence makes them less likely to be exploited.

Sharpening your memory skills and improving grades. Understanding how memory works can produce significant alterations in study style. For example, the popular technique of highlighting textbooks as you read does little to enhance your ability to recall or apply concepts on exam (Dunlosky et al., 2013). Psychology majors recognize that cramming is not going to produce long-term learning and arrange their study environments to maximize their success (e.g., few or no available distractions, quiet, well lit). They are more inclined to test themselves on material until they achieve a level of mastery and they can usually judge accurately when they have studied or prepared sufficiently to turn in their best performances.

Strengthening your financial management strategies. Psychology majors understand the importance of making short-term sacrifices for long-term gains. They recognize that the fun of acquiring new shoes, the latest video game, or a new cell phone is temporary and pales in comparison with the rewards of investing that same money in an account that compounds interest over time.

Engaging in healthier behavior. Psychology majors learn tools for managing healthy lifestyles. They often study the deleterious effects of poor nutrition, drug abuse, smoking, and sleep deprivation. They are systematic and disciplined in pursuing wellness because they know optimal physical condition predicts optimal performance. They can implement behavior-modification strategies to make more effective choices about their health and live longer, healthier lives.

All of these are some of the side benefits of majoring in psychology, but we also recommend that you consider the possibility — even if it seems remote — that psychology might not be the best major for you.

Some Reasons *Not* to Major in Psychology

Although we are blessed and grateful to have worked with an abundance of talented and committed psychology majors over time, we also know that some students who declare the major and unhappily stick it out to the end probably would have fared better by going in another direction. Here is our typology of students who should consider some other options.

The Clinical-or-Bust Major

Perhaps fueled by images of clinical psychologists in the media, many students commit to the psychology major, but not to the major as it really is, rather to the major they wish it were. These **clinical-or-bust majors** envision being immersed in clinically oriented courses, solving problems with clients, and making life better for those who seek their expert advice. They choose psychology because of their powerful desire to help others and tend to see a psychology major as their best or only option. Typically, these students are startled and perhaps even disgruntled by how little clinical coursework the undergraduate major involves. Similarly, they aren't thrilled by the many requirements (e.g., statistics, research) that appear to them to have nothing to do with clinical service.

We applaud students who want to devote themselves to helping others; it is a noble goal. However, psychology represents just one avenue for achieving that goal and just one of many distinctive pathways represented in the helping professions. The person who flourishes in a psychology career is one who is conversant in research and who learns to rely heavily on existing research in picking and choosing clinical interventions. If the rigor of psychological research is not attractive, then other help-ing disciplines may have greater appeal. For example, majors in social work or educa-tion may be more likely to lead to fulfilling careers as professional helpers and their research practices may be a better fit as well. There are many ways to enter helping or human service professions and a major in psychology is not required for most of them.

The Anti-Science Major

Declaring a science major means committing to prescribed scientific protocols as well as the values and ethics that support good scientific practices. It means learning how to exercise creativity in predicting or defining relationships among variables, demonstrating patience in working out procedural details, imposing disciplined con-trol over extraneous matters, and executing research plans with precision. Good sci-ence majors tend to be conscientious and attentive to matters of detail.

Anti-science majors are psychology majors with no real feel for science. They begin to struggle in the major when the research and statistics sequence begins. They may fret that they can't come up with appropriately creative ideas. They often select problems that are too large to explore (e.g., "I want to cure child abuse") for the time-frame of a course project. They may find statistical analysis a time-consuming and even frightening burden.

Failure to embrace psychology as a science simply means the major won't be very much fun since the bulk of the major is geared toward scientific rather than applied training. Students who struggle with the science components of psychology might want to pursue majors that emphasize social rather than scientific elements.

The Avoidant Reader Major

An unfortunate trend in college life that has been attributed to students being overscheduled is a dramatic decrease in reading and studying academic material (O'Brien, 2010). Ironically, students are voracious readers when it comes to process-ing information from the Internet, especially in social media, but their natural curi-osity and enthusiasm just doesn't typically extend to college reading assignments.

Research findings suggest that contemporary college students don't put in the time required to become masters of subjects they are pursuing (Weir, 2009). Although it may be reasonable to assume you can get by in some subject matters without doing the reading, we make the case that this is harder to do in psychology. Why? Because without doing the required reading, students have to navigate using common sense. As we discussed earlier, common sense and psychology don't reliably lead to the same conclusions. Therefore, the student who doesn't do the reading will perpetually struggle in the absence of a deep understanding of the course content.

If you don't enjoy reading most college-level assignments, we recommend that you spend some time thinking about the kinds of reading that feel less onerous. Those content areas might help you find a major that would be a better fit. Alternatively, if no reading holds any attraction for you, you might reconsider whether a college degree is the right path for you. Acknowledging that you hate to read may be just the liberating conclusion to help you find another meaningful goal to guide your future.

The Refuge Major

Students change majors quite a bit in college (Lederman, 2017). On average, one third of all college students change majors within their first three years of study. As many as one out of every 10 will change majors at least twice. We've met many individuals who just couldn't settle in, changing as many as five or six times before walking across the stage at graduation. According to Lederman, 31% of social science majors change majors at least once. Many students move into psychology because exposure to psychology content just feels right and may be intrinsically motivating. The first major just may not have been a good fit, and psychology fills the bill.

However, one pattern we have become aware of in changes of major is students' tendency to declare psychology as a major after washing out in another major. Many students select psychology for their second run because they think it will be easy. They take refuge in psychology but may not have the intrinsic interest in the discipline that will sustain them through the challenging times. Having failed at their first choice, they want a major that is safe, pleasant, and unchallenging. On the surface, psychology seems to satisfy those criteria.

Whether you are transferring to the psychology major after having had a bad experience with another major of you are just in need of some professional advising expertise to make the most of your experience, it is a great idea to sit down with an academic advisor, particularly one well versed in the demands of the psychology major, to talk over your plans. Describe what you expect from psychology courses and discuss your aspirations. How do you see psychology helping you to get where you want to go? It may be that other majors are better suited to the goals you have in mind.

The Driftwood Major

The vast majority of students with whom we work thrive in the major. They are energized by the challenges presented in the courses and rise to them by doing their best work. However, a substantial number of students are **driftwood majors** — they declare the major and then attempt to float their way through to graduation. Their creative ideas are uninspired. They don't develop assigned projects completely and often attempt to submit them past deadlines. They regularly let their project group members down. In general, they are an unexcitable lot. Ironically, they often try to negotiate for extra credit at the end of a course to salvage grades that may be beyond repair. They graduate with low GPAs and tend to have few ideas about how to apply what they have learned toward their future. They often show up in faculty offices two weeks before graduation and ask, "How do I get a job in psychology?"

To us, this lack of fit is the saddest situation of all. Students possess the ability but simply never engendered the kind of enthusiasm that makes the work less like work. Instead of embarking on a new path that might be more intrinsically satisfying, they rationalize that they should stay in the psychology major since they have already invested so much time in it. This situation represents the *sunk cost* scenario, in which a person settles for a path that is expedient rather than pursuing a better alternative that might prove more engaging.

Adrift students should analyze whether problematic fit is the primary reason for their lackluster performance. Overscheduling, learning disabilities without appropriate compensating strategies, uneven performance due to emotional challenges, food insecurity, problematic study habits, and an absence of motivation or drive can all contribute to academic performance that will result in poor grades. These qualities will also potentially alienate their professors, the very people on whom they might be counting for a strong letter of reference. Student services usually provide access to skilled counselors who can evaluate whether another pathway might lead in a different direction, one in which the student might perform better.

You Are What You Do: Why You Should Major in Psychology

Choosing a college major is an important decision, one of the most important ones you will make in your life — so why not select a course of study that you can be enthusiastic about? Why not choose psychology? Psychology is a wonderful, exciting, and ever-expanding area of study. What could be more interesting or revealing than learning about why people — including you — behave as they do? You will quickly learn that you get out of psychology as much as you put into it. Although it's possible to muddle through almost any academic major, why would you want to? Choose a major that satisfies your heart, soul, and mind. We think psychology might just be the right choice for you.

Thought Questions

1. Do you know another myth about psychology that is not covered in this chapter? Can the material in this chapter help you to dispel it?
2. What concerns, if any, do you have about majoring in psychology?
3. What excites you about majoring in psychology?
4. Are there any other majors you are considering? Are they similar to or different from psychology?
5. Besides those we discussed in this chapter, do you have any other motives for choosing to major in psychology?
6. What goals and values underlie your rationale for choosing a psychology major?
7. What will you say to well-meaning people who try to dissuade you from pursuing a major in psychology?
8. What are some options you can pursue if psychology turns out not to be a good fit?
9. How will you embrace psychology? List some reasons that psychology is apt to be the right choice for you.

CHAPTER 4

Building Psychology-Related Skills and Attitudes

The cure for boredom is curiosity. There is no cure for curiosity.

~Dorothy Parker, American writer and satirist

Although there is no standard curriculum for psychology (Stoloff et al., 2010), there are standard expectations about the kinds of skills and attitudes students should acquire or refine during their pursuit of a psychology major. The major will probably involve taking 12 to 15 psychology courses. Lower division classes provide a general introduction to a broad array of concepts and theories in psychology. Upper division courses cover specialized areas of psychology in greater depth.

It can be all too easy to get caught up in ticking off your list of required courses and forget that your primary goal in obtaining a degree in psychology is to build a knowledge base, refine the strategies you use in psychology to solve problems, and hone the attitudes and habits that will serve you well after graduation.

■ ■ ■

Jane and Dana both have regular opportunities to serve as psychology program reviewers. As a routine part of their visits to other departments, they interview students who are just about to graduate and ask, "Now that you are almost ready to finish, what have you learned to do as the result of your study of psychology?" Sometimes students react with a wide-eyed speechless pause. They can often readily tell us their GPA and list the courses they have taken but they don't know how to describe how their thinking and attitudes have changed as a result of being in the psychology major. They haven't really thought through how what they have learned will be useful to them in the future. How can this be?

There is a simple explanation. The focus of higher education has historically been on transmitting the content of the various disciplines Professors tended to frame their jobs as lecturing, assuming that students' relevant skills would change implicitly as the result of learning about the discipline and completing the course requirements. More recently, professors have come to realize that students do not necessarily recognize or have a thorough understanding about how their thinking and values will change based on their learning. Without any informal assessment or even acknowledgment of the changes that their professors expect, it is no wonder that so many students are unable to describe, or fail to grasp, the cognitive changes that they have undergone from their major.

In 1995, Barr and Tagg proposed that it was time for a new paradigm in higher education. They characterized the traditional way of teaching classes in higher education as a **content-centered approach** and described many problems involved with using this strategy. Chief among the concerns was that the learning that students did in a content-centered approach tended to be geared toward passing content tests and didn't produce learning that endures. An unfortunate by-product of this is that it encourages students to care substantially more about the grade they receive than the transformative possibilities of their learning. Barr and Tagg argued that a **learning-centered approach,** in which the professor's job moves beyond sharing content to explicitly focus on skill development, would produce much longer-lasting learning.

Many important stakeholders in higher education have embraced the idea that an undergraduate degree should produce transformative effects not just in what student know but in how they think. The implications of the paradigm shift are huge. First, learning-centered courses move the teacher from being the **sage on the stage** to being the **guide on the side** (King, 1993). This approach often substantially increases student engagement and promotes persistence to complete the degree. Higher education scholars refer to such activity as **high-impact practice (HIP)** (Kuh, 2008). Consequently, universities have a stake in getting more faculty to use active-learning or high impact strategies because these correlate to more success (Kuh, 2008).

Academic departments now experience pressure to conduct formal assessment planning as part of accreditation processes. Accreditors oversee and validate the quality of academic programs across the country to ensure that universities have evidence that they are fulfilling the mission and vision they advertise to students. Accreditors can be part of regional associations that make judgments about the academic fitness of institutions or they can be affiliated with professional organizations, including those affiliated with such disciplines as chemistry, engineering, nursing, and even theatre, in which case the focus is on accrediting specific disciplinary programs.

To comply with accrediting mandates, faculty members participate in assessment planning that typically goes beyond the grading of tests. They must articulate explicit learning goals, design assignments that give students ample opportunity to achieve those goals, and use the results of their findings to improve their programs. Mature programs not only collect data on how well students are learning the content but tend to focus on how well students exhibit the expected learning skills (Stanny & Halonen, 2011). This helps the programs move toward continuous improvement. Ideally, students should also receive feedback about how effective they are in demonstrating the skills.

In this chapter, we help you answer the following important questions: What are you learning to do, and what attitudes or values are you developing in your major? First, we look at the popularity of the psychology major and explore more deeply the emerging concept of psychological literacy. Next, we discuss the American Psychological Association's (2013) *Guidelines for the Undergraduate Psychology Major*, which most departments have adopted to guide their curriculum and assessment planning. We correlate undergraduate student-learning outcomes to the workforce skills that employers appreciate. We conclude the chapter with a discussion of the metacognitive changes—in effect, how you think about your thinking and what you learn to value—that are likely to happen in your outlook and attitude as the result of studying psychology.

The Status of the Undergraduate Psychology Major

Psychology is a wildly popular undergraduate degree. It is typically among the top five majors on any campus and in some schools, it is the most popular major. See **Figure 4.1** to understand the substantial growth that has taken place in psychology at all levels, but particularly note the dramatic growth in psychology at the bachelor's level. Consider this: Out of the 1.92 million bachelor's degrees that were conferred in the 2016–2017 academic year, 124,497 (6.2%) went to psychology majors (American Psychological Association, 2018). Nationally, that percentage made psychology the fourth-most popular college major, after business, health professions and related programs, and social science and history.

Speculations abound as to why the major is so popular (Halonen, 2011). On the negative side, substantial numbers of students choose psychology because they are under the false impression that the major is an easy one. They are usually disabused of this perception when their first exams are returned. On a more positive side, psychology is accurately seen as providing added value to a liberals arts degree. For example, McGovern et al. (2010, p. 25) found that "undergraduate psychology — whether

FIGURE 4.1 Growth of psychology degrees from 1950–2017

Data from: Norcross, J. C. (2015, August 7). Undergraduate study in psychology: What APA's national survey tells and warns. American Psychological Association convention. Toronto, Canada and NCES, Digest of Education Statistics, 2017.

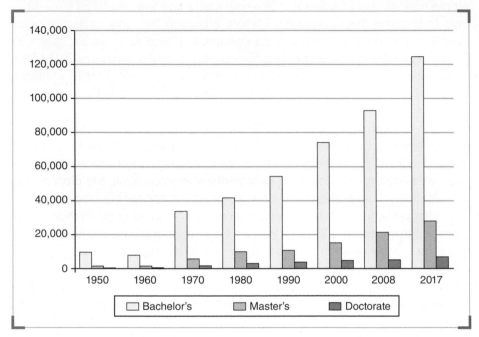

one course, several, or a full major — offers the very best potential of liberal learning. It is at the juncture of the humanities and the sciences where students gain the human-focused values and the scientific tools necessary to see and to care about the human condition and to improve it." A somewhat more succinct description of the value of studying psychology comes from one of our colleagues, who suggests that you should "study psychology so you won't be a jerk!" Both approaches point to the practical value of the major in navigating increasingly complex contemporary life.

The Emergence of Psychological Literacy

We introduced the concept of *psychological literacy* in Chapter 1. Boneau first coined the term in a classic survey published in 1990 in the journal *American Psychologist*. He surveyed textbook authors to determine whether he could identify the 100 psychology concepts that were most important to an undergraduate education. (Note that this research represents a perfect example of the idea that the curriculum is primarily about content.) Cranney and Dunn (2011a) defined psychological literacy as an adaptive and intentional application of psychology to meet personal, professional, and societal needs. The broadening of the paradigm takes into account what students learn to do, how they learn to think, and what they value in the major (e.g., Cranney et al., 2014).

The APA sponsored the Puget Sound Conference on Undergraduate Education in 2008, in part to develop a blueprint for an undergraduate curriculum that would effectively train students to become psychologically literate (Halpern, 2010). McGovern et al. (2010, p. 11) described the contemporary components of psychological literacy as including:

- having a well-defined vocabulary and basic knowledge of the main subject matter of psychology;
- valuing the intellectual challenges required to use scientific thinking and the disciplined analysis of information to evaluate various courses of action;
- taking a creative and amiably skeptical (friendly, but critically constructive) approach to problem solving;
- applying psychological principles to personal, social, and organizational issues in work, personal, and civic matters;
- acting ethically;
- being competent in using and evaluating information and technology;
- communicating effectively in different modes and with many different audiences;
- recognizing, understanding, and fostering respect for diversity; and
- being insightful and reflective about one's own and others' behavior and mental processes.

People developing the knowledge base and capacities described in the list fulfill the Puget Sound Conference's goal of fostering psychologically literate citizens. One person who personifies psychological literacy is discussed in *A Major Success Story: A Daily Dose of a Psychology Major*.

National Guidelines on Undergraduate Psychology

In 2000, the American Psychological Association appointed a task force to develop some guidelines to determine the appropriate learning goals for undergraduate psychology programs (Halonen, 2014). The first set of guidelines, originally published in 2002 and formally approved by the APA in 2007, proposed ten goals to accomplish the job. The guidelines differentiated goals for the foundation of effective psychological thinking from those that more generally contribute to the development of liberal arts skills.

The APA requires an official review and revision of policy approximately every ten years. A new task force gathered information about the utility and helpfulness of the first set of guidelines, which prompted the revision group to make some important changes. They collapsed the original 10 goals into 5:

- Knowledge base in psychology
- Critical thinking and scientific inquiry
- Communication
- Ethical and social responsibility in a diverse world
- Professional development

Jon Stewart
Bachelor's Degree

FIGURE 4.2

A Daily Dose of a Psychology Major

Former psychology major Jon Stewart, who was both the host of and a writer for the very popular *Daily Show*, managed to revolutionize the way people stay current with contemporary events. Jon provides a superb example of the characteristics of the psychologically literate citizen and how those characteristics prepare people for workforce success. Critics called Jon "the most trusted name in fake news." His satirical approach to the news helped him capture a shelf full of Emmys and several Peabody Awards for excellence in broadcasting.

After graduating from the College of William and Mary, Jon held numerous jobs. He was a contingency planner for the New Jersey Department of Human Services, a contract administrator for the City University of New York, a puppeteer campaigning to sensitize people about learning disabilities, a high school soccer coach, a Woolworth's shelf stocker, a bartender, and a busboy. Jon mustered his courage and tried stand-up comedy, earning the 2 A.M. slot in a New York comedy club. From his 7 years in stand-up, he branched into other entertainment ventures, including acting in movies and televisions shows and authoring best-selling books.

Despite the fact that Jon tends not to give much credit to his psychology major, many critics of his interview style see clear evidence of a background in psychology. His self-deprecating style put his guests at ease. He is a careful listener and exercises expert interviewing strategies. He is insightful about motives, both those of other people and his own. He retired from the *Daily Show* in 2015 to spend more time with his family at their farm in New Jersey where the family cares for rescued farm animals and promotes a foundation called "Do Unto Animals (Stewart, 2015).

Best Advice? "Love what you do. Get good at it. Competence is a rare commodity in this day and age. If you don't stick to your values when they're being tested, they're not values; they're hobbies."

Information from: Columbia Journalism Review guide. New York, NY: Routledge.

The task force identified relevant student-learning outcomes for each of the goals and made suggestions about how the outcomes differ between 2- and 4-year programs. The goals of the guidelines and their corresponding learning outcomes can be found in **Table 4.1**. At the time of this writing, APA is appointing a third task force to conduct the 10-year review and revision.

TABLE 4.1

APA Guidelines for the Undergraduate Psychology Major, Version 2.0

Goal 1: Knowledge Base in Psychology

Students should demonstrate fundamental knowledge and comprehension of the major concepts, theoretical perspectives, historical trends, and empirical findings to discuss how psychological principles apply to behavioral problems. Students completing foundation courses should demonstrate breadth of their knowledge and application of psychological ideas to simple problems; students completing a baccalaureate degree should show depth in their knowledge and application of psychological concepts and frameworks to problems of greater complexity.

1.1 Describe key concepts, principles, and overarching themes in psychology

1.2 Develop a working knowledge of psychology's content domains

1.3 Describe applications of psychology

Goal 2: Scientific Inquiry and Critical Thinking

The skills in this domain involve the development of scientific reasoning and problem solving, including effective research methods. Students completing foundation-level courses should learn basic skills and concepts in interpreting behavior, studying research, and applying research design principles to drawing conclusions about psychological phenomena; students completing a baccalaureate degree should focus on theory use as well as designing and executing research plans.

2.1 Use scientific reasoning to interpret psychological phenomena

2.2 Demonstrate psychology information literacy

2.3 Engage in innovative and integrative thinking and problem solving

2.4 Interpret, design, and conduct basic psychological research

2.5 Incorporate sociocultural factors in scientific inquiry

Goal 3: Ethical and Social Responsibility in a Diverse World

The skills in this domain involve the development of ethically and socially responsible behaviors for professional and personal settings in a landscape that involves increasing diversity. Students completing foundation-level courses should become familiar with the formal regulations that govern professional ethics in psychology and begin to embrace the values that will contribute to positive outcomes in work settings and in building a society responsive to multicultural and global concerns. Students completing a baccalaureate degree should have more direct opportunities to demonstrate adherence to professional values that will help them optimize their contributions and work effectively, even with those who do not share their heritage and traditions. This domain also promotes the adoption of personal and professional values that can strengthen community relationships and contributions.

3.1 Apply ethical standards to evaluate psychological science and practice

3.2 Build and enhance interpersonal relationships

3.3 Adopt values that build community at local, national, and global levels

Goal 4: Communication

Students should demonstrate competence in writing and in oral and interpersonal communication skills. Students completing foundation-level courses should write a cogent scientific argument,

Continued

present information using a scientific approach, engage in discussion of psychological concepts, explain the ideas of others, and express their own ideas with clarity. Students completing a baccalaureate degree should produce a research study or other psychological project, explain scientific results, and present information to a professional audience. They should also develop flexible interpersonal approaches that optimize information exchange and relationship development.

4.1 Demonstrate effective writing for different purposes

4.2 Exhibit effective presentation skills for different purposes

4.3 Interact effectively with others

Goal 5: Professional Development

The emphasis in this goal is on application of psychology-specific content and skills, effective self-reflection, project-management skills, teamwork skills, and career preparation. Foundation-level outcomes concentrate on the development of work habits and ethics to succeed in academic settings. The skills in this goal at the baccalaureate level refer to abilities that sharpen student readiness for post-baccalaureate employment, graduate school, or professional school. These skills can be developed and refined both in traditional academic settings and in extracurricular involvement. In addition, career professionals can be enlisted to support occupational planning and pursuit. This emerging emphasis should not be construed as obligating psychology programs to obtain employment for their graduates but instead as encouraging programs to optimize the competitiveness of their graduates for securing places in the workforce.

5.1 Apply psychological content and skills to career goals

5.2 Exhibit self-efficacy and self-regulation

5.3 Refine project-management skills

5.4 Enhance teamwork capacity

5.5 Develop meaningful professional direction for life after graduation

Keep in mind that the revised version of the guidelines, published by the APA in 2013, delineates what you should know and be able to do upon graduation. Some psychology programs may adopt *Guidelines 2.0* to discern how to evaluate their students who are completing the degree. The guidelines also suggest how skills each individual course should contribute to the overall program. Most undergraduate syllabi stipulate the skills that the course should foster; however, these are not always laid out systematically using the APA framework. **Table 4.2**, which shows an example of the desired outcomes for an introductory psychology class, illustrates how using the guidelines can help departments develop goals for individual courses.

In designing their classes, not all faculty focus on skill development. However, students who don't get a skills infrastructure in their courses can examine *Guidelines 2.0* and identify the ways in which a course might be having an impact on how they are learning to think. ***Measuring Up: How Courses Build Skills*** offers an opportunity to assess yourself so that you can practice identifying how your courses contribute to the development of these important skills. Self-assessment skills become especially important as you near graduation and contemplate job interviews.

TABLE 4.2

Introductory Psychology Student-Learning Outcomes Based on the *APA Guidelines 2.0*

Introductory Psychology Course Goals

All students in an introductory psychology course should be able to do the following upon completion of the course, consistent with the department's assessment plan and coherent with the *APA Guidelines 2.0.*

Content

Acquire basic knowledge of theories, concepts, and principles in psychology

- Characterize the development of psychology as a scientific enterprise
- Discuss classic research in psychology, including its historical and cultural contexts
- Explain the principles of psychological literacy

Critical Thinking

Apply knowledge of sound research procedures to solve problems

- Use evidence to develop and evaluate claims about behavior
- Evaluate the quality of research designs and the validity of research claims
- Look for alternative explanations in evaluating the validity of claims

Communication Skills

Refine communication skills related to psychological science

- Begin using APA conventions in scientific writing
- Verbally express ideas precisely and persuasively in multiple formats
- Assess the strengths and weaknesses of their collaborative style as a group member

Ethical and Social Responsibilities in a Diverse World

Discuss the role of ethical practices in psychology

- Identify relevant ethical issues involved in psychological research and practice
- Discriminate ethical from unethical practices
- Describe why ethics matters in psychology

Professional Development

Refine skills to complete projects

- Develop strategies for completing assignments in a timely fashion
- Evaluate the strengths and weaknesses of their performance
- Identify applications of psychology that produce career opportunities

↑
▭▭▭ **Measuring Up**

How Courses Build Skills

Find the syllabus from a course you have taken in psychology.

Step 1: Examine the syllabus for clues about whether the class was learning centered or content centered. Was the emphasis on tests or on other, more active-learning strategies? Did the syllabus emphasize skill development or focus primarily on the concepts or theories in the course?

Step 2: Look at the student-learning outcomes in the syllabus. Which, if any, of the five APA goals are represented? (If no outcomes are apparent, speculate about what outcomes might be addressed from the course description.)

Step 3: Speculate about how well you met those outcomes. How did your experience in the course improve your ability to think like a psychologist? As a result of taking the course, what can you do now that you couldn't do before you had the course?

Step 4: Consider making this process habitual. Even if a professor doesn't articulate skills-related objectives, you may be able to apply the APA goals to monitor how your thinking is changing. Specifically, using *Guidelines 2.0* to shape how you characterize your own learning can dramatically improve your answer to the question "What are you learning to do in your major?"

Linking Undergraduate Goals to Workplace Objectives

Any effective liberal arts major should provide a path into the professional work world. We believe that psychology provides one of the strongest and most adaptable majors that higher education has to offer. The content of much of the undergraduate curriculum is uniquely suited to supporting strong performance in the professional world. The skill set of the psychology major also readily translates into workforce demands. As such, we think that the undergraduate major confers a **psychological advantage** in the workforce over other liberal arts programs. The psychological advantage should also have a positive effect for those headed to graduate school.

A standard undergraduate psychology curriculum offers workplace-related content that can't be found in other disciplines (cf. Landrum et al., 2010):

- How are attitudes formed and how can they be changed? (Social psychology)

■ What strategies are best for selecting and developing employees? (Industrial psychology)

■ What factors make people more or less effective in processing information? (Cognitive psychology)

■ What variables motivate top performance? (Psychology of motivation)

■ What are the best ways to promote learning new skills? (Psychology of learning)

■ What environmental designs help people do their best work? (Environmental psychology)

■ What stress levels are optimal for effective performance? (Psychology of emotion)

In addition to learning their course material within the major, psychology students gain skills that give them a competitive advantage as they enter the workforce (Halonen, 2011). Workplace-related skills refined by the psychology major could include:

■ accurately describing and predicting individual and group behavior;

■ understanding and using data to support an argument;

■ interpreting research data and graphs accurately;

■ evaluating the legitimacy of claims about behavior;

■ synthesizing information from diverse sources;

■ having insight into problematic behaviors;

■ demonstrating the capacity to adapt to change;

■ operating effectively in informal and formal channels of an organization;

■ managing difficult situations and high-stress environments;

■ communicating effectively in oral and written modes;

■ starting and executing projects with limited information and experience;

■ exhibiting persistence in challenging situations;

■ working effectively in teams that include people from diverse backgrounds;

■ engendering trust through personal integrity; and

■ writing reports that follow directions and use appropriate conventions.

To help you think more about what you have learned to do in the psychology major, take a look at **Reality Check: If They Could See Me Now**.

Metacognitive Changes

Some changes that will happen to you in the course of the major will be *metacognitive*, meaning that your understanding of your own thoughts and attitudes will change. Successful psychology majors take on the characteristics of those who

Reality Check

If They Could See Me Now

Assume you are applying for a tutoring job on campus. (Actually, it's a good idea to try to become a tutor; research suggests that working on campus helps contribute to academic success; Kuh, Kinzie, Schuh, Whitt, & Associates, 2010.) Your interviewer asks you to write down 10 abilities or strengths you have that would make you a good tutor. List these skills below. Review the frameworks described in this chapter (e.g., psychological literacy, APA learning outcomes, and workplace skills) to help you frame your develop your approach. Once you have written the list, identify any specific learning contexts (e.g., introductory psychology, involvement in a psychology club) that have helped you develop a particular skill. What evidence can you offer that you meet a qualification from your experiences in psychology?

No.	Skill	Evidence from Psychology Context
1		
2		
3		
4		
5		
6		
7		
8		
9		
10		

value a psychological perspective on the world. These characteristics include the following:

Intellectual curiosity. Psychological thinkers relish the opportunity to think deeply about behavior. They enjoy asking questions to get to a deeper understanding of behavioral motives. They like being able to predict outcomes. They enjoy solving puzzles. One clear advantage of being a major is the likelihood that you will rarely be bored, since people's behavior can always inspire your curiosity.

Expectation of complexity about the origins of behaviors. Psychological thinkers surrender the notion that the world is simple. They don't just settle for one simple causal agent when a host of influences may be involved. They enjoying teasing out the variables that may explain behavior and find research on such questions to be a satisfying way to address the complexity.

Tolerance of ambiguity. Psychological thinkers understand that behavior is complex and embrace the fact that we may never account for all the factors that influence some behaviors. They are not daunted by complexity, but are inspired by it. Consequently, they can also tolerate very high levels of frustration and tend to be patient when answers aren't readily forthcoming. In fact, when beginning psychology students work on writing assignments that involve synthesizing research findings, they often feel frustrated when they can't find the exact studies they need to make the argument they are trying to develop. However, by the time they near graduation, they tend to get excited and inspired when those answers aren't easy to find because it means there are unknowns yet to be discovered.

Humility. Psychological thinkers tend to be humble about the limitations of what they know. We may never know all the explanations for some complex behaviors; some phenomena can never be put to an empirical test. Therefore, we often must make decisions using incomplete information. Psychological thinkers do the best they can and are not surprised when new information emerges that changes how we think about a phenomenon.

Amiable skepticism. Psychological thinkers can be hard to persuade. They are aware that anecdotal evidence is a flimsy form of justification. At the very least, they are likely to respond to simplistic explanations about particular behaviors with the question, "What's your evidence?" They are comfortable adopting a skeptical stance until they can find persuasive evidence.

Enthusiasm for the value of human diversity. Social psychology fosters an appreciation for the value of group problem solving. Consequently, when group members bring perspectives that reflect differences in sociocultural background (e.g., race, gender, ethnicity, nationality, regional affiliation), the caliber of problem solving is likely to improve. Psychological thinkers don't just respect human diversity, they welcome it because they understand that differences in perspective can enrich the process and produce better outcomes.

Recognition of the value of ethics and integrity. Doing the right thing for the right reason is not always an easy course of action. In fact, psychology's history does have some ugly exemplars in which ethical concerns were not prominent. Contemporary ethical practices and oversight through institutional review boards and codes of ethics have dramatically affected this aspect of the discipline. Psychological thinkers follow formal ethical codes and also understand the importance of building trustworthy relationships with others. They resist temptations to take questionable or inappropriate shortcuts. They do the right thing for the right reason, even when people aren't observing their actions.

Engagement in civic and social responsibilities. Psychological thinkers tend to consider the broader impact of their actions. They recognize the satisfaction that comes from making constructive contributions. They tend to be particularly sensitive to people who function at some disadvantage, which explains the inclination of some psychological thinkers to work in a service-oriented capacity. Regardless of their occupation, they enjoy feeling a part of something bigger than themselves.

In Conclusion

When it comes time to write a letter of recommendation for you, your professors are likely to draw their descriptions of who you are and what you can do from among the lists addressed in this chapter. The more conversant you are about what constitutes the skills of the psychology major, the more likely you will be performing at a level that will make those letters from your professors persuasive.

Even if a professor doesn't hold you to any skill-development performance standards, it's a good idea to adopt reflective practices that help you understand how you are changing as your make your way through the psychology major. Try to avoid the trap of focusing on the grade. Instead, attend to the following:

1. How have your thinking skills and attitudes changed as a result of taking the course?
2. What did you do in the course that prompted those changes?
3. How satisfied you are with how your thinking skills and attitudes are changing as a result of taking the course?
4. How do you think these skills will help you in future psychology courses?

With a little practice, chances are good you won't ever be confused or tongue-tied if someone asks you what you have learned to do in the psychology major.

Thought Questions

1. What is the difference between a learning-centered approach and a content-centered approach in a course?
2. How popular is the psychology major in contemporary higher education?
3. How would you describe the characteristics of a psychologically literate person?
4. What is a high-impact practice and how does it affect student learning?
5. What are the five major learning goals of the APA *Guidelines for the Undergraduate Psychology Major 2.0*?
6. What should you be able to do as the result of completing an undergraduate major in psychology that would be appealing to an employer or would help you to be admitted to professional postbaccalaureate programs?
7. Why might completing a psychology major give you an advantage in competing for jobs in the workforce compared to other majors?

5

Hitting Your Stride as a Student

I never lose.
I either win or learn.

~Nelson Mandela

Four years sounds like a long time, but your undergraduate years will go quickly. Successfully completing a major requires a thoughtful, serious, and sustained effort from start to finish. To succeed academically, you need to refine skills, develop routines, be persistent, and avoid being discouraged when you have the inevitable setback. Approaching challenges with an open mind and a good sense of humor helps, too. The goal is to hit your stride as a student, to be intentional about what you do to produce the best outcomes from your efforts. In this chapter, we examine all of the areas that influence how successful you will be in the major. Let's turn to practices that work, beginning with the one that mystifies most people: time management.

Managing Your Time

When Dana was in college, he noticed a couple things about his fellow students. Those who did well in the courses for their major seemed to be interested in what they were studying (recall Chapter 2). Those who did less well often didn't like what they were studying and seemed overwhelmed by their workload. His friends who left before completing their degree did so not because they couldn't do the work, but because they did not fit into the rhythms, requirements, and social norms at that particular university. They either transferred to other colleges or universities that were better suited to their goals (or had the major they wanted), or they took time off from college to regroup and figure out their next moves. Few flunked out calamitously or completely.

No matter how smart they are, college students are not immune to the cognitive biases that make it easy to mismanage time. For example, humans regularly suffer from the *planning fallacy*, which entails underestimating how much time really must be devoted to a task to complete it successfully (Buehler, Griffin, & Ross, 1994). They assume that a complicated task — writing a detailed research paper, preparing a clear oral presentation — will take less time to complete than it actually will. They may not understand the true complexity of the demand or they may have forgotten related experiences they have had that they can use to help them assess the time required more accurately. When pinched for time from bad planning, they *satisfice* — that is, they settle for performing less than stellarly and probably shortchange what they could have learned in the assignment.

In general, people also tend to exhibit *positive illusions* (Taylor & Brown, 1994). They optimistically evaluate themselves more favorably than they truly should. This optimistic bias can contribute to an expectation that tasks are going to be easier than they really are simply because good outcomes naturally follow when people believe in themselves. To preserve the illusion, when these students perform poorly, they tend to blame "tricky questions" or bad luck rather than owning up to their own deficiencies.

Finally, the *overconfidence effect* (Kahneman, 2011) contributes to poor planning. Sometimes people tend to have a strong belief that things will work out in their favor, regardless of indicators that they might be wrong. A good example of academic overconfidence is illustrated by the student who does poorly on the first three examinations in a course but vows to do well on the final, trusting that a strong performance on the final will neutralize their earlier bad performance. It won't. Given the ways that most professors assign points, it is unlikely that a person can recover if they bomb three out of four exams.

Those who succeed in college learn to manage their time wisely and well — they are time savvy. They know which assignments require lots of time and which need less time. They learn how much time, for example, to budget to write a paper or study for an exam. They keep up with the work in their most challenging courses while knowing what is happening in their less demanding classes. They finish their reading before class meets so that they are prepared for discussion or a pop quiz.

Students who fare less well miss deadlines, submit work late or not at all, fail to prepare for exams, and routinely pull draining all-nighters to stay afloat. Many suffer sleep deprivation and end up receiving poor grades despite their academic abilities. Success in college does not depend on what you know or don't know but on how well you juggle all your course responsibilities and your extracurricular life — how well you manage your time.

Even bright and interested students can fail if they don't learn to manage their time well. They may never learn to transition from the demands of high school to those of college, which are steeper: more reading, more writing, more tests and papers, and more self-reliance. Today's students often have competing responsibilities, too, including jobs. Many value their social activities a great deal and spend a considerable amount of time with their peers. And then, of course, they have the

TABLE 5.1

College Student Use of Time in a 7-Day Week (168 hours)

Activity	Percent of students' time
Attending classes or lab sessions	9
Studying	7
Work/volunteer work/club participation	9
Sleep (estimated)	24
Socializing and recreation	51

Data from: Arum & Roksa (2011).

constant lure of online life and social media — they are connected to friends and family so much so that they often communicate with both groups several times a day.

How do students tend to divide their time in a typical college week? **Table 5.1** shows how students in one noted research project on the challenges of the first 2 years of college life spent their typical week (Arum & Roksa, 2011). Drawing conclusions is easy: Students in this sample spent the majority of their time engaging in leisure pursuits (partying, playing video games) and the least amount of time studying (and they spent almost *twice* as much time relaxing as they did sleeping!). This report represents only one study, but it did include a variety of students from a mix of colleges and universities.

Take a few minutes to figure out how you divide your time, using the activities list in Table 5.1 and the **Reality Check**. Feel free to add any activity you routinely do that is not included there. The main questions for you are these: Are you spending enough time studying to do well academically? Are you managing your time well?

What kind of a time manager are you? Let's see how you do in a typical week. In **Measuring Up: Do You Manage Time or Does Time Manage You?**, you will keep a time diary to track where you spend your time in a typical week.

We now turn to a common problem shared by many students: Not getting enough sleep.

Don't Forget Sleep

How much sleep do you usually get each night? How much sleep do you need?

For some reason, many students like to brag about how little sleep they get, as if going without is a badge of honor or an indication of their fortitude (less rest makes me the best!). But the fact is that most people need between 6 and 8 hours of sleep per night to do their best thinking. All-nighters tend to produce very fragile learning that may not be easy to retrieve under stressful testing circumstances.

Ample research shows that when we do not get sufficient sleep, our work suffers (Dement & Vaughn, 2000; Maas & Robbins, 2011). People — students as well as working adults — who get enough sleep accomplish many more tasks quickly and

☑ Reality Check

Managing Time Like a Pro

Which of the following recommendations are part of your time-management routine?

- ☐ I do not miss class unless I am ill.
- ☐ I prioritize my studies by doing the most challenging work first.
- ☐ I allocate time across my classes rather than studying for just one class per day.
- ☐ I start planning projects and assignments when they are assigned, not at the last minute.
- ☐ I stay current in my reading and meet the due dates for my assignments.
- ☐ I work backward from due dates to identify reasonable blocks of time in which to complete my projects.
- ☐ I devote more time management to online than face-to-face classes because online courses require more self-direction to complete the work.
- ☐ I schedule classes over the length of the school day to increase study time between classes. (I don't sleep in!)
- ☐ I concentrate my studying during daylight hours to avoid late-night distractions.
- ☐ I study in quiet places that provide little interruption.
- ☐ I shut off my phone and don't constantly check social media.
- ☐ I never study on my bed.
- ☐ I take short breaks to stay attentive and engaged.
- ☐ I adhere to an established routine whenever possible.

Which recommendations do you need to explore to improve your time-management strategies? Which recommendations do you reject with a reasonable rationale?

efficiently while feeling less stressed, less harried, and less tired. Getting a reasonable amount of sleep also turns out to be associated with better health. Ask yourself this: How many people do you know who routinely get sick when midterms, final exams, and holiday breaks roll around? Are you likely to crash and burn as stress and work mounts across the semester? One psychologist who studies sleep, James Maas, suggests that sleep is like a bank account: The less you get, the more you suffer a **sleep deficit**, which undermines your performance, your well-being, and your health (Maas & Robbins, 2011). So, try to avoid having a low sleep balance in your account by aiming to get as close to 7 or 8 hours of sleep per night as you can.

Sleep experts recommend several strategies to produce optimal sleep conditions. Avoid overstimulating activities late in the day. Don't exercise or eat heavily before you go to bed. Read materials that are not too engaging at bedtime. Strive to develop a routine time to retire. And don't take your phone to bed — checking your social media and restful sleep are incompatible.

Of course, you might not find it possible to get that many hours each night. You may have a noisy roommate, early classes, late work hours, or child-care issues, among other possible challenges. Fit in a nap at some point during the day — say, between classes. Short naps (about 20 to 30 minutes) can improve your alertness, enhance your performance on tasks, and reduce your mistakes without causing you to feel

↑ 📏 Measuring Up

Do You Manage Time or Does Time Manage You?

Step 1: For one week, keep a 24-hour time log. Write down everything you do in 15- or 30-minute segments. Your log should include things like commuting, sleeping, attending class, watching television, surfing the Internet, working at a job, athletic practice, studying, hanging out with friends, being on your phone, eating, and so on — everything. This record will provide you with a realistic snapshot of how you choose to use your time.

Step 2: Once the week is up, review the log. How do you use your time? Do you spend it wisely? What are the main causes of your lost time or the feeling that you don't have enough time to do all that needs to be done? Analyze your use of time and the habits you have developed about how you spend your time.

Step 3: Reflect on these questions: What changes could or should you make to better use your time? Are you wasting any time? What are the major time-sucks in your week? For example, if you are spending more time in the gym each week than you are studying for your classes, then something is wrong. If lunch with your friend always stretches to 2 hours, you might want to arrange another time — say, a weekend evening — to catch up. Are you reserving enough time for studying, doing homework, writing papers, and so on? What is your plan to better manage your time in the future? Were you surprised by how you actually spend your time?

Consider this: Not every minute of your day needs to be focused and productive; relaxation and leisure are important components of a healthy and balanced life. Still, time for playing should be scheduled and it should not interfere with necessary responsibilities (studying, sleeping, working).

---

groggy or adversely affecting your nighttime sleep (National Sleep Foundation, 2015). A well-timed nap can leave you refreshed and ready to go.

Oh, one last point: Too much sleep (that is, far more than 8 hours — some students sleep 12 hours or more in a night) is just as counterproductive to your efficiency and success. A routine, moderate amount of sleep in a very dark and quiet place will produce the best results.

We now turn to ways to improve study skills.

Improving Specific Study Skills

Ahmad was enrolled in a class on the psychology of adjustment. The material was engaging because it covered a lot of ups and downs he was experiencing in his academic, social, and personal life. He never missed class and was an active participant, asking and answering questions. He took the first exam with confidence and thought he did pretty well — until he received his exam grade in the next class. It was well below the class average and one of the worst test grades he'd ever earned. How could he do so poorly on material that spoke to him the way this did? He went to see his professor, who asked some questions about how he studied. After a few minutes, it became clear that while Ahmad did the reading and reviewed the course material, he didn't read strategically. He just assumed that if he read the chapters and the section summaries he would do well. The professor suggested some ways to prepare for the next exam and Ahmad followed them. When he took the next test, he received a much higher grade than on the first. He decided to use the techniques the professor suggested when studying for his other classes and soon noticed his grades improving in those as well.

By the time students get to college, most are confident — probably too confident (recall the overconfidence effect) — that they know how to study. Many students rely on the system they have always used, and some were lucky enough in high school to get by without really studying. The demands of college require much more effort, and while some people end up succeeding, many others do not. They discover that college-level work is more rigorous and detailed, that courses cover material more quickly, and that the competition among students — whether obvious or not — is more pronounced. In this section, we review some techniques and offer suggestions to help you study more efficiently and effectively so that you retain more of what you learn.

Reading

Technology has certainly made our lives easier and more entertaining, but the emphasis on short messages — texting or tweeting — may have a cost. Students become used to reading shorter, briefer bits of writing. Fewer students seem to be reading for pleasure these days, which means that college-level reading will feel much more like work than perhaps it used to. Reading chapters in textbooks, especially densely written technical material or highly detailed introductory texts, becomes a real challenge for some students because they simply don't have the practice. Some students do **drive-by reading**, which means that they read too fast at too shallow a level. By not allowing any time for reflection, they cannot create personal meaning about the readings. Developing that personal meaning makes it easier to learn.

How should you approach reading to retain information? The best way to read entails using your time effectively by actively thinking about what you are reading. If you are intrinsically interested in the material, it will be easy to stay engaged throughout the reading. However, if the content doesn't have natural appeal, you will need to be more strategic. Don't try to read an entire chapter (or book) in one sitting. Divide the chapter into segments and read one per study session. If you try to read the whole chapter at once you risk getting tired or bored.

As you read a section, use the **SQ4R method** (e.g., Robinson, 1970), which you may have learned sometime in your past. This acronym stands for the key steps in reading for meaning and retention: **s**urvey, **q**uestion, **r**ead, **r**ecite/relate, **r**ecord, and **r**eview. Each step is summarized in **Table 5.2**. The steps are easy, straightforward,

TABLE 5.2

The SQ4R Method for Effective Reading

Survey: Before you begin to read, get a feel for what's to come. Look over the chapter or section headings to get a sense of the material. Once you begin to read, you will know where the chapter is headed.

Question: Examine the headings in the chapter or section. Turn them into questions ("Conformity" becomes "What is conformity?") that you can later answer when you complete the reading.

Read: Get started reading the chapter or section. Answer the questions you just asked as you read and after you are done reading. If you have finished and still aren't sure your answers are correct, go back and reread sections as needed.

Recite/Relate: Recite your answers—that is, say them out loud and in your own words. You want to own the concepts by putting them in your own words, which will make them easier to recall later for a quiz or test.

Record: After you've said them out loud, write them down in your notes so you can study them later. Writing your thoughts downs also allows you to put your ideas into words, which increases the likelihood you will remember them in the future.

Review: After you finish the chapter or section, do a memory check by asking yourself about the key questions you posed earlier. Try not to look at your written answers unless you absolutely must.

Information adapted from: Robinson (1970).

and surprisingly effective. Once SQ4R becomes routine to you, you will be able to approach all of your reading systematically.

Nota Bene: Highlighting Doesn't Work So Well

Nota bene is Latin for *note well* or *take note of this important point.* Take careful note of this important fact about highlighting and underlining: It does not promote learning. That's right, it doesn't work. Generations of students who have relied on yellow or pink highlighters to mark up their texts and notes and whatever else have lulled themselves into a false sense of security. Controlled research demonstrates that highlighting does not work, largely because it prevents students from adopting other, more practical techniques that actually help them learn (Dunlosky, Rawson, Marsh, Nathan, & Willingham, 2013). Highlighting has been shown to be an empirically ineffective study tool. "Say it isn't so," we hear you cry; alas, all those thick, colored markers you bought in the college bookstore will have to find some other purpose.

Note Taking

The availability of portable devices like smartphones, tablets, and laptops is changing the college classroom. Many students no longer bring traditional paper notebooks to class. Instead, they type their notes into whatever device they prefer, which not only saves space and paper but seems to be easier than using a pen or pencil. Unfortunately, what seems like a great solution may present problems for learning.

Let's begin with handwriting or, rather, how handwriting is slowly but inexorably being replaced by typing on a keyboard. Is moving a pen across paper really so different than tapping keys? According to some psychologists and neuroscientists, the answer is yes — compared to typing, handwriting is intimately tied to deeper learning, the generation of ideas, and information retention (Konnikova, 2014).

Two researchers wondered whether relying on electronic devices might lead to more shallow information processing and reduced learning than the pencil-on-paper approach (Mueller & Oppenheimer, 2014). They conducted a series of studies, most of which followed the same structure: Researchers assigned students to classrooms and had the students take notes using either laptops or traditional notebooks. The researchers presented the same lectures to both groups, who were told to use their usual approach to note taking. Half an hour or so after the lectures, the students took an in-class exam on what they heard. The questions were both factual ("Who was shot in Ford's Theatre?") and conceptual ("Explain how a true democracy differs from a representational democracy").

Although the students who used the laptops took more copious notes, the notes were usually **verbatim** — that is, the students recorded exactly what they heard. By failing to put the ideas into their own words, they acted like stenographers. In contrast, the notebook group transformed the lecture content, turning it into information that was meaningful to the individual note taker. Not surprisingly, the laptop group did much worse on the recall test compared to the traditional notebook group. Despite the fact that the traditional notebook group wrote fewer notes, they engaged in higher-order thinking and deeper processing than the laptop group because they wrestled with the concepts instead of just transcribing them.

The bottom line is clear: Writing — not typing — is linked with better information retention. To maximize your learning, take a traditional notebook to class with you. If you have virtually illegible handwriting, then transcribe your notes into digital form later. Your initial learning — wrestling with key concepts via handwriting — will already have occurred. Subsequently translating your written text into a more readable (typed) form might help you rethink and further clarify what you wrote earlier.

How to Study

During high school, Martina routinely waited until the night before any big test to prepare. Usually she spent a couple of hours memorizing her notes and flipping through whichever chapters were going to be on the test. This method worked pretty well, as Martina usually earned A's and B's. When she got to college, she decided she would continue to rely on this approach. When she got back her first exams in each of her classes, she was shocked at how low her test grades were. She didn't fail any of her tests, but her scores were mediocre at best. Martina realized that the volume of material and detail associated with each class was greater than anything she had encountered in high school. She needed to find a better way than "cramming and jamming" the night before tests to succeed in her classes. Studying *hard*, then, is a very different thing from studying *effectively*.

Students like Martina use what we might call the **binge method**: They spend several hours reading, rereading, and reviewing notes — often trying to memorize terms or concepts — the day before an exam. This practice is ineffective for several reasons. Studying the same material for hours and hours at a stretch gets dull. Ironically, it is anxiety provoking to try to learn when dealing with last-minute pressure. Doing so also means that you might neglect studying or keeping up with your other classes. Isn't there a better system?

Psychologists have long suggested using an evidence-based approach to studying (Dunn, Saville, Baker, & Marek, 2013). One of the most thoroughly researched findings concerns what is known as **spaced learning**, or the *spacing effect*. Students who distribute their studying of particular material across a period of time — say, studying for a set interval of time (30 minutes to 2 hours or so) every day for an exam that is 2 weeks away — learn and retain more information than those who cram just before the exam. Space your learning and make it a routine to perform better than you would if you were cramming at the last minute. Students who do this tend to be less stressed about their coursework because they are almost always caught up.

A related finding on study efficiency deals with where people study, or **contextual cues**. Research shows that people who study in different venues have an easier time recalling what they need to know during exams than those who always study in the same place (Smith, Glenberg, & Bjork, 1978). Mixing up where you study allows you to develop what psychologists call **multiple retrieval cues**; if you always study in the same place (your desk, a particular carrel in the library, or the same table in a coffee shop), you will develop cues associated only with that place. Study your material in different places to make your learning sturdier. Being flexible about where you study is apt to pay a variety of academic dividends. Studying will be easier to initiate. **Table 5.3** lists some additional steps you can take to improve how you study. Consider trying one or more of them.

TABLE 5.3

Steps to Improve How You Study

Always attend class: Sit where you can get to know the instructor and other students. Avoid sitting in the back of the classroom.

Schedule time to study for each of your classes: Set aside two 3-hour blocks per class, twice a week, for doing reading and homework.

Write down important dates: Know when your homework and papers are due and the dates of your exams. Put this information in your phone, calendar, or planner.

Start assignments, including reading, early: Working ahead allows you to pace yourself and to avoid cramming or doing everything at the last minute.

When you get tired, take a break: Go outside for a brief walk, check your email, get a drink, whatever. You can also switch your study to a different subject to avoid fatigue or boredom.

Review any key terms and complete any practice tests in your reading: Use the end-of-chapter exercises to get a sense of what you know and don't know.

Celebrate your achievements: Reflect on what you are learning as well as your progress toward meeting your academic and professional goals.

Test-Taking 101

We now turn to the main event of most students' academic careers — test taking. As you likely know, tests are a big part of college life. You can use some of the following straightforward strategies, in addition to studying for your exams consistently and in advance, to increase your chances of doing well.

Look over your exam before beginning it. Too many students just write their names on the exam and then plunge in without knowing what will come later in the test. Take a couple of minutes to flip through the exam so you know what kinds of questions or problems there are, how many points they are worth, and if there are any questions that will require much more time than the others. Doing so allows you to budget your time better. You might want to start by answering longer questions first, saving the quicker ones (often multiple-choice questions) for last. If nothing else, looking through the exam will reduce your anxiety — there won't be any surprises or, if there are, you will have time to think about how to handle them.

Do well on multiple-choice questions. The basic strategies for answering multiple-choice questions — test questions that require the test-taker to select the best possible answer from an array of possibilities (usually 4 or 5) — are as follows.

First, make sure you read the entire question. It is easy to get tripped up on a question if you stop with answer A only to find out later that the options you didn't read were also right and the correct answer was "All of the above."

Once you have read all the choices and you know the answer to a question, mark the answer right away and move on to the next question. When you come to a question you don't know, skip to the next one and answer it and any remaining questions. You can answer those multiple-choice items you don't know last — just don't forget to come back to them! When you return to a question you initially could not answer, try to identify which of the answers are not at all plausible. Doing so will often narrow your choices from 4 or 5 options to 2 or 3. If you still cannot reason out the answer, choose the one that "feels" best — and then move on.

If you have time at the end of the exam to review your answers, you can circle back to check the questions you weren't sure about. It is quite all right to change answers, as research shows that review often motivates students to alter incorrect answers to correct ones (Benjamin, Cavell, & Shallenberger, 1984).

Answer essay questions effectively. The best approach to answering essay and open-ended questions starts with putting your pen down for a moment. Think about what the essay question entails. Then, pick up your pen and jot down a brief outline of the points you want to make. (You can write this on the test itself or on the exam booklet.) The outline keeps you from forgetting key issues as you write your answers and prevents you from writing too much. Some professors may give partial credit for an outline that verifies your understanding even if you didn't allow enough time to write out your complete answer.

Avoid the regurgitation method of essay writing. There is no need to tell the instructor everything you know about a topic; just answer the question being asked. Whenever possible, use concrete examples to illustrate the points or argument you are making in your essay. Being specific is almost always better than being general or worse, vague. Once you finish an essay, look over the prompt one more time and go back through what you wrote to make sure that you responded to all parts of the question.

Check how much time has passed and how much is left to complete your exam. Pace yourself during an exam. Don't rush, but don't work at a leisurely pace, either. When half the test period is done, for example, you need to be more than halfway through the test so you can allow some time to review.

Never, ever leave a question blank. Even if you have no idea what an answer might be, write something. Just don't be obnoxious or silly in your answers because that will produce a toxic effect on your professor's judgment of you. Return to a blank question after you've completed the rest of the test. The answer to the question — or a possible answer — may come to you as you answer other questions, or you might see a cue or a clue in another question. Remember, if you leave a question blank, there is no opportunity at all for the instructor to give you partial credit for what you do write. Always write something.

Don't leave an exam early unless you have thoroughly reviewed your answers. Far too many students race through their exams to finish them as quickly as possible. Such speed can lead to skipped items (forgetting to come back to that multiple-choice question, for instance), incomplete answers (forgetting to address one of the points in an essay question), and flat-out wrong answers. If you finish before time is called, go back through your exam to make sure you have answered all the questions and have done so to the best of your ability — there is no prize for being the first one done and certainly no problem with being the last person to finish.

Stay relaxed. Sometimes performance anxiety, from worrying about how you'll do to having a full-blown panic attack, can get the best of you. Concentrate on staying relaxed during the exam. Dress for comfort. Avoid caffeine and other substances that can overstimulate you at just the wrong time. Take some deep breaths.

Anxious About Math?

Many students (even psychology majors) become anxious when they are confronted with math problems. Statistics and data analysis, both of which are important aspects of understanding and carrying out research methods, are integral to psychology. Psychologists of all types need to be comfortable with the language of mathematics; so do students of psychology.

If you have math anxiety, you may shy away from completing your math and statistics requirements by postponing taking them until late in your college career. Doing so is a mistake for several reasons. First, math skills (particularly the logic required to do math and the step-by-step nature of solving problems) are useful in a variety of courses, not just those that are explicitly quantitative. Second, the longer you wait to complete even basic math requirements, the rustier your high school math foundation will be. Third, if you know you get anxious about quantitative work, you need to try to overcome your fears sooner rather than later because completing your degree will require becoming fluent in math.

Many math and statistics departments offer problem-solving sessions or tutoring. Taking advantage of these will help, as will always completing your homework and regularly meeting with instructors or teaching assistants during their office hours. Once students who are anxious about math or statistics break through their fear and concern, they approach the course material with a fresh and open attitude, one that makes it easier to understand and learn new skills.

If at first you don't succeed, seek help. If you are struggling with one of your classes, ask your instructor if any tutoring services are available. Among psychology students, seeking tutoring for learning statistics is popular, and many psychology departments provide stats tutors — often senior majors who did well in the class. Many schools also have writing centers that can offer help with writing papers and learning to effectively answer essay questions.

Suggestions for students with disabilities. If you have a documented disability that might influence your test performance, inform your professors at the start of the semester. Generally, students with disabilities are entitled to extra time to complete exams or can have access to specific testing conditions (e.g., a non-distracting space). Find out whether your college or university has a disability resource center. If it does, you can use it to learn about your school's resources and policies. If your school doesn't have one, it will likely have policies to help students with disabilities. Be sure to follow university policies in order to secure accommodations.

Having a disability doesn't limit the professional success you can have in a psychology-based career. See *A Major Success Story: Applying Psychology to Customer Service* for a great example.

About Grades: Review Your Successes and Struggles

When one of our colleagues returns graded material to her students, she always tells them they are permitted 15 minutes of joy, ambivalence, or self-pity — and no more. In other words, if they get a good grade, they are only allowed to revel in the success for a short while, and if they do poorly, they can only feel sorry for themselves for a brief time. If their grades are just okay — not great, not bad — they should not spend too much time being distracted by it.

Why does she impose this limit? Because students are apt to focus exclusively on their grade or score. In so doing, they ignore important information, such as what material they knew well and what they knew less well. Learning from successes and mistakes is important. You should always conduct what's called a *postmortem* on your quizzes, tests, papers, and the like. By reviewing the answers you got wrong, you have a second chance to learn the material, which will likely appear in some form on a later exam or

A Major Success Story   **‹‹‹**

Pensacola News Journal\Part of
the USA TODAY NETWORK

Julian MacQueen
BA, Hotelier

FIGURE 5.1 Hotelier Julian MacQueen prepares to take off on a business trip from his private hangar.

Applying Psychology to Customer Service

Not many people would think of a learning disability as a blessing, but Julian's life story demonstrates just how far one can go with a great education in psychology, a plucky spirit, and a different point of view. Diagnosed with attention deficit disorder (ADD) later in life — coincidentally, at the same time his daughter received a similar diagnosis — Julian came to recognize that ADD actually allowed him to make new and interesting connections that might elude someone with more typical processing skills. His capacity for thinking outside the box gave him significant advantages in solving problems and he found the perfect outlet — hotel management — for his unique talents.

Before he even started college, Julian began working with a local chef in a beach resort. His character and work ethic were so impressive that by the time he graduated from college, he had 8 years of experience in hotel management. He was mentored by a successful hotelier and absorbed the information he learned. He was able to parlay his knowledge and energy into building a thriving hotel management and marketing company with more than 1,800 employees.

What advantages did being a psychology major contribute to his professional success? Julian has been surprised by how much his psychology background has helped to set him apart. Understanding people provides a real advantage in his competitive industry. He credits psychology with enhancing his listening skills and his power of intuition. He is tickled when people describe him as being able to "see around corners." He also believes that the compensating strategies he developed to help him focus despite the distractions of ADD helped him become a better problem solver.

Best Advice? "Be willing to be wrong and to laugh at yourself. Expect answers from the most unlikely places, and open yourself up to the infinite possibilities around you. Recognize that you can't control the world. It's how you react to it that's going to define you."

Information from: Salley (2014).

other assignment. The questions you answered correctly tell you what you know well. All too often students only look at their grades and ignore all other comments from the instructor. Don't do that! Take the time to read and learn from them. Whatever you do, don't throw graded materials away — save them and review them before the next such assignment or test so that you avoid making the same errors (e.g., writing a too brief conclusion to a paper, forgetting to answer all parts of an essay question).

It is a very good idea to get into the habit of using exam wrappers every time you get back a test. **Exam wrappers** are questions aimed at getting you to review your performance and on any comments from instructors on a test (Lovett, 2013). By answering these questions and examining the test, you can see what worked and what didn't so that you can adjust your study habits and approach to test taking for the next time:

- How did you prepare for the exam? Are there things you might want to do differently next time?
- What sorts of errors did you make on the exam? Is there any pattern or commonality among them?
- What can you do differently to prepare for the next exam?

Personal Ethics

You are a professional in training, and part of that training is building trustworthy character. The habits you adopt now will affect you and how you act in the future. Part of your responsibility as a student is to be ethical; that is, to follow a moral code. In the context of college and university life, this code generally reflects three areas of emphasis:

1. **Do your own work.** As a student, you are responsible for undertaking and completing your own assignments, taking your own tests, writing your own papers, and so on. This means that you do not submit other people's work as your own. To do otherwise is to lie and to cheat.

   No doubt your school has clear rules about what constitutes academic lying and cheating, and you should familiarize yourself with them. Your school's student handbook is a good place to begin. For example, quite a few handbooks specify an honor code that requires students to turn in fellow classmates whom they believe have cheated on a test or an assignment. If doing this makes you uncomfortable and you see someone cheating, you might consider submitting the person's name anonymously.

2. **Do not plagiarize.** Plagiarism is the act of taking another person's ideas — usually in written form — and passing them off as your own without properly attributing the ideas to their original authors (that is, without citing supporting references). Plagiarizing the work of others is a form of academic theft. Some people plagiarize by knowingly copying phrases, sentences, and even whole paragraphs from published works or sites on the Internet. This is known as *intentional* plagiarism. In *unintentional* or accidental plagiarism, the perpetrator is unaware of having plagiarized. When summarizing some set of ideas, for example, they may incorporate quite a bit of the original language into their writing without using proper supporting citations. It sounds right because it turns out to be more or less verbatim from the original source.

The facts are these: College students don't write like psychology professionals. Professors easily spot plagiarized writing because the voice in the writing doesn't correspond to the way most undergraduates speak or write. In addition, most professors have access to technology that can provide formal estimates of unoriginal writing in submitted assignments and direct the professor to the actual lifted material.

Although the risk of getting caught and penalized should deter plagiarism, a more important reason to do your own work is to maximize your learning and the development of your communication skills. Table 5.4 provides some concrete steps for avoiding plagiarizing textual materials.

Like most adults, college students feel harried, so they often rush to complete their tasks, including their assignments. Unfortunately, such hurrying often leads to academically dishonest behavior. Some students

---

TABLE 5.4

Simple Steps for Avoiding Committing Plagiarism

1. Review the material you intend to paraphrase; that is, rephrase and summarize in different words.
2. Put the text away where you cannot see it, or close your document or web browser.
3. Draft a summary in your own words.
4. Compare your summary with the original text to make certain you are conveying the main message.
5. Repeat the above steps as needed.

Other suggestions:

■ Never cut and paste material into your writing from online sources; instead, paraphrase it using the above instructions.

■ Rely on your own ideas as much as possible; use the ideas of others to support your arguments or observations.

■ Keep a detailed list of any references you are using (as a psychology student, your citations should be written in APA style).

■ Cite these references by author last name and the date of publication — for example: (Jones, 2014). This will give your instructor information about the source you are using so they can consult it as needed.

■ Use quotes sparingly. Selecting only high-impact quotations will force you to develop your paraphrasing skills.

One last thing: If you must quote from an article, chapter, book, or other source, select a brief quote, use quotation marks, and indicate the source in the text and in a list of APA-style references.

end up justifying plagiarizing material when they are rushing to finish a paper or other assignment. They assume no one will notice, that they will only do it this one time, and thus they believe (hope) they can get away with it. Managing your time — planning how and when you will do your course work — reduces your risk of plagiarizing. And remember, it's always better to turn in a late assignment, even with late penalties, than it is to plagiarize the work of others.

3. **Avoid behaviors that will tarnish your reputation.** Appleby (2011) recommends that college students be aware of the full range of academically dishonest behaviors, including:

Cheating. Some forms of cheating are using another's work with or without the student's consent, such as copying answers from a test or homework assignment; sending a substitute to take an exam; collaborating on projects that are supposed to be independently created; or altering grades.

Submitting the same work to multiple classes. Some students submit the same assignment, often a paper, to more than one class. It's fine to write two different papers on the same topic for two different classes, but it is unethical to turn in the same paper twice.

Fabricating. Fabricating is falsifying or inventing information in order to appear to have done library or other scholarly research. Making up a source is foolhardy because faculty members can often detect the deceit — and what will happen when an instructor looks for the reference or asks for it?

Misusing materials. Although this may not happen very often, sometimes students obtain advance copies of quizzes or exams or they use a calculator when it is against the rules. Using unauthorized materials is cheating, plain and simple. Not only does it represent an unfair and unearned advantage over other students, it is a clear lapse in personal integrity.

Interfering. Any actions you take that obstruct a fair assessment of another student's work constitute a violation of integrity. Similarly, attempting to influence your teacher through bribes or threats is unethical.

Facilitating academic dishonesty. **Academic dishonesty** includes any attempt to help another person violate standards of academic integrity. You may believe you are being a good friend by letting a peer copy your homework, but what you are doing is enabling cheating. Doing so makes you as culpable for the dishonest act as the person who engages in the actual cheating.

Making false excuses. One final area deserves some attention: misrepresentation. Many students feel overwhelmed by their workload at times but only a minority of them choose to deal with this by telling what they believe to be little white lies to their instructors ("I had to miss the exam because I woke up with a fever" or "I couldn't turn in my paper during the last class because my car broke down on the way to school" or — the perennial favorite — "My grandmother died"). Using any form of deception or misrepresentation to postpone, delay, or otherwise avoid completing your schoolwork is academic dishonesty. Don't be surprised if your professor asks for some form of evidence (e.g., a car repair bill, a note from your physician, even an obituary) before they accept your explanation for your failure to deliver your work on time.

Getting into the habit of doing the right thing for the right reason helps to build positive character. You can take pride in being someone who can be trusted. Later you will find that your professors are more enthusiastic about writing letters of recommendation for you if your character is unblemished.

Navigating Cyberspace

We now want to focus on a very important and sometimes overlooked topic: your **cyberidentity** — your presentation of yourself to other students and to professionals (including your instructors and academic advisor) in the online world. We believe this is important because so much of our lives now revolve around social media and our individual online presence.

Here are some rules for the (virtual) road:

Whatever you put on the Internet is there FOREVER. Anything you post on a website — a comment, a picture, whatever — is permanent. The website may shut down, but it's quite likely there is a copy of your post elsewhere, possibly many other places. Think very carefully about what you share with others because it could come back to haunt you. Off-color language or jokes, snarky or rude comments, and inappropriate photos of yourself or others have the potential to embarrass you later in life. Important people in your life (friends, family, college faculty, current or potential future employers) may not appreciate or understand your post.

Do not leave your social media accounts open to everyone. If you use Facebook, Snapchat, Instagram, or other social media, be sure to set your security settings appropriately. For example, you might only want your friends but not strangers seeing all of your posts. Would you want a potential employer or a graduate school admissions committee to see everything you have posted, including the comments and links that your friends have added? If your answer is "no," then you may want to make some changes to the kind of information you allow to be seen.

Communicate appropriately. Many faculty members have received email messages from students like this one:

> Hey, are you in your office? When are your office hours? Please respond immediately. Dude, I need to see you like right now! (From beefcake69.)

The level of presumed familiarity and informality in this sort of message is not appropriate for a message sent from a student to a faculty member. Such messages inevitably create a negative impression.

Think before you send that email. For example, look at the course syllabus to see when the professor holds office hours. That saves you writing an email and avoids wasting your professor's time. However, if that doesn't work, a better email would be:

> Dear Professor Hanson:
> Do you have any office hours today? If not, would you be able to meet with me another day this week? I'd like to talk about my grade in your social psychology class. I probably need about 5 minutes of your time.
> Thank you.
> Justin Jenner

Address the email using the appropriate designation. The safest strategy is to address your email to Professor Hanson. You may prefer to use Dr. Hanson if you know the professor holds a doctoral degree. Avoid using terms that don't recognize special status, such as Mr., Ms., or Mrs.

Naturally, pay attention to the content of email messages you send not just to your professors; you should carefully construct and vet any communication you send, whether to peers or professionals. A colleague suggests to her students that they write any email message as if they were contacting the boss of the job they hope to obtain after graduation. Developing good email habits now will serve you well once you leave college.

Be reasonable about waiting for a response. Most professors receive copious amounts of email each day and may need some time to work through the queue to get to your comment or request.

Finally, as great as email is for quick connections, it doesn't always work well to express to communicate effectively. For example, if you are having a conflict, it is better to deal with it face-to-face so that you can get more informational cues to help you navigate the conflict. As well, emojis may not be sufficient to get your message across.

Closing the Loop

This chapter has provided guidance aimed at helping you to develop into a solid and confident student of psychology. We've covered key issues — from managing your time and sleep quality, to getting the most from your reading, to study skills, test-taking strategies, the importance of being an ethical student, and managing your presence in cyberspace. We want to close our discussion of student skills by offering a few final suggestions.

Learn from your mistakes. No one goes through college without a few mishaps. Even a spectacular blunder can be informative. When you make a mistake, allow yourself to learn from it. React with grace rather than with anger, upset, or regret. Then move on to the next challenge. One of the great things about life during college is that you get to reinvent yourself at the start of each quarter or semester. If you did not like how things turned out in one term, you have the opportunity to redeem yourself, to change your ways, to study harder, or whatever, in the next. Resolve to learn from your mishaps or mistakes instead of trying to forget about them.

Adopt a growth mindset. Social psychologist Carol Dweck (2016) observed that many people — including too many students — display a *fixed mindset* when it comes to their beliefs about learning skills, intelligence, and academic abilities. For example, believing that you can't improve your problem-solving skills is an example of a fixed mindset ("I've never been very good at math and that's not going change — my parents weren't good at math, either"). In contrast, when students exhibit a **growth mindset**, they believe they can become smarter and can learn new things and refine old skills. They also understand that exerting effort makes them academically stronger. As a result, putting in more time and effort increases the likelihood that they will do better in any academic domain. So, don't assume your academic skills and abilities are fixed. Instead, adopt a growth mindset and see them as plastic, malleable, and always ripe for improvement.

Overcome wishful thinking. A mark of a maturing mind is the wisdom to recognize that imagined or desired outcomes — our hopes and dreams — don't always turn out as we plan. We have to learn to face those facts with understanding and good humor. It can take some time, effort, and experience to reach such a point.

One common delusion that students express, driven by **wishful thinking**, is that they will still be able to get an A in a class by doing well on the final when their earlier work was clearly unsatisfactory. They may assume that a strong final performance will impress their professor, or that a professor is too nice to flunk someone who tries hard. This is called wishful thinking for a reason. Just because we want a certain outcome doesn't mean it will — or even can — happen. Being positive is important but you cannot ignore concrete performance indicators like grades. Working hard while moderating your expectations is usually wiser than assuming that things will simply fall into place for you. For the future to turn out as you hope, you need to work hard and to be responsible in the present.

Always do your best work. It is very easy to convince yourself that next time you will do better on whatever academic task presents itself — that you will get a higher score on an exam or write a better paper. But what if next time never comes? Too often we promise ourselves we will fix our problematic behaviors only to engage in them again later. Our final suggestion is not divinely inspired but based on common sense: Always try to do your best work. Treat each responsibility, whether great or small, as if it is worth doing well. If you do your best, you can avoid feelings of regret when things don't go quite as planned, just as you can relish your little victories when things go well.

Thought Questions

1. How can you manage your time more effectively? Identify three changes you can make and try them out.

2. Are you getting enough sleep? If not, what can you do to ensure you get a sufficient amount each night?

3. Identify your study techniques. Are you sure they are effective? How do you know?

4. Do you always study in the same place? If you do, can you try to study in a few other places in order to develop more retrieval cues?

5. What new test-taking strategy presented in this chapter would you like to try?

6. How can you become a stronger student and hit your academic stride? List some concrete steps you can take.

7. What is your current cyberidentity like? What changes should you make to it?

CHAPTER

6

Charting Your Course in the Major

You have brains in your head. You have feet in your shoes.
You can steer yourself, any direction you choose.

~Dr. Seuss

One of the great joys of pursuing a college education is being able to exercise autonomy in making decisions about how to build your major. The freedom to choose when and what you want to study can be a heady experience but it can also tempt you to make decisions that may not always be in your best interest. For example, Samantha loved the freedom she had in designing her schedule, but after 3 years of study she was distressed to discover that she didn't know her graduation requirements quite as well as she thought she did—she was missing a general education course and might end up having to delay graduation.

Even though there is not a standard set of courses across colleges and universities, the psychology major should be manageable over a 4-year period (Stoloff et al., 2010). This means that achieving the degree is possible even for students who transfer to other institutions.

But 4 years in college can go by quickly, and the 4 years sometimes stretch into 5 or 6 due to a variety of challenges, including lack of access to needed classes and funding shortfalls. When you don't understand the long-term consequences of your plans, you may create delays that will impede your progress. Even if you finish your degree in 4 years, you will want to make sure that you take advantage of all of the opportunities available to you.

■ ■ ■

The goal of this chapter is to help you become more intentional in your decisions and actions so that you can get the most out of the major. We also want to underscore the importance of seeking expert help along the way to minimize risks and delays. We provide a map of the terrain that must be navigated during your years as a major. We offer some guidance to help you optimize both your enjoyment of and your efficiency in college. We first examine the common stages of student development in the undergraduate years, highlighting the cognitive changes students are likely to undergo. We recommend strategies for reaching optimal outcomes that will help you have the best options after you graduate. We conclude this chapter by addressing some of the questions that often come up when students are working their way through the degree, in the hopes that you will see the value of expert advice and seek professional advising to help you chart the wisest path for yourself.

Stages in the Psychology Major

Students often tend to think about their courses in a compartmentalized fashion; they take school one course or term at a time and don't always look at their academic career as a whole. From our vantage point as professors, we see some stages of change that students go through during their time in college that are not necessarily linked to the completion of any given term (Halonen et al., 2003). In this section, we take a look at those stages.

The Novice Stage

The **novice**, or first, stage takes place when students are new to the discipline. Although we focus here on the changes that students undergo when they take introductory psychology, the characteristics of the novice learner tend to be the same among students in other classes early on, when they are just learning about the nature of the discipline.

Years ago, students could not take psychology until they reached a college campus, but with the advent of Advanced Placement (AP) and dual-listed classes, many students now come to college having already taken their first psychology class. Regardless of where the novice student initially encounters psychology, the experience in that first course can profoundly impact them. For example, on the strength of her Introduction to Psychology course, Jane switched from a journalism major to psychology and found her calling.

Characteristics of the novice learner. We love working with beginning students. They show enthusiasm for acquiring new concepts and theories that help explain behavior, but even the best students are surprised by how much of psychology doesn't fit readily with what they think they already know about psychology. Students struggle to understand why psychologists insist on **objectivity** in describing behavior and often confuse behavioral description with far more elaborate inferences about the behavior. Novice learners are more likely to interpret the meaning of behavior rather than just stick to the measurable facts; for example, on observing a physical altercation between two people, a novice learner might focus the causes of behavior rather than quantify the number of punches or negative comments made. They aren't particularly interested in evidence to support claims about behavior and tend to instead trust their own experience and believe the testimony of trusted others. They are often big fans of pseudoscience, systems about cause–effect relationships that don't have much, if any, scientific support, such as astrology or handwriting analysis; novice learners actively resist having those beliefs challenged (Lilienfeld, 2004).

Novice learners wrestle with accepting the trappings of science as part of the discipline they are learning to explore. They find having to adopt the conventions of **APA format** in their writing and speaking projects to be cumbersome, bewildering, and even tedious. They struggle to distinguish independent from dependent variables in simple research designs and often aren't very excited about learning the significance of the difference of those terms.

Students who are just starting out in psychology show many of the characteristics of the **dualistic learner**, a concept developed by William Perry (1970). Beginners tend to dislike **ambiguity**, prefer simple answers to complex questions and expect their professors to have all the answers. There is very little gray area in how they think about problems. They can be easily frustrated by questions that don't yield easy or quick answers, but through their study of psychology, they begin to recognize nuances and to understand that the causes of behavior are often subtle.

Recommendations for the novice learner. Several tips can help novice psychology students settle into the major and distinguish themselves as serious, intentional students. Our goal in this section is to help students move away from the mentality of merely getting through their beginning courses. The strategies that follow will enrich the experience in courses and lead to longer-lasting learning.

1. *Actively look for ways to apply what you learn.* Not only will your learning stay with you better, but considering the material in a personal way may help you identify areas that you might be interested in pursuing later in independent studies and projects.

2. *Embrace the breadth of the discipline.* Many students begin their major with the expectation that psychology will primarily focus on helping people. As noted earlier, clinical concerns represent very little of the discipline you will explore in beginning courses. Be patient. You will be able to choose electives that fit your interest as you progress in the major, but by being open to the full range of specialties psychology has to offer, you may discover new areas of interest. Being curious about the broad range of content that psychology encompasses will serve you well throughout the major.

3. *Start to winnow the broad subtopics in psychology to the ones that you are most enthusiastic about studying.* Knowing that you prefer "social" topics over "perception" topics can help you make choices about which classes to take as you go along. You may begin to develop some themes that

reflect your specific interests in the discipline and may shape the nature of projects you pursue in advanced coursework. For example, suppose your interests focus on sustainability concerns. You can look at persuasion tactics in social psychology, develop surveys to assess public sentiment in research methods, examine cognitive traps that encourage misuses of resources in cognitive psychology, and so forth.

4. *Invest yourself in class discussion.* If you aren't participating at all when you have the opportunity, take a deep breath and then take the risk of speaking up. It is rare that bad things will happen if you try to contribute. You will get more out of the class if you share your ideas and perspectives because doing so facilitates your understanding and retention. You will also have more to say if you come to class prepared to engage in discussion. Talking about the ideas that the class covers will help consolidate your learning even if you are speaking just to a partner in class in a pair-share exercise.

5. *Be careful about participating excessively in class discussion.* Participate, but monitor the frequency and the depth of your disclosures in class. The content of psychology classes may tempt you to say too much about yourself that may be inappropriate or stray off topic. It is not a good idea to dwell on aspects of your own mental health history to illustrate course concepts. Your classmates are likely to think "TMI!" (too much information!) when they hear private, highly personal disclosures.

6. *Visit your professor during office hours.* Very few students take advantage of an individual professor's attention during his or her office hours. Think of it this way: You have already paid for this resource through your tuition and most professors enjoy having students seek their help. For many professors, having teaching moments during office hours is the best part of the job. Going to office hours will set you apart from other students, encourage the professor to get to know you, and add to your comfort about being in and participating in the class. Such visits can sometimes lead to other important opportunities, such as learning about relevant extracurricular activities or being invited to join a professor's research team. See **Reality Check: Finding an Academic Mentor** for more pointers that can lead to a profitable mentoring relationship.

7. *Get comfortable with conceptual messiness.* Not much about psychology is tidy. The sooner you can begin to think of ambiguity as interesting rather than frustrating, the more fun you'll have in the discipline. When there isn't a crisp explanation for a particular behavioral phenomenon, it means that that area may be ripe for research and discovery.

8. *Hang out in the psychology department or wherever students gather.* Some of your lifelong friendships may be waiting for you in the student lounge. Informal connections can also help you identify faculty who may be looking for hardworking student volunteers to be part of their research team.

Reality Check

Finding an Academic Mentor

Some students are more likely to be successful in academia if they can develop a special relationship with a professor. A student may be drawn to a faculty member because of the faculty member's personal charisma or a shared passion for particular ideas; regardless, having a professor who is accessible and supportive can make all the difference in helping students stay the course through to graduation. Mentors can also be instrumental in helping students achieve their goals following graduation.

How do you know a faculty member might be open to taking on a mentoring relationship? It helps to do some observational research. Size up the student traffic in the professor's office. If students are regularly present during office hours, the faculty member welcomes the presence of students and probably has some mentoring relationships underway. If no one is visiting a faculty member during office hours, that faculty member might be more available to be a mentor. Most faculty members genuinely enjoy working with students, which is why they got into teaching in the first place.

What's the best way to engage a faculty mentor? Visit your professor during office hours and ask for a few minutes of his or her time. Mentoring relationships tend to grow out of positive interactions. Which of the following would you feel comfortable exploring with a prospective mentor?

- ☐ Clarifying something confusing in the professor's lecture
- ☐ Getting specific recommendations on next semester's courses
- ☐ Asking your professor to look over your notes to see if you are capturing the key information
- ☐ Requesting test-preparation tips
- ☐ Inquiring about the professor's academic background
- ☐ Asking how the professor balances work and family life
- ☐ Determining whether the professor collaborates with students on research
- ☐ Volunteering to be part of the professor's research team
- ☐ Seeking advice on potential career options

What's the best way to nurture the relationship once it has been established? Be completely reliable in performing any tasks you have agreed to take on for the professor. Demonstrating a strong work ethic in fulfilling your obligations not only solidifies the relationship, but it makes it much easier for your mentor to write a glowing letter of recommendation when the time comes.

9. *Attend student events to get to know the faculty and other people in the major.* Many departments host a psychology club that schedules social and service activities to enhance student experience. Students with a strong academic record may also be invited to join one of the national honoraries, Psi Chi or Psi Beta, if their department sponsors a chapter. Volunteer for committee work in psychology-related interest groups to help refine your leadership skills. Be sure to follow through on any commitments you make so that faculty and your peers know that you are reliable.

The Developing Stage

In the middle stage, which we refer to as the *developing* stage, students focus on how to think about behavior as a scientist. At the outset of this stage students should be taking the courses that serve as the backbone for scientific inquiry — research methods and statistics. Departments use a myriad of strategies to build students' research skills. In a typical sequence, students take a statistics class, sometimes taught by the mathematics department, either before or while taking a class in research design. Some programs have instead a two-semester research sequence that combines methods and statistics. Ideally, you should finish your statistics and research methods courses before taking higher-level core classes (e.g., cognition, social, developmental, neuroscience) and advanced courses so that you have a framework for thinking empirically (Dunn et al., 2010). Indeed, students learn more rapidly in advanced classes in specialized topics of psychology when they already have a thorough background in research methods.

Characteristics of developing learners. Developing learners become more sophisticated in describing behavior and inferring meaning or motivation as they go along. They start to become comfortable with measurement and precision as necessary elements of good science. Developing learners begin to explore theoretical frameworks, including recognizing that any theory has strengths and weaknesses. They can manage small-scale research projects and also select and properly apply statistical analysis to determine whether their hypotheses were successful. They begin to display some vigilance regarding the ethical constraints that characterize well-designed research.

Developing learners begin to have major changes in attitude during this stage that help them move in the direction of becoming apprentice psychological thinkers. In Perry's (1970) framework, they become **relativistic learners**, recognizing that hard and fast truths are fairly elusive. They start to grasp how two individuals can share the same space but not experience the same subjective reality. They show more appreciation for precise definitions and crisp procedures because of the degree of control these practices provide in determining valid research conclusions. Although they still prefer simpler over more complex answers, they begin to show enthusiasm for targeting as many variables as possible that might influence a particular behavior The **amiable skeptic** (someone who challenges conclusions to be helpful rather than harshly critical) begins to emerge in this stage.

As developing learners face demands to become more sophisticated in their use of APA format, their communication skills grow. When seeking information, they typically want to use every reference they examine rather than recognizing the importance of being selective to produce the strongest argument. They haven't yet mastered writing for a psychology-oriented audience but are less likely to protest about having to use APA communication conventions. As project managers, they can take on more complex tasks and feel more comfort in sharing the workload even with people they wouldn't have chosen for their team. They can give and take criticism but tend to be satisfied with superficial ("That was really great!") rather than in-depth evaluations, even though a deeper approach to feedback is more helpful and promotes better learning.

Recommendations for developing learners. During this stage, developing learners become even more intentional about getting the most from their learning and serious students begin to set themselves apart from majors who are just slogging through. They strive to master the conceptual frameworks of many subspecialties in psychology. They should be actively identifying the specific kinds of psychology that they find most appealing, upon which they can build future plans.

Here are some tips about this stage for the developing learner:

1. *Follow the recommended sequences of courses.* Course curricula, whether comprised of general education requirements or those for a major in psychology, are usually laid out in a particular manner for specific reasons. Generally, introductory requirements should be completed before intermediate courses, which in turn should be taken before advanced and capstone classes. Sometimes students decide they want to put off some requirements as long as possible. Bad idea. For example, many psychology students try to postpone taking research and statistics for as long as they possibly can (recall our earlier discussion about math anxiety). Doing so, however, is counterproductive because basic skills in methodology and analysis are important for getting the most out of intermediate and advanced psychology courses. By taking classes in the recommended sequence, you maximize the opportunity to learn the most from the material. The skills acquired in earlier courses will lay a foundation for what will be expected in later courses, refining both your knowledge and your proficiency in the major in the process.

2. *Give time and attention to identifying the path that you would most like to follow after you graduate.* At this stage, it is very useful to determine in which area your interests are strongest: research/academic; clinical/human services, or practical/work related. This will help you decide which advanced electives to take. If research or clinical work draw you, the path you look at might include graduate school. To prepare, pursue research opportunities, lab courses, and other activities that can show your intellectual rigor and fitness for graduate school.

   Students who are interested in practical applications of psychology should focus on workplace-simulating experiences through internships, field placements, service learning, or volunteer activities. Every student should build a strong **résumé** (a brief description summarizing not just what you have done but what your skill sets are) that will interest future employers.

3. *Actively consider your personal connections to the coursework you take in this stage to maximize the impact of the material.* One of the advantages of studying psychology is that it feels so personal. Not only do developing

learners mine their personal lives for relevant examples that make concepts come to life, they think about the ways in which a given course could connect with their future plans.

4. *Identify research questions that can sustain your interest through the rest of the major.* Students who want to go to graduate school can benefit from identifying some core concepts or theories that might be similar to the demands they will face in undergraduate research. For example, Tina recognized early on that she liked social psychology more than other specialized areas and was especially drawn to the factors that prompt people to help one another. She took a related course in positive psychology and got excited about doing research on empathy for her term paper. In her capstone project, it was easy for Tina to come up with an associated topic — charitable-giving patterns — in the area in which she had already developed some expertise. Concentrating her undergraduate interests then helped her identify graduate programs where she could continue doing the research that she found so stimulating.

5. *Nurture helpful relationships.* As you develop proficiencies in some more specific topics, make strong connections with people who can help you in the higher-level projects you will be undertaking. Professors who share your interest may be able to identify experts in the subject, which can shorten your search for resources. Consider making the librarian on your campus who specializes in social science research your new BFF (best friend forever).

6. *Identify professors who will be good references for the steps that follow graduation.* Letters of reference sound more compelling when written by professors who know their students well. If you ask professors whom you admire at an early stage of your schooling whether they would be willing to write a strong letter of recommendation when the time comes, they will appreciate how thoughtful you are being about your future. That favorable reaction can contribute to a praise-filled recommendation. See **A Major Success Story: The Power of Professors Who Know You Well** for an example of how important the right letter of recommendation can be to opening doors.

7. *Join an active research group.* In the developing stage, you should be learning firsthand about the fun and frustration of research projects. Ideally, you should try to conduct your own research or be a member of a research team by the end of this stage. If you are trying to get into graduate school, evidence of your independent research will improve your chances; if you want to move into the work force, conceiving and running a research project will provide evidence of your project management skills.

8. *Seize opportunities to talk about psychology in academic settings.* If you are like most students, you will have to complete quite a few projects in

A **Major** Success Story

Nadine Kaslow
PhD, Clinical Psychology Professor

FIGURE 6.1 Psychologist Nadine Kaslow works out with the Atlanta Ballet.

The Power of Professors Who Know You Well

Nadine Kaslow knew she wanted to be a clinical psychologist from early on and was prepared to do the hard work required as an undergraduate to get where she wanted to go. She had a stellar grade point average, developed her leadership in appropriate extracurricular activities, and became an active contributor in a faculty member's research group, resulting in having publications even before she graduated. There was just one hitch: Nadine was one of the legions of psychology majors who typically don't test well. If graduate faculty used the usual criteria to determine whether she should be admitted, she may not have been able to get into graduate school.

However, Nadine's development of her resources as an undergraduate included building mentoring relationships with people who wrote effective, attention-getting letters of recommendation that ultimately made a persuasive case regarding her fitness for graduate work. Her mentors were able to write wonderful descriptions of her capacity to do high-level research and her exceptional abilities in solving clinical problems. Nadine's relationships with her mentors reaped huge dividends. She was accepted to multiple graduate programs. She completed her PhD at the University of Houston and launched her career. Her research is impressive for its breadth, depth, and originality. She has made a lifelong commitment to mentoring future generations of psychologists, especially psychologists who are still early in their career.

Her research interests include women's mental health, suicide and family violence, culturally informed interventions, and psychology education and training. She is a member of multiple academic departments—psychiatry and behavioral sciences (primary), pediatrics, psychology, and emergency medicine—at Emory University School of Medicine. Due to her long-standing service at the American Psychological Association, she was enthusiastically elected as president, serving in 2014. In her limited spare time, she consults for—and works out with—the Atlanta Ballet.

Best Advice? Don't let a bad GRE score block your goal of graduate school. Compensate for this one troubling aspect by distinguishing yourself in all other areas of consideration.

your advanced courses. Presenting the results of those projects is a great way to practice speaking like a psychologist. You might volunteer to do a presentation in class or present your research findings at a student research symposium; doing so will help you overcome the anxiety that tends to accompany learning how to become an effective public speaker.

9. *If you plan to go to graduate school, dedicate some time at the end of the developing stage toward making that happen, including scheduling the GRE, securing reference-letter writers, and identifying possible careers that might be most satisfying.* This stage is also the time to target graduate programs that are appealing to you and to start the application process. If your research passions have crystallized, narrow your focus to programs that feature faculty whose interests match your own.

10. *Build a portfolio.* A portfolio can be online or hardcopy (paper). Consider pulling together samples of your best work electronically into a **portfolio** so that you can easily access evidence of the quality of your thinking. A portfolio can come in handy for graduate school interviews and can set you apart in a job search. **Table 6.1** shows an example of what a psychology portfolio based on the **APA's** *Guidelines* **2.0** might include.

11. *Play like a psychologist.* Find out whether your department has social outings or attends conferences together. If possible, try to join in the travel to begin to see what might be expected in that professional lifestyle. Socializing with other students whose postgraduation interests are similar to yours can reap academic as well as social rewards.

12. *Be your own best critic.* The best developing students begin to evaluate the quality of their own work conscientiously and strive not to turn in anything but their best efforts. Before you submit work for evaluation, think about its strengths and weaknesses. When you receive feedback, read it with the idea of improving your learning.

TABLE 6.1

The Psychology Portfolio

Construct your portfolio to correspond with a specific set of performance standards, such as the **APA's** *Guidelines for the Undergraduate Psychology Major 2.0*, or use the standards that have been adopted by your own department. Here are some examples that are based on the APA performance categories:

Psychology Content
- A transcript highlighting your undergraduate courses and grade point average
- A copy of a capstone project
- A discussion of your preferred framework or theory

- A brief paragraph explaining any clusters of courses (e.g., human resources, human development) that reflect your special interests
- A description of how your minor has informed your psychology major

Scientific Inquiry and Critical Thinking

- A list of all projects you completed during your undergraduate career that demonstrate critical thinking
- Abstracts of successful research projects you've completed
- Acceptance letters or awards for research projects
- Grant proposals
- Theoretical reviews

Ethical and Social Responsibility in a Diverse World

- A copy of an institutional review board approval
- Service-learning project descriptions
- Letters attesting to high-quality volunteer work that you have done

Communication

- A copy of your best paper, along with feedback from the professor
- A PowerPoint of your best class presentation
- A videotape of a speech you've given
- Recommendations that address your interpersonal effectiveness

Professional Development

- A formal career plan
- A résumé
- A list of people willing to serve as references
- An analysis of the strengths and weaknesses in your project management skills
- Testimonials regarding the effectiveness of your teamwork skills

The Advanced Learner

Toward the end of the major, strong programs offer **capstone courses** that facilitate integrating learning across courses (Dunn & McCarthy, 2010). Capstone courses typically are smaller-sized seminar classes that may be devoted to a specific topic (e.g., history); or capstone work may involve internships, participation in a research team, or any other high-level activity that integrates learning across courses in the major. Our discussion focuses on the nature and quality of student capstone performance.

Characteristics of the advanced learner. Advanced students in psychology should have a comfort level that derives from having chosen the major wisely. In Perry's (1970) framework, advanced learners can be described as **committed learners** — learners who make reasonable decisions despite the presence of ambiguous conditions. As apprentice psychological thinkers, they enjoy complexity and more readily rely on empirical data than on personal experience. They have become *variable minded* because they assume that behaviors stem from a variety of factors and they enjoy the work involved in making tentative speculations about cause and effect. They can pick and choose from an array of strategies, selecting specific approaches that best suit the questions being considered.

As advanced learners, psychology majors are genuinely enthusiastic about the power that comes from working with empirical evidence. They have more ease with using an approach of amiable skepticism, which helps them more thoroughly consider matters under discussion. They are vigilant about complying with the ethical requirements of the discipline.

Particularly in their capstone projects, advanced learners concentrate on developing **coherent arguments** (positions that hold together). They read the literature selectively. Advanced learners pay attention to the reputation of publications, the credibility of the authors, and the plausibility of the authors' arguments. Their presentations in front of professional audiences are less anxiety inducing. Advanced students also tend to be more comfortable in leadership roles; they are conscientious about involving all group participants to help ensure that contributions from all members are of high quality. They are also more reflexively self-critical in ways that can help them generate the best possible projects. They are likely to seek feedback on their performance to help them optimize their learning and promote enduring improvement.

Recommendations for the advanced learner. Before their senior year, advanced learners should have developed a plan for the period after graduation. Think about your final courses, especially your capstone, as an opportunity to improve your professionalism. If you plan to go to graduate school, you will already have established a track record, so you can devote your senior year to preparing for graduate school. If you don't plan to go to graduate school, then your primary consideration should be getting ready to enter the workforce.

1. *Capstones should represent your best work.* Strive to make your project a good indication of your capacity for producing solid work. Pay attention to the quality both of the product and of the process through which you produce the work. Be prepared to talk about what you have accomplished, recognizing that your description may vary depending on whether you are trying to impress prospective graduate school representatives or potential employers.

2. *Consolidate your faculty fans.* When approaching faculty for letters of reference, look your prospective letter writer in the eye and inquire about whether they can write you a strong recommendation. Go with the ones who enthusiastically say yes. To ensure candor and demonstrate your confidence, waive your right to read what the faculty member has to say. If a faculty member hesitates or cannot reassure you that their recommendation will be helpful, be gracious, thank them, and move on to someone

whose enthusiasm will increase the likelihood that they will write a persua-sive and positive letter. Lukewarm letters do little to make a strong case for your fitness for a job or graduate school placement.

3. *Show off your public speaking skills.* If you have a chance to appear in a research showcase, participate! It will help you practice explaining psy-chology to the public and will strengthen your résumé. Such opportunities signal your seriousness as a scholar. Some student research exhibits also have prizes for the best student research projects, which would provide even more evidence of your high caliber for future employers or graduate admissions committees.

   You might be asked to help with prospective student recruitment by describing the quality of your undergraduate experience. By all means, accept this opportunity to help build your résumé and demonstrate your ability to be a responsible representative of the university. Doing this service will give you public speaking practice, improve your ability to handle impromptu questions, and build your confidence about working with the public.

4. *If you took the GRE and weren't thrilled with your score, work on your backup plan.* Consider creating a study group to prepare for retaking the exam, or signing up for a review or prep class. However, if you don't make additional effort, don't expect a better score if you take the test again. Your plan B can also include figuring out a way to find a job that can either help you gather more experience to reapply to graduate school or to launch your career.

5. *If you are hoping to start working, use the resources of your campus career center.* Connect with the staff member who knows the most about placement for students with psychology or social sciences degrees. Complete the inventory tests that help you identify fields that are most suited to your interests. Write a compelling résumé and be prepared to tailor it for specific audiences. (See pages 171–176 for a discussion of résumé writing.)

6. *Gain experiences in applying psychology in different kinds of contexts.* Ser-vice learning, internships, field experiences, volunteer activity, and even psychology-related jobs can add depth to your résumé. Supervisors can expect that you will ask them for a letter of reference so it is important to do your best and most reliable work in any activity where you are applying what you have learned in the major.

7. *Compete for special designations.* Most departments have activities that dis-tinguish high-achieving students from their peers. Don't be shy. Strive to achieve distinction. Volunteer for leadership positions. Submit your papers to competitions. Every award you receive and leadership position you accept provides a new and impressive entry on your résumé and demon-strates the seriousness of your intentions.

8. *Solicit feedback on nearly completed works to help ensure your strongest performance.* Even professional psychologists take advantage of peer review to make sure that they communicate their key ideas as effectively as possible. Being able to absorb constructive criticism is a valuable skill in the workforce or graduate school.

9. *Keep your ethics squeaky clean.* You are not just building expertise about psychology; you are building your reputation. How your peers and faculty feel about you can be permanently altered with even a single ethical misstep. If you make promises, keep them. One of the strengths of the psychology major involves the ability to build and maintain trust, which will be important in any setting.

10. *Don't complete your graduation requirements by taking throw-away courses.* Eight hours of advanced yoga to fulfill your graduation requirements may help your spirit. However, taking advantage of the opportunity to enroll and succeed in more rigorous courses will help you make a stronger argument for your work ethic and intellectual rigor. Take challenging electives as these may enrich the content in psychology you can apply in professional settings after graduation.

Frequently Asked Questions Regarding Advising

In the second half of the chapter, we have tried to anticipate typical challenges that students face as the major unfolds. We have organized the advice around the typical dilemmas we have heard from students during our careers as advisors.

We encourage you to develop a solid relationship with your own major advisor, whether that person is a faculty member or a professional advisor, because consulting with a local expert will most likely produce the best outcomes related to the specific problems you will face. What works on one campus may cause inadvertent challenges on another. Your tuition covers the cost of expert advising help so it is silly not to use this resource for optimal benefit.

Navigating Declaration of the Major

What's the best time to declare the major? As a general rule, declare the major as soon as it feels right. Although psychology courses are not always tightly sequenced in the major, some classes are **prerequisites**, courses that have to be taken before other, more challenging classes. Indeed, you will have the best opportunity to accommodate sequenced class requirements if you declare early.

On the other hand, we discourage you from declaring before you genuinely know that you have found an academic home. Ronan (2005) suggested that 50% of students change their major at least once. Some students change two or three times before settling into an academic home. If you make frequent changes to your major, you may protract your time in college and add significantly to the cost of your schooling. In fact, some states (e.g., Florida) charge higher tuition for students who exceed the target number of undergraduate hours, in order to move students efficiently through a 4-year program.

I started out in a different major but I've been told to find another. I'm good with people, so is psychology a good bet? It might be, but doing well in the major requires much more than good interaction skills. People who fare best in the psychology major are those who appreciate science, who like numbers and statistics, and who can handle complex explanations of behavior. Being good with people is helpful but not sufficient to be successful as a psychology major.

My program has a minimum GPA to be considered an official major. My GPA isn't high enough yet to declare. What should I do? Because funding for academic programs is typically not as generous as most departments would like, many departments have designated psychology as a *limited-access* program by specifying a minimum GPA to enter. If your GPA isn't high enough for you to be officially admitted, make an appointment with an advisor to discuss your options. If your GPA is close to the minimum, consider taking lower-level courses in which it may be easier to bring up your GPA. If your GPA is substantially lower, you might retake courses (using what is called *course forgiveness*, which allows you to replace an earlier bad grade with a better one when you retake a class) to improve your GPA. Alternatively, you might want to rethink whether the major is really the best place for you to flourish.

Navigating Registration

Must I see an advisor to plan my course list? Many programs require oversight by a professor or advisor on students' schedules. This tends to reduce costly errors and curbs students' impulses to register for courses that are not in their long-term best interest. Other programs allow students to make their own schedules but may not be too accommodating if students make mistakes in their planning. It is always a good idea to find someone in a position of authority whom you trust who can give you objective suggestions about the most effective ways to make your choices. Some programs ease the challenge of getting registration advice by offering peer advising programs in which more seasoned students help identify the potential pitfalls of newer students' plans (Nelson & Fonzi, 1995). Expert advising advice can save you time, money, and frustration.

I often don't get the courses I really want. How can I improve my chances of getting the schedule I want? Courses close out and popular courses fill up quickly. We often hear about classes filling up within hours of the opening of the registration period. Obviously, getting advice about your schedule early enough so that you can be among the first registrants is the best strategy. You might also consider looking for some online classes that fulfill course requirements if you need more flexibility to follow the path you are most interested in.

Am I out of luck if a course I want is closed? Maybe. Find out whether the class has a wait list; if it does, recheck the list regularly. It may help to talk directly with the professor, but she may not be able to exceed the limits set by the registrar (the limits are often related to classroom capacity as dictated by fire codes). You might also go to the class the first day in case some registered students don't come and spots open up. Be polite and persistent but understand that you may not get into the class.

My advisor seems disinterested. Should I ask for another one? Yes. Some departments may not allow for changes but if the chemistry isn't good between you and your advisor, do all you can to get someone who seems genuinely interested in your future and your well-being. If you can't officially change advisors, then identify a knowledgeable mentor who can fill in that gap and rely on your official advisor to sign off on the choices you make using input from others. Ask for help from the head of advising or the department chair.

Navigating the Faculty

Should I ask a professor if I can get into a class once it has already begun? Most colleges will allow you to join a course in progress if you haven't missed too many classes. However, missing the first hours of class will mean that you miss hearing the context set for the course. A better decision might be to defer registration for that course until you can join the class on the first day. If you do get into the class, do not expect the professor to recap the lectures you missed. Develop a relationship with a high-achieving student in the class from whom you can borrow notes to catch up on what you missed.

If I miss class, should I talk to the professor about what I missed? We don't advise it. Not all professors pay close attention to attendance because they operate on the assumption that they are dealing with adults. The professor might not have noticed you were missing. But professors also can be offended if you obviously prioritize other activities, especially if they are trivial, over attending class (Kuther, 2014). If you miss a class, it is your responsibility to do the make-up work. Anticipate this by sharing your contact information with another strong student in the class who can provide you with details of any class you might miss.

Whatever you do, don't ask the professor, "Did I miss anything important?" [One of the best answers we have ever heard was from a quick-thinking professor who responded, "Yes, that day was the day we gave away the Porsche in class and you had to be there to win."] Professors are rankled because the inference is that you think the class doesn't usually cover important things, even if that isn't what you intended to convey.

What's the best way to ask a professor for help? Professors keep office hours and respond to email as part of their job. That doesn't mean that all professors will be thrilled to hear from you or be responsive to your requests, but it helps for you to know that part of their responsibilities includes time spent answering students' questions. Alert the faculty member that you'd like some help and, if possible, estimate how much time you might need. Prepare a set of questions to make the most efficient use of the professor's time. Don't overstay your welcome and be sure to express your appreciation for the time the professor spends with you.

What's the best way to get invited to join a professor's research team? Excel in the classroom. Visit the professor during her office hours. Read what the professor has written so that you are informed when you talk with her. Ask her directly if there are any roles you can play to assist in the research. If she says no, ask her if she knows of any other possibilities that she can recommend. Most faculty members will try to help you secure access to undergraduate research opportunities even if they can't accommodate you as part of their team.

I want to avoid a professor in the department because his ratings are so low on Rate My Professor. Is that reasonable? Not really. First, recognize that social media evaluations of professors tend to pull opinions either from extremely happy or extremely unhappy students, so the ratings might not be an accurate characterization or correspond well to the standard you have in mind for great teaching (Otto, Sanford, & Ross, 2008). In addition, even unpopular teachers make a connection with some students in the class. Strive to be one of those with whom any teacher can make a more positive connection. We recommend taking time to visit the professor during his office hours to demonstrate your good intentions.

I'm in a course that feels toxic. Should I drop it and take it later from someone else? It is rare that a course is hopeless. However, especially if you have in mind braving a high-stakes competition (e.g., admission to graduate school) in the future, you may need to drop the class to protect your GPA. Before you do, be sure that there will be other faculty who offer the course or you may simply be postponing rather than avoiding the toxic situation. In the worst-case scenario, consider taking the course elsewhere and transferring it in if your perception is that the faculty member's performance is unacceptable or damaging to your academic record.

My professors don't ever respond to my emails. Am I doing something wrong? Maybe. Professors can sometimes receive over a hundred emails per day. It is easy to get swamped or miss specific requests for help because of the amount of email they receive, so some nonresponsiveness may be accidental. However, sometimes students can be pretty uncivil when making requests by email since the medium itself tends to promote casual responses. In *Measuring Up*, we give you an opportunity to troubleshoot ineffective email requests.

What if a professor treats me unfairly? We hope you don't experience the disconcerting challenge of having a professor treat you unfairly or disrespectfully. Nearly every college graduate has a memory of at least one professor who was not ideal. Most of the time the best course of action is to ride it out, do your best, and move on. However, if the maltreatment reaches levels that cause you serious distress or poses a serious threat to your well-being or your future, you may need to take some protective action.

Arrange to visit the professor with another person you trust (a potential witness if things go awry) and lay out your concerns. Be specific about the behaviors that have

⬆ 🔟 Measuring Up

Sharpen Your Impression Management

Email has become a standard way to communicate with faculty members. It is easy and efficient to connect with your professors using email, but many students don't recognize that a badly constructed email can have a long-lasting effect on the impression that a professor has about a student's professionalism. What follows is an example of a badly written email. See if you can identify all of the problems contained in this request for help. Then draft a more professional version that might produce a more positive response.

> Mrs. Thompson:
> Missed class yesterday. Was there anything important from class that will be on the next exam? Need to know right away so I can plan my weekend. Catchya later.
> Badass98@student.mail

What problems can you identify?

1.

2.

3.

4.

5.

Key:

1. The approach is too informal, including incomplete sentences and colloquial language ("catchya later").

2. The salutation fails to convey respect for the professor. In addition, female faculty members who hold PhDs usually prefer to be called professor or doctor, not Mrs. or Ms.

3. The request does not identify who the student is.

4. "Badass" may be offensive to the professor.

5. The message implies the professor may spend class time on unimportant material.

6. The student appears to pressure the professor about a response for the student's convenience.

7. There is no class identified so the professor would have to waste time asking or looking up which course the student is in to be able to answer.

8. The student doesn't apologize for missing class, which would have been a more civil way to engage the professor. Nor does the student offer an explanation for the absence.

What would a more effective email look like?
Professor Thompson: I apologize for missing Cognitive Psychology on Tuesday. I had last-minute car troubles. I read the syllabus so I know what I missed and I'm current in my work, but is there anything else that happened in class that I need to know about to prepare more effectively for the next exam? I appreciate any feedback you can provide. Thank you.

Jamie Simpson

---

led you to conclude that there is a problem that needs to be addressed. Recognize that professors tend to hold more power than students, so your evidence will need to be compelling if you hope to have a positive outcome. If the problem cannot be fixed informally, you may need to move up the hierarchy in the department and speak with the department head. Some serious problems may even require the intervention of a dean. Your college may also have a specific officer in charge of investigating discrimination complaints, and your complaint may need to start in that office. However, a good guideline for problem resolution is to attempt to resolve difficulties at the lowest level possible in the organizational hierarchy.

I'm uncomfortable because one of my professors seems too friendly. What should I do? Sometimes professors have poor boundaries (Halonen, 2002). For example, they can show preferential treatment toward a student based on interests that are personal and romantic rather than academic. If you think a professor is coming on to you, take some steps to protect yourself. Redirect unwanted attention back to the class. Do not meet alone with the professor behind closed doors or off campus. If the attention is unrelenting (and sadly both of us have seen professors who have created such situations), then consider reporting your concerns to the head of the department. Happily, predatory faculty members are rare, but their actions can be extremely damaging to successful completion of the major.

If you are tempted to develop a relationship with your professor, be aware that most campuses prohibit professor–student romances. Becoming entangled romantically with a professor is rarely something that can be kept secret and will dramatically distort the relationships you develop with your peers. To avoid a variety of negative consequences, wait to begin a romance with a professor after that professor no longer has grading power over you.

Navigating the Curriculum

Can I put off taking the experimental psychology class as long as possible? (I hear it's hard!) This is one of the worst strategies you can use. Don't do it! Because research constitutes the backbone of psychology, you will have a big advantage if you take the research class as soon as possible. Many schools require that students complete this course before taking any upper-level classes. Understanding what good research involves will make it easier to begin to make connections among your advanced classes.

I'm not good at math. Why do I have to take statistics? Psychologists emphasize description and measurement in their work. Statistics is a powerful tool that helps us determine whether or not the manipulations we design will produce the outcomes we intend. Most curricula require a basic statistics class that helps students learn the most familiar and useful tools in the psychologists' statistical toolbox: correlations and analysis of variance. Becoming comfortable knowing when and why one uses these tools and being familiar with R or **SPSS**® (powerful statistical programs) to manage masses of data should empower you to conduct studies that have some impact. If you believe you will struggle in a statistics class, participate in study or review sessions before your exams and use whatever tutoring services are available.

Take some solace in that fact that you are not alone in your distaste for the mathematical side of psychology. It may be useful to think of statistics as an interesting game that helps us pinpoint patterns and build confidence in our conclusions. Or think about statistics as a distinctive form of communication; the more adept you are with numbers, the more persuasive you can be in mustering evidence to strengthen the psychological arguments you will develop.

Can I take courses if I haven't completed the prerequisites? You may be able to persuade a professor into waiving a prerequisite, but it usually isn't a very good idea. Why? Because those who design the program curriculum recognize that students need to have prior experience with certain concepts to be successful in the next classes in the sequence (Dunn et al., 2010; Stoloff et al., 2010). Prerequisites help students build their knowledge base through **instructional scaffolding** by providing a sequence of challenges that increase in difficulty over the major. Although it's possible to do well in a course without taking its prerequisite, a course taken without a prerequisite will almost inevitably require more work than it ordinarily would. In addition, those students who abided by the rules will have an advantage in the class — they can focus on the concepts being presented instead of spending time doing background reading to catch up.

Do I need to have a minor? And if so, what should it be? A minor may not be a requirement for your program. But if you do want to have an additional concentration, think about the areas that may be useful for the future you have in mind. Courses in business and management can make you more attractive in the workforce. Graduate schools like to see rigorous minors, such as philosophy, biology, or another science. Plans to enter the helping professions can be improved with additional social sciences. If writing has a place in your future, courses in communications or English literature will be helpful. A foreign language minor can make it easier to get into study-abroad programs as well as broaden your employment options.

Should I double major? Many students can manage a double major in the confines of a 4-year program. However, you must recognize that having two areas of study means the faculty of both majors will expect you to be hardworking in each of your respective majors. Finishing advanced coursework in two majors at the same time can be especially taxing: Think about completing two capstones in the same challenging semester, for example. For those who are committed to graduate work in psychology, a double major does not confer a particular advantage and potentially can delay your graduation. On the other hand, if you truly love the second major, then pursue it — but do so with your eyes open, knowing that you will need to work hard to stay on track and graduate on time.

Should I pursue a certificate if one is available in my program? Some programs offer certificates, which show evidence that a student has taken a concentration of electives in a certain subject area. Certificates are sometimes available in child development, human services, human resources, and industrial-organizational psychology, among other psychology subfields. Certificates provide a little something extra to impress potential employers but don't tend to carry much weight for graduate school. However, receiving a certificate does not guarantee that your investment of time and energy will produce more of a payoff than simply completing the major.

I have to do an independent study. How can I come up with an idea to research? It seems like everything that is important has already been discovered. Grab an introductory textbook. Open it up to the table of contents. Pick the chapter that is the most appealing to you and skim it to see which concepts pique your interest. Take a list of two or three concepts and visit your professor during office hours to see if a conversation about those ideas might inspire an interesting idea and help you develop a manageable design.

Navigating Disappointing Performance

What if I get a D in a core class? First, make absolutely certain that your grade was calculated properly. Mistakes do happen, and when professors are shown that something went wrong on their end, they will usually apologize (with some embarrassment) and correct it. Make every effort to calculate your own grade accurately rather than expecting the professor to do the math on the spot. Don't be offended if the professor recalculates your estimate; it is just part of the job.

If the grade is accurate, analyze what prompted you to turn in such a lackluster performance. Not enough sleep? Taking too many credits? Long-winded roommates? For your performance to improve, you will need to fix the conditions that sabotaged your potential.

If your program has grade forgiveness for poor performance, file the appropriate permissions as you register to take the class again. Don't make the mistake of thinking that you already learned a lot the first time so you won't have to work hard when you retake the course. A bad grade means that you didn't learn the concepts well enough the first time. Making a half-hearted effort on a second try almost always fails to result in a better grade the second time around.

Can I ask to be assigned to a more functional group in my class? You can try, but it probably won't work. Professors who assign group projects as part of the class are helping you build your teamwork skills. When you graduate, you won't always get to pick and choose the people with whom you will work. Try to adopt the attitude that you are learning not only about the content of the project but also about refining your project management skills. Actively strategize about how to help the group function better. If this doesn't work, ask the professor to help the group figure out better ways to collaborate.

Some of my friends cheat whenever they can. How do I withstand the pressure to join them? It can be hard on a person's morale to observe so much undetected academic misconduct but taking the easy way to pass classes can taint your school years for you, producing some lifelong regrets. If you engage in academic dishonesty, you take a risk that can cost you your degree. An earned degree is a proud accomplishment; a stolen one is tarnished and will never feel completely legitimate.

Navigating Your Future

There are several important questions you should ask and answer in order to plan for your future career or education. These include the following.

How do I secure the best letters of recommendation? When you ask your professor for help, bring with you a one-page summary of your key achievements so the professor has enough detail to write an informed letter. Remind her of how you did in her course and explain why you have chosen her in particular to write your letter. Ask if there is any other information that would be useful for writing a strong letter. Be sure to follow up with a thank-you note and with news of the outcome. The latter is especially important if you need to ask for another letter in the future.

If the professor turns you down, don't protract the conversation. You want letter writers who are enthusiastic and positive. Move on until you find someone who is happy to help you. Obviously, if your performance has been lackluster, your options may be fairly limited.

How can I find a mentor who can assist me with career planning? If your assigned advisor is reluctant to help you chart your path, ask your advisor or the head of the department for some assistance in identifying a **mentor**, someone who takes special interest and offers guidance in your professional development, who might be able to serve in that role. One of the alumni of your school or a current graduate student might be just the person to help you talk through your options.

How important is extracurricular activity in getting where I want to go? Having a lot of extracurricular activity doesn't have as much impact on your future as a strong academic performance does. It isn't useful to spread yourself thin with too many outside activities, as they can detract from the more important indicator of your capability as a student — your academic performance. But the by-product of extracurricular activity — the development of leadership skills — should strengthen your job or graduate school applications. Be sure to talk about the effect of what you did in your extracurricular activities.

Is a field placement a good idea? Absolutely. Field placements and internships provide practical experiences in which you can apply principles of psychology. If the field placement comes close to the kind of workplace you envision for yourself, it can help you see whether that type of work will be satisfying. In our experience, some students perform so well in field placements that they receive job offers because the host agency is so pleased with their work and wants to continue the relationship. If the field experience is not satisfying, though, you may be able to rule out work of that particular kind for the future.

When should I take the Graduate Record Exam? The deadline for taking the **Graduate Record Exam (GRE)** depends on the schools to which you will be applying. It is usually best to take the exam early in the fall of your final year. Receiving your results in early fall can help you then be considered for assistantships or grants in many programs.

Does it help to prepare to take the GRE? Usually. Using a practice exam book or online resource allows you to develop the pace necessary to deal with the huge number of multiple-choice questions on the GRE. The practice questions may also cover specific content that is on the exam. Another strategy for preparing is to systematically review a current introductory psychology textbook the summer before you take the exam. Study groups are also useful for building your confidence about the exam.

If I do poorly on the GRE, should I retake it? Analyze what caused you to not do well. See if you can determine whether you didn't really know the material well or whether anxiety got in your way. If the former, refer to the strategies we will describe in preparing for the GRE and try harder (see pages 221–222). If anxiety was the problem, consider making use of whatever counseling services might be available on campus to help you figure out how to reduce your anxiety. Happily, if you take the GRE more than once, you can choose the score that you want to be forwarded to your prospective graduate programs.

What if I don't get into graduate school? It happens. Jane didn't get in the first year she applied. It's not the end of the world. Psychology graduate programs are remarkably competitive, especially in the clinical arena. Plan to strengthen your application by doing some work in research or clinical settings. If possible, attempt to stay aligned with an active research team as a volunteer.

Looking Back

At the conclusion of your major, you will want to feel satisfied that you chose your major well and did all you could to make the major work for you. If you practice an intentional and thoughtful approach to your decisions, we can virtually guarantee that you will not just be a happy major but a valuable one.

Thought Questions

1. Why should you strive to be an intentional student?
2. What are the hallmarks of students' thinking when they are just starting out in the study of psychology?
3. Why are research concerns so prominent among the milestones of the developing student?
4. How do the pathways differ for majors who plan to enter the workforce versus those who want to go to graduate school?
5. Why should you seek help when you are registering for your courses?
6. What are the risks of taking statistics and/or research methods late in your major?
7. What should you do if you start having serious difficulties with a professor?
8. What advantages might you realize if you can avoid engaging in academic dishonesty as you complete your degree?

7

Doing Psychology Research From Start to Finish

One of the first rules of science is if somebody delivers
a secret weapon to you, you better use it.

~ Herbert A. Simon, Cognitive Psychologist and winner
of the Nobel Prize in Economics

Smita enrolled in a research methods in psychology class because it was required for all psychology majors. During the first class, the instructor announced that everyone was going to come up with an original research idea. They would all be designing and executing their own **experiments** that semester. Smita started to panic. She had no experience doing research, wasn't sure what the instructor meant by "experiments," and had no idea how to use the library to locate information on psychology. She was thinking about dropping the class until the instructor explained that she didn't expect the students to be familiar with the research process; they would all learn about it together in a gradual, incremental way. Smita breathed a sigh of relief. In a flash of insight, it occurred to her that she might be able to do something in the area of student stress and academic anxiety for her research project. She certainly had a head start in understanding the phenomenon and she thought her research could be personally helpful in the adventure ahead.

■ ■ ■

Psychologists are critical thinkers and researchers. They know how to pose research questions and create plans for carrying out investigations. They also know how to present their findings in different ways to different audiences. We designed this chapter to help you review the fundamentals of research design;

find good, researchable ideas; develop an appropriate strategy for answering questions; and present your findings in written and oral formats.

We begin this chapter by setting the context for research in psychology. You were probably introduced to research fundamentals in your introductory psychology course, so many of the terms described will likely be familiar. This quick review should help you be more conversant in an important function of the discipline—the generation of new knowledge. We explore how to make the best use of available resources in psychology to develop your own ideas about the underpinnings and causes of behavior in humans, animals, or other organisms. To help you develop critical thinking and research skills, we offer guidance on sources that work best, followed by information on how to use the library to explore the available psychological literature. We discuss the importance of using the resources of cyberspace wisely and constructively. We then introduce the writing style psychologists and psychology majors use to communicate their ideas and research findings with each other. We also take a look at other kinds of writing you may be asked to do as a major. We close with tips on how to make presentations to professional audiences.

Reviewing Research Fundamentals

Psychological research is empirical, meaning that research generates objective evidence to describe, explain, or predict behavior. Psychologists use a variety of different strategies to address both basic (explaining the fundamental "laws" of behavior) and applied (practical) concerns. They use both quantitative (numbers-based) and qualitative (narrative-based) research to conduct their scientific explorations.

Experiments tend to dominate the attention of psychologists because they have the greatest power to explain the causes of behavior. Experimental research involves controlled comparisons in which researchers manipulate certain **variables** while measuring other variables. When doing research with humans, for example, one group — the **experimental group** — gets a *treatment*, that is, an experimental level of the manipulated or independent variable that represents the researcher's hunch regarding what factors lead to a particular behavior. Another group serves as the **control, or comparison, group** in that they don't experience the other level of the **independent variable**, one that is not anticipated to change behavior. Instead of merely measuring behavior, experiments tend to influence people by subjecting them to test conditions that are identical with just one exception: exposure to different levels of the independent variable. In a well-designed study, researchers strive to find a significant difference in the **dependent variable**, that is, how participants behave regardless of whether they are in the experimental condition or the comparison condition.

A simple example of this type of research design is a clinical trial in which researchers are testing the effectiveness of a new medicine. Volunteers are randomly assigned either to receive the drug of interest (similar to a treatment) or they receive what is called a **placebo**, a sugar pill that should produce no medicinal effect. **Random assignment** refers to a process that ensures that all volunteers in an experiment have an equal chance to be assigned to either the treatment or the control condition. The placebo group constitutes the control condition. If there are differences in the two groups, researchers will know the drug (independent variable) causes the effects (dependent variable) since everything else has remained the same due to the **controlled conditions** used in the experiment.

How might that strategy apply when studying behavior? Suppose we want to know whether studying is more successful if a person studies against a backdrop of classical music. Researchers might require experimental subjects who have been randomly assigned to the experimental condition to turn on Mozart during every study session. The people in their control group study in quiet conditions. In this case, the independent variable is type of sound exposure (Mozart in the experimental group vs. quiet in the control group). Comparing the groups to look for any differences in the academic performance (the dependent variable), such as the exam or quiz scores, of the two groups allows the psychologist to discern cause-and-effect relationships based on manipulated variables. As students of the discipline, psychology majors will get a lot of practice identifying independent (manipulated) variables and dependent (measured or outcome) variables in various research designs found in published literature.

Like psychologists, psychology majors are also critical thinkers and (budding) researchers. The focus of a research methods class typically is on helping students learn how to use experimental methods to establish cause-effect relationships. Of course, not all psychological research is experimentally based. Although space constraints prohibit us from exploring other approaches in detail, we list some of the common research alternatives to experiments in **Table 7.1**.

Students should also be able to interpret literature related to a topic of interest and even to add to that literature by designing and possibly executing their own research projects. Part of the learning curve in becoming a psychology researcher involves getting familiar with relevant peer-reviewed sources

Creating Research Ideas

Based on the literature (instead of on personal experience), researchers learn to make scientific claims and write stylistically appropriate research papers and lab reports that other psychologists and students of psychology can readily understand. Let's start by addressing an important question: Where do students of psychology get ideas for research papers and projects? The origins of psychological questions that spur research can appear to be a mystery to some students, especially the first time or two they have to think of a researchable project topic. There are many ways to develop ideas. Here are some popular guidelines that both psychologists and students routinely use (for other ideas, see Dunn, 2013a,b; Martin, 2007).

TABLE 7.1

Some Alternative Research Approaches to Psychological Experiments

Approaches That Emphasize Observation

Observational research represents a form of nonexperimental research in which an investigator carefully observes and often records the ongoing behavior of humans or other organisms. Investigators target specific behaviors using operational definitions and report their results both qualitatively and quantitatively.

- **Case study research** relies on a detailed, in-depth examination of a person. Case studies are qualitative rather than quantitative, and usually a narrative description of the person's behavior (or life experience) is presented.
- **Naturalistic research** involves researchers making careful records of behavior in nonexperimental contexts.

Approaches That Establish Correlations (but Not Causality) Among Variables

Correlational research is a nonexperimental approach aimed at identifying the nature of associations (positive, negative, or nonexistent) between or among several variables. Correlational results are not causal results; in order to determine whether a causal relationship exists between two or more variables, an experiment must be conducted.

- **Survey research** entails having a sample of people from a larger population answer a set of standardized questions in order to infer what most people in the larger population feel or think about a given topic or issue.
- **Archival research** involves using existing records to determine patterns among variables. Measures of academic achievement, work performance, and traffic citation records each can serve as an archive that provides data on human behavior.
- **Quasi-experimental research** uses the general format of experimental research with one key difference: There is no random assignment of participants to either a treatment or a control group. Thus, investigators are never entirely sure whether an observed result is due to an independent variable or to some quality linked to the participants themselves.

Approaches That Focus on Published Information

- **Literature reviews** summarize peer-reviewed information about a particular topic. A researcher investigates existing scientific literature, whether in journals and books or online, pertaining to some research topic to make a claim about it or to frame what is already known in a novel way.
- **Meta-analyses** synthesize trends across related studies to determine where the weight of evidence may lie in explaining behavior. For example, a meta-analysis might report the percentage of studies that confirm positive outcomes from the use of a new clinical technique from all the experiments that have examined the technique's effectiveness.

Look around. Rely on your observation and intuition — what interests you about what you see around you? Why do people on your campus behave as they do? Are there any common or unusual behaviors displayed by students or other members of the campus community that are worth examining more closely? For example, why do some people sit in the same seat every day in class? How do professors differ in how they decorate their office or what they hang on their office door? What attitudes shape whether students cheat or stay honest when taking exams?

Extend already published research. If a psychological topic you learned about in class or in a course reading piqued your interest, consider extending what is known about it. Research psychologists often test the limits of experimental effects by changing conditions, adding new variables, or employing different groups of participants. Locate a published work (you will learn how to do this shortly) and think of ways to alter its hypothesis by looking at it from a different angle. When you find an article that fascinates you, look through its Discussion section; there you can find ideas for new directions in published research.

Find a paradox. People love information that contradicts expectations. Consider romance: Many people assume that attraction occurs most strongly when a person finds someone whose personality type is completely different from his or her own — in other words, when opposites attract. Although this sounds reasonable (and may well be in a few cases), generally people actually prefer to become partners with similar rather than dissimilar others — in effect, birds of a feather flock together (Luo & Klohnen, 2005). Such everyday paradoxes make excellent starting points for researchable questions and they always draw people's interest.

Identify a real-life problem. Everyday life is filled with problems that could be constructively addressed by simple psychological interventions. Many college cafeterias have done away with trays, for example, a change that has prompted students to take only the food they really want to eat (Curry, 2008). These *natural experiments* reduce food waste and cost while promoting student health.

Here's a real-life problem to mull over: How can you motivate students to use the stairs in academic buildings (thereby getting valuable cardiovascular exercise) instead of taking the elevator? What sort of message (say, on a sign) or modeling would encourage and persuade rather than offend or annoy students? These and other practical ways to change attitudes on campuses are common; it's just a matter of identifying and exploring them. What is happening on your campus right now that could serve as your inspiration?

A research program can flourish and become a way of life. See **A *Major Success Story: Sound Decisions*** for a great example of one psychology major's journey into a professional life in auditory research.

What about you? What psychological issues puzzle you, either about yourself or those close to you? What do you think about when you evaluate the choices and actions of close friends, peers, or perfect strangers? Or consider the social or political issues on campus. Do any issues bother you or cause you to wonder about them? Is there anything there you can capitalize on in the form of an interesting research question?

Once you have a topic in mind, you need to flesh it out with supporting evidence. What sources should students like you use when conceiving papers or projects?

A **Major** Success Story   «««

Jim Bashford
PhD, Research Professor

FIGURE 7.1 Professor Jim Bashford demonstrates principles of sound wave conductance in a perception class.

Sound Decisions

Jim declared a psychology major at the outset of his college career. He first was drawn to psychology when he worked on his high school senior thesis, in which he began exploring the work of Sigmund Freud. Although he thought Freud's observations were both extraordinary and important, he concluded that Freud's theories were not just arbitrary but maybe "a little insane." However, working on his thesis inspired Jim to want to be a clinician in part because he thought there must be better ways of explaining and improving human behavior.

During graduate school, Jim got sidetracked by experimental psychology, especially by **psychophysics**, the branch of psychology that deals with how sensation and perception define human experience. In particular, he was fascinated by auditory perception, in part due to his love of music and sound. He liked how work in the physiology of hearing blended with the experimental methods he had learned in psychology. He joined his university's perception lab and happily reports that he never left. He currently serves as the director of the lab, writes grants to secure funding for the lab operations, publishes his findings, and teaches on the side.

His primary work focuses on digital methods of altering speech signals so that communications can be more intelligible. For example, his lab was able to determine the voice pitch that can be most easily understood in a noisy cockpit. His work has specific implications for helping people with hearing impairments who need modifications to the signal quality for sounds to be audible to them.

Being in a profession that involves asking and answering questions satisfies Jim's curiosity. He especially enjoys designing experiments and analyzing the results. Sometimes he feels some strain from the pressures of getting the results written up for publication when what he really enjoys is getting to run more experiments. Writing grant proposals is a necessary evil to support the work of the lab, but the economic necessity of this aspect of his role "wonderfully concentrates the mind," he says.

Best Advice? "As a writer of science, try to be concise, absolutely clear, and compelling, so the reader doesn't wander off until you've made your best case. Being compelling shouldn't be that difficult if you keep it personal. We're talking about psychology. What's more personal than that?"

                                          »»»

Check out *Measuring Up: Brainstorming Your Way to Research Topics* for some pointers on generating great research ideas.

Sources for Developing Psychological Claims

Marcus took a course in developmental psychology during his freshman year. One of the first assignments was to write a research paper on birth-order effects on child development. For example, do firstborn children differ in some psychologically meaningful and measurable ways from their later-born siblings? Are firstborns more introverted than siblings born later? Do later-borns engage in more risk-taking behavior than do firstborns? Are there any other birth-order effects? Marcus wrote a draft of his paper and sought feedback on it from his instructor a few days before it was due. In the draft, he mined his personal experience, describing the ways his older sister and younger brother's attitudes and actions were distinct from his own.

 **Measuring Up**

Brainstorming Your Way to Research Topics

Besides considering the sources listed in the text above, you can also learn to develop ideas for psychology research papers or projects through a creative technique known as **brainstorming**. Many thinkers rely on brainstorming as a way to come up with unusual or even radical solutions to questions or vexing problems.

Generate ideas. The instructions are actually rather straightforward: Identify an area of psychology that interests you (e.g., clinical psychology, social psychology, developmental psychology, cognitive psychology, biological psychology) and write down as many things that come to your mind related to the area you chose as possible. Here's the important part of brainstorming: Don't censor yourself. Your ideas can be ridiculous, wild, zany, silly, difficult, impractical, or whatever — don't worry about how they seem, just put them down on paper. At this point in the exercise, the goal is to generate as many ideas as possible without ruling anything out by thinking "That's crazy — it will never work" or "I'm sure this has been done already" and so on. Remain open to possibilities.

Evaluate ideas. After you run out of ideas and you have a list of possibilities to consider, now you can be more critical. Which idea or ideas might be worth developing into a topic? Why?

If you are working with two or more other students on a project, you can do group brainstorming to develop research ideas. Here, one person serves as the leader, whose responsibility is to keep the generation and sharing of ideas flowing. A recorder writes down all the ideas the group generates without judging their worth. After the group runs out of potential topics, each of the topics on the list is considered. Friendly discussion and editing whittles the long list down to a few possibilities.

The instructor explained that research papers need to incorporate published research found in the psychological literature rather than casual observation or personal stories, no matter how compelling and interesting these might be. The instructor cautioned Marcus about making subjective assumptions and conclusions, encouraging him to use library resources to make objective arguments about what developmental psychologists already know and to identify what they still don't know about birth-order effects. Although he had to rewrite most of the paper, Marcus was glad he shared the draft with his instructor. When he left her office, he went to the main library on campus and worked with a reference librarian who helped him locate four helpful journal articles on birth order. He ended up earning a good grade on the paper and thereafter relied on library sources (as well as the helpful assistance from librarians in the reference department) rather than on his personal and highly subjective experience when writing papers.

When they first arrive at college, many students are like Marcus: understandably prone to using their own experiences when they are unsure about which sources to use for writing and research projects. Some instructors specify the sources that are appropriate for assignments but others do not, so it's always a good idea to ask teachers for clarification about their preferences. Generally, professors in psychology and the other social sciences expect that the data will be scientifically reliable rather than based on personal experience or opinion, casual observation, or hearsay. Popular sources such as newspapers, magazines, social media, television programs, YouTube videos are not usually considered scientifically reliable. No matter how interesting it might be, information from *Psychology Today*, the *Huffington Post*, or the *Onion* does not meet academic standards. These sources can sometimes be used to introduce or illustrate an idea but are usually not considered to provide sufficient or valid support by themselves.

Like professional psychologists, psychology students should rely first on journal articles as their primary sources, then on chapters and books that summarize empirical evidence. What follows are descriptions and rationales for why this is so.

Journal articles. Journal articles are peer-reviewed scientific or scholarly articles that make claims supported by agreed-upon theories, research methods, and public evidence. The process of **peer review** involves evaluating the ideas and arguments in a manuscript or other work by professionals working in the same field. These peers often remain anonymous and expend serious effort to be objective when assessing whether to accept or reject a submission for publication. Peer-reviewed journal articles tend to make one main argument and to provide supporting evidence in the form of a review of the relevant psychological literature and typically an experiment or series of experiments that support the author's claims. Major journals tend to be published monthly or on some regular schedule, which means that articles appearing in them discuss what is currently known about the topics presented therein.

Your institution's library probably has a periodical section with print journals. If it does, browse through a few psychology journals to get an idea of what has been published recently. **Table 7.2** lists journals published by the American Psychological Association (APA) and the Association for Psychological Science (APS), both excellent sources of top-quality research.

TABLE 7.2

Journals Published by the American Psychological Association (APA) and the Association for Psychological Science (APS)

APA Journals

American Journal of Orthopsychiatry

American Psychologist

Archives of Scientific Psychology

Asian American Journal of Psychology

Behavior Analysis: Research and Practice

Behavioral Development

Behavioral Neuroscience

Canadian Journal of Behavioural Science

Canadian Journal of Experimental Psychology

Canadian Psychology

Clinical Practice in Pediatric Psychology

Clinician's Research Digest: Adult Populations

Clinician's Research Digest: Child and Adolescent Populations

Consulting Psychology Journal: Practice and Research

Couple and Family Psychology: Research and Practice

Cultural Diversity & Ethnic Minority Psychology

Decision

Developmental Psychology

Dreaming

Emotion

Evolutionary Behavioral Sciences

Experimental and Clinical Psychopharmacology

Families, Systems, & Health

Group Dynamics: Theory, Research, and Practice

Health Psychology

History of Psychology

The Humanistic Psychologist

International Journal of Play Therapy

International Journal of Stress Management

International Perspectives in Psychology: Research, Practice, Consultation

Journal of Abnormal Psychology

Journal of Applied Psychology

Journal of Comparative Psychology

Journal of Consulting and Clinical Psychology

Journal of Counseling Psychology

Journal of Diversity in Higher Education

Journal of Educational Psychology

Journal of Experimental Psychology: Animal Learning and Cognition

Journal of Experimental Psychology: Applied

Journal of Experimental Psychology: General

Journal of Experimental Psychology: Human Perception and Performance

Journal of Experimental Psychology: Learning, Memory, and Cognition

Journal of Family Psychology

Journal of Latinx Psychology

Journal of Neuroscience, Psychology, and Economics

Journal of Occupational Health Psychology

Journal of Personality and Social Psychology

Journal of Psychotherapy Integration

Journal of Rural Mental Health

Journal of Theoretical and Philosophical Psychology

Journal of Threat Assessment and Management

Law and Human Behavior

Motivation Science

Neuropsychology

Peace and Conflict: Journal of Peace Psychology

Personality Disorders: Theory, Research, and Treatment

Practice Innovations

Professional Psychology: Research and Practice

Psychiatric Rehabilitation

Psychoanalytic Psychology

Psychological Assessment

Psychological Bulletin

Psychological Methods

Continued

Psychological Review	Rehabilitation Psychology
Psychological Services	Review of General Psychology
Psychological Trauma: Theory, Research, Practice, and Policy	Scholarship of Teaching and Learning in Psychology
The Psychologist-Manager Journal	School Psychology
Psychology & Neuroscience	Spirituality in Clinical Practice
Psychology and Aging	Sport, Exercise, and Performance Psychology
Psychology of Addictive Behaviors	Stigma and Health
Psychology of Aesthetics, Creativity, and the Arts	Training and Education in Professional Psychology
Psychology of Consciousness: Theory, Research, and Practice	Translational Issues in Psychological Science
Psychology of Men & Masculinities	Traumatology
Psychology of Popular Media Culture	
Psychology of Religion and Spirituality	**APS Journals**
Psychology of Sexual Orientation and Gender Diversity	Advances in Methods and Practices in Psychological Science
Psychology of Violence	Clinical Psychological Science
Psychology, Public Policy, and Law	Current Directions in Psychological Science
Psychomusicology: Music, Mind, and Brain	Perspectives on Psychological Science
Psychotherapy	Psychological Science
Qualitative Psychology	Psychological Science in the Public Interest

Information from: American Psychological Association (2019) and Association for Psychological Science (2019).

Chapters and books. Book chapters often summarize a psychologist's research on a question or the available research of many investigators dealing with a topic. Peer-reviewers or editors who are experts in the relevant topic usually review chapters before they are published as a book. A book might deal with one topic — there are many books on birth order and psychological development, for example — or the book might contain work on a variety of topics including birth order, such as a handbook on issues in human development. Because chapters and books may take much longer to publish than journals, the information in them is often less timely. Nonetheless, chapters and books on psychology can be a solid source of psychological information.

Start your literature review with recent journal articles dealing with your issue of interest and then supplement those articles with relevant chapters or books, if needed. All else being equal, articles, chapters, or books that have been published recently (within the last 5 or so years) are apt to be preferable over those that are older, unless a resource has been recognized as classic or markedly significant. Naturally, these decisions depend on the topic and its current scientific popularity; sometimes you may rely on older works but it is always best to look for recently published sources. Where to look for these sources? The best place to begin is in an academic or research library.

Doing Efficient Library Research In Psychology

Academic libraries are social and cultural hubs that connect users to all kinds of information from an incredible variety of disciplines and fields of study. Our focus here is a narrow one — navigating the psychology literature — but when you can, familiarize yourself with your school's library, as its resources will help enrich your learning in all of your undergraduate courses.

Using PsycINFO

Locating the psychological literature requires you to use library resources; whether you do so by physically visiting the library or by going online is up to you. Searching the literature entails the use of databases, many of which are found online through most college and university libraries. The most useful database for students is **PsycINFO**, a reference tool maintained and continuously updated by the APA. This database contains citations and abstracts (brief research summaries) from journals, book chapters, books, book reviews, and other materials published in psychology since 1887. PsycINFO also allows users to search for research sources from sociology, nursing, psychiatry, and education. Another APA database, **PsycARTICLES**, gives users access to the complete text of electronic articles that were originally published in APA journals. Because PsycINFO is generally available and used by students, we will center our discussion on how to use this database. (Other helpful databases include PubMed and Bio Abstracts.)

To begin searching a database, you will need to use **search terms**, the key words that are linked to a given topic. If you choose a topic from a textbook, for example, you can try some of the terms that are discussed in the chapter or chapter section that interests you. For example, if you are interested in prejudice, you could focus on a particular type, such as racism or sexism. Alternatively, you can use an encyclopedia of psychology, selecting search terms from entries of interest in the encyclopedia. **Table 7.3** lists several common encyclopedias. Your library may have others; any one of them will provide you with viable search terms. For college-level assignments, rely on discipline-specific encyclopedias and dictionaries rather than general ones.

After you have a working list of search terms, you can expand it by accessing some of the index terms in PsycINFO. Once you are in the database, you can look for and then click on *PsycINFO's online thesaurus of psychological index terms*. Other search terms can be found in the thesaurus and added to your list.

PsycINFO's main search screen is very straightforward. You can insert a search term to begin looking for references, for example, or you can refine your search by selecting one of many field options, which narrow the search for a term. You could, for instance, look for the titles of works that include the search term "birth order" or you could search for abstracts that include the specific phrase "birth order." Perhaps you have learned that a particular psychologist publishes about birth order; you can also search by name to find all the articles published by that author.

TABLE 7.3

Some Common Encyclopedias of Psychology: Good Sources for Search Terms

Baumeister, R. F., & Vohs, K. D. (Eds.). (2007). *Encyclopedia of social psychology* (Vols. 1–2). Los Angeles, CA: Sage.

Corsini, R. J. (Ed.). (2010). *The Corsini encyclopedia of psychology and human behavior (4th ed., Vols. 1–4).* Hoboken, NJ: Wiley.

Eysenck, H. J., Arnold, W., & Meili, R. (Eds.). (1982). *Encyclopedia of psychology.* New York, NY: Continuum Press.

Harré, R., & Lamb, R. (Eds.). (1988). *Encyclopedic dictionary of psychology.* Oxford, England: Basil Blackwell.

Kazdin, A. (Ed.). (2000). *Encyclopedia of psychology* (Vols. 1–8). Washington, DC: American Psychological Association.

Ramachandran, V. S. (Ed.). (2012). *Encyclopedia of human behavior* (2nd ed., Vols. 1–4). San Diego, CA: Academic Press.

The point is that PsycINFO is extremely flexible; in fact, the only challenge you are likely to face is that it often provides too many research citations — you may want 5 but you get 500. If it returns too many results, narrow your search further by looking at only empirical articles, those that were published in the last year, and so on. If you are unsure how to refine your search, ask a reference librarian to help you. These professionals are trained to search for and find material for users — working with one can only help you to develop quicker, more effective search strategies.

Once you find some references about your topic, collect them to begin to build your research argument. If the reference is available electronically, print or download it. If it isn't available in digital form, go to the periodicals section of the library, locate the bound journals and make a photocopy of the article. If your school's library does not have a subscription to a particular journal and you cannot obtain a copy through some other online database, you can probably order a copy through what is known as **interlibrary loan** (you can probably do so online; ask a reference librarian for assistance). Once you have copies of the articles, you can read them and take meaningful notes from them at your leisure.

Check the Library's Catalog

Virtually all college and university libraries are searchable online. You can search by author, title, or keyword. You can also use the **Library of Congress Subject Headings** (LCSH; Library of Congress, 2012), a six-volume alphabetized guide often found in a library's reference department. Use the LCSH by looking up one of your search terms to see what other search terms are related, then continue your catalog search using those terms. If you find promising books listed in the online catalog, look for the subject headings associated with them, which will be hyperlinked. Click on one of the headings to start a search of all the available books in the library linked to that particular subject heading.

If your PsycINFO search suggests chapters or books, you can check the library's catalog to see if the library has a copy of the book (either a physical copy or an online version). If it doesn't, you can likely borrow a copy of the book by ordering it through whatever interlibrary loan service your school uses.

One important suggestion: As you search the catalog, keep a record of the call numbers of the books you intend to consider. Many catalogs are hooked up to printers, making keeping track of titles easy, or you can download your list or simply write down the call numbers in a small notepad or on your phone before you head to the stacks. Don't erase the numbers or throw them away; you may need to refer to them again before the project is done.

Use Known References to Locate Other References

Another good way to obtain sources for your assignments and writing projects is to look through the reference sections of the works you already have in your possession. Reading reference sections will not necessarily inform you about the most recent publications but will usually provide you with the major or classic references on a topic. As you examine the reference sections of the articles, chapters, or books you find, you will readily recognize those sources that are cited frequently, an obvious clue to their relevance and importance to the topic.

Use the reference lists to identify the names of the main authors working within a research area. As noted earlier, you can search by author in PsycINFO to make certain you have found the author's publications that are relevant to your topic. You can even search for their publications within a particular journal or that appeared during some time frame (a year or range of years).

Always Ask for Assistance

What happens if you are unable to locate useful sources in your initial search? Allow yourself a half an hour or so of searching on your own. If you cannot find published material on a topic, assume that you are probably not using the right approach. Lack of success is perfectly normal. Figuring out how to pick and choose appropriate resources for an academic paper is not easy. Don't despair; do as Marcus, the student who was interested in research on birth-order effects, did: Ask a reference librarian for assistance. You can dramatically shorten your search process with the help of campus librarians, who are expert at finding peer-reviewed sources. You won't be imposing or bothering them; reference librarians treat student requests as mysteries that they not only can solve but love to solve. They relish the opportunity to help students find exactly the right sources to build the most solid argument. Reference librarians, in particular, know how to search effectively for information no matter how obscure it might be. Don't be afraid to ask for help — they can be very helpful when it comes to searching multiple databases, narrowing search parameters, and suggesting new search strategies. They also know your school's library intimately, including what is and is not available, so they can locate sources quickly. There is never any shame in consulting an expert, especially one who wants to help! It takes a little time to develop search expertise. Since your tuition costs help pay her salary, why not consult with a librarian to optimize your search?

Many academic libraries offer tutorials on using reference, technical, and other resources. If your library does, take the time to sign up for this valuable instruction.

Searching the Internet

The Internet is an amazing tool, one none of us would want to do without. However, it should be used with moderation and care because the way it performs searches is not selective or necessarily intelligent — no guiding filters focused on quality are involved. The nanosecond results of a web search for "birth order" or "prejudice" will not rate the relevance or accuracy of the listed results. Unless a website's content is valid or peer reviewed, using it for college-level work is problematic. Whatever your information source is — *especially* when it comes from the Internet — evaluate it critically and find independent verification of its veracity. It pays to be a skeptical consumer and user of the Internet.

Here are some questions to ask yourself when evaluating evidence from the Internet:

- Who is the author? What are the author's credentials?

- Was it published by an established organization? Was there any peer or professional review involved? Self-published documents or books are rarely considered to be reliable sources and should be avoided in scholarly work.

- Is the evidence from the Internet clearly placed within the established research tradition? Is the material informed by existing evidence? If not, then it is highly suspect.

- Science strives to be a neutral enterprise even if scientists don't always achieve neutrality. In contrast, the Internet doesn't foster neutrality. Does the Internet site have a point of view, particular perspective, or even an agenda? Is the site at all politicized or biased?

- How up to date is the source? Is there a date of publication? When was the website updated last?

Using established websites maintained by professional organizations in mainstream psychology is always a good idea. Consider visiting those sites maintained by the APA, the APS, and Psi Chi. Websites from college and university psychology departments and those maintained by specialty organizations in psychology (see the list of APA divisions in Table 2.1) are apt to be useful sources as well.

Table 7.4 summarizes the steps in the search process we reviewed in this section. Refer to this table to carry out your search of the psychological literature efficiently when you get a new paper or project assignment.

Once you locate some sources to use for your research, you will need to evaluate whether they are useful to you. The questions provided below can help you assess whether a source is appropriate for your needs. Use the **Reality Check: Evaluating Psychology Sources** to assist you in developing the right critical-thinking approach to references.

TABLE 7.4

Recommended Steps for Searching the Psychological Literature

Step 1: Identify your research topic by using one of the topic-generation strategies or choose a topic from a course, psychology book, or a reading.

Step 2: Gather search terms for the research topic (consider using a source from Table 5.2) and search for them in PsycINFO.

Step 3: Collect copies of journal articles from periodicals at the library and from downloadable sources, books, book chapters, and interlibrary loan.

Step 4: Search the reference lists in the sources you collect; repeat step 3 as needed.

Step 5: Consider consulting a reference librarian who can help you expand or focus your search of the literature.

Step 6: If needed, carefully search the Internet for additional sources, but be appropriately critical and skeptical about what you find.

✓ Reality Check

Evaluating Psychology Sources

When reviewing a source ask yourself the following questions:

Accuracy
- ☐ Is this an original or primary source?
- ☐ Are facts provided?
- ☐ Are they supported with sources?
- ☐ Was the research peer-reviewed by other experts?

Authority and Credibility
- ☐ Is the author an expert in the field?
- ☐ How do you know if the author is an expert?

Objectivity
- ☐ What are the goals of the research?
- ☐ What opinions are expressed by the author?
- ☐ Who is the intended audience?

Currency
- ☐ When was the research published?
- ☐ Has it been updated since then?
- ☐ Are there new studies being conducted by others on the same topic?

Coverage
- ☐ How narrow and detailed is the research topic?
- ☐ Does the author give any background about or context for the research?

Overall Evaluation
- ☐ Is the research helpful to you? Is it believable?
- ☐ Would the research be useful in helping you form a reasonable opinion or decision?

One final piece of advice: You will have to review many more sources than you will actually use in your paper. If your paper requires 10 sources, don't be satisfied with the first 10 articles you read. You will end up struggling to construct an argument that is forced and unsatisfying. A better goal is to locate two to three times more articles than you need so you have a rich landscape from which to build a compelling argument.

Writing About Psychology

Besides being critical thinkers who rely on the scientific method, psychology majors are also good storytellers. They develop narratives exploring the implications of *hypotheses* (empirically testable questions) and research findings. Before we explore the two types of papers that psychology professors are most likely to assign — lab reports and literature reviews — we first review the writing conventions that psychologists practice using APA style.

APA Style in Brief

APA (American Psychological Association) style is an agreed-upon set of rules for communicating the results of scientific research in psychology. By using these shared rules for writing and presentation, all psychologists and psychology students can understand one another more easily; that is, what appears in APA style is predictable, consistent, and accessible to educated readers. Moreover, the writing is sufficiently clear that anyone could take the directions found in an empirical article and repeat what was done in a given research project (psychologists and other scientists refer to this as being able to *replicate* a study) to verify the validity of the original author's arguments.

Specialists in the discipline read and analyze research claims carefully to determine if the arguments are sound. Ultimately, if the report is plausible, they verify the claim and regard the work as valid. If the report is not plausible, they instead may challenge the conclusions drawn by the investigators because of flaws in the logic, design, or clarity of expression. This professional give-and-take advances science because it makes theories, methods, and explanations as open and objective as possible (as this book was being written, the discipline of psychology was moving to make all published research data open, available, and accessible to anyone via the Open Science Initiative).

The most complete summary of APA style can be found in the ***Publication Manual of the American Psychological Association*** (APA, 2010). Our review in this chapter is necessarily compact. Still, the information here is sufficient for crafting an APA-style lab report or literature review. If you have more specific questions, you can find the answers or guidelines you need in the *Publication Manual* or in one of the various available books on how to write about psychological research (e.g., Dunn, 2011).

The Research or Lab Report

Sometimes students will conduct an experiment or **correlational study** from start to finish — collecting data, analyzing it, writing it up, and presenting it orally. Other times they will propose a study and describe the results they anticipate finding if the project were actually conducted.

Research reports usually follow the conventional outline of APA-style papers and published empirical studies, including a format that has four main sections: the introduction and three sections entitled "Method," "Results," and "Discussion," respectively.

Introduction. The **Introduction** section of any APA-style paper gives readers a focused and detailed review of the literature related to the question or issue being explored. A thorough introduction provides a concise overview and then addresses the following points:

■ What scholarly evidence is already known about this topic?

■ Why is the current study being conducted? What question does it address?

■ How can any new findings extend what is known about the topic?

■ What variables were measured and manipulated in this study?

■ What **hypothesis** was tested? Why?

An introduction begins broadly, identifying the topic being researched and then increasingly narrowing the focus by reviewing relevant prior studies and leading up to the rationale for the current work's hypothesis.

Method. The **Method** section provides a specific road map or guide for understanding exactly what was done in the study from start to finish. The level of detail must allow a reader to recreate the study from scratch if desired. When reading a good Method section, a reader should be able to envision herself taking part in the study, answering questions, and engaging in the various behaviors required by the experimenter.

The Method section of a research report usually features three subsections. The **Participants** subsection describes the people who took part in the research, including whatever demographic information (e.g., sex, age, education) might be relevant to the study. The **Materials** subsection describes any equipment, surveys, questionnaires, and the like that were employed in the research. A chronology of what took place, who said and did what, and when they did so is in the **Procedure** subsection, as are any important details about the experimental design and the ethical debriefing of the participants at the study's conclusion.

Results. APA-style **Results** sections describe the research findings clearly and concisely, indicating how participants behaved, along with supporting statistical analyses. Readers get a clear sense of whether the research supported the hypothesis, but there is no interpretation included in this section. Results are factual and focused; researchers may include tables or figures displaying data or graphing findings for clarity. A full account of the findings, their implications (if any) for understanding the larger research literature pertaining to the topic, waits for the Discussion section.

Discussion. Discussion sections put findings into perspective: What do the results mean for understanding behavior? Why do they suggest one interpretation over others? Where should future research turn to next? This last main section of the research paper or lab report represents an opportunity for the author to consider the broader context of the research topic, to interpret what was found and place it in proper perspective. Researchers often use the Discussion section to explain which aspects of the methodology worked well and which did not, as well as to qualify any observations and to highlight the limits of the study and what could be improved upon in any future investigations. All studies have limits; no single research project can address or answer all questions.

Although **Table 7.5** outlines all sections of the APA-style paper, the four main or central sections are indicated in **boldface**. The table also includes additional information about layout and content.

TABLE 7.5

Characteristics of Sections, Layout, and Content of the APA-Style Manuscript

Title page—Appears on page 1 of the manuscript

Title explaining the nature of the work (12 words or fewer)

Author name and academic affiliation (name of your college or university)

Running head (an abbreviated title), with page numbers beginning on the title page in the header; see the sample paper in Appendix A for formatting

Any author notes, which are added to the bottom of the title page

All information on the page is centered

Abstract—Appears as page 2 of the manuscript

This short summary in one paragraph (not indented) notes the hypothesis, method, results, and implications of the work; 120 words or fewer

Keywords (5 or fewer words that connect the research to the psychological literature; these should be double-spaced and centered under the last line of text)

Introduction—Begins on page 3 of the manuscript

The centered title of the paper appears above the first line of text

Includes an overview of the research question, a review of relevant studies, and the purpose and hypothesis of the present experiment

Method—Immediately follows the end of the manuscript's introduction

Participants (who took part, how many, their sex, and any other pertinent demographic information)

Materials used (surveys, questionnaires, personality measures, equipment, tools)

Procedure (a step-by-step narrative description from the beginning to the end of the study, including what participants were told, what they did, and what information was gathered and recorded for analysis)

Continued

Results—Appears immediately after the Method section

Describes behavioral outcomes and any statistical results of the study but *not* any interpretation; tables and figures are included as needed to explain what was found

Discussion—Appears immediately after the end of the Results section

Addresses questions such as: Did the results support the hypothesis? Did the investigation broaden what is already known about the research area?

What do the findings mean? What do they imply about our understanding of the research question? How should future research proceed? Can improvements be made? What's next?

References—Begins on a new page following the last page of the Discussion section

Follows APA citation style: List of authors alphabetized by author's last name (no first names, initials only)

Any citation in the body of the paper must be listed in the references

Table(s)—Begins on a separate page after the last page of the references

Figure(s)—Follows any table(s) on a separate page

Information from: APA (2010).

Papers in correct **APA format** must be typed. Here are the basic formatting requirements (others are noted in Table 7.5):

- Double-spacing is used throughout the paper. There are no exceptions to this.
- Each page has a 1-inch margin on all four sides.
- The right margin should not be justified, that is, it should be jagged in appearance.
- Only a 12-point font should be used, one that is clear and easy to read (Times New Roman is the default font).
- Every page is numbered in the top right-hand corner and inside the 1-inch margin (only the Figures pages do not include a page number).
- With the exception of the Abstract paragraph, the first line of every paragraph is indented (use the tab key, which usually indents 0.5 inches).

The best way to understand the layout, structure, and function of an APA-style paper is to look at some examples. Appendix A in this book contains an annotated APA-style student paper that will serve as a helpful template when you are drafting and writing your own paper. You might also go to the periodicals section of your library and look up one of the APA journals from the list in Table 7.2. Open the journal and pick an article to review. Pick a second article at random in the same journal and compare it to the one you already reviewed. Although they are structured the same, the subheadings that create meaning and order in the introduction, Results, and Discussion will differ from one another. However, the overall outline — title, abstract, Introduction, Method, Results, Discussion, and references — will be the same.

References. As with the other sections, the style and presentation of citations in the **References** section of an APA-style paper are standardized. Although all citations are similar, the most recent edition of the *Publication Manual* (2010) lists 77 categories of references — from the basic journal article to video blog posts (vlogs). **Table 7.6** provides common reference formats that students are likely to use when writing lab reports or literature review papers. These samples will serve you well (note that the entries in Table 7.6 are not double-spaced — they would be in a student paper or a research manuscript). You can also consult the References section of this book for other examples. If you have a more exotic reference to cite (say, a photograph or a film), look up the formatting guidelines in the *Publication Manual*.

One important note: References appear in what is called a hanging-indent format (see the entries in Table 7.6). That is, the first line of each reference aligns with the left margin; however, any text on the second and subsequent lines is indented five spaces.

TABLE 7.6

Basic Examples of APA-Formatted References

Journal Articles

Bem, D. J. (2011). Feeling the future: Experimental evidence for anomalous retroactive influences on cognition and affect. *Journal of Personality and Social Psychology, 100,* 407–425. doi: 10.1037/a0021524

Mehl, M. R., Vazire, S., Holleran, S. E., & Clark, C. S. (2010). Eavesdropping on happiness: Well-being is related to having less small talk and more substantive conversations. *Psychological Science, 21,* 539–541.

Books

Bruyère, S. M., & O'Keefe, J. (1994). *Implications of the Americans With Disabilities Act for psychology.* Washington, DC: American Psychological Association.

Pennebaker, J. W. (2011). *The secret life of pronouns: What our words say about us.* New York, NY: Bloomsbury Press.

Edited books

Fiske, S. T., Gilbert, D. T., & Lindzey, G. (Eds.). (2010). *Handbook of social psychology* (2 vols.). Hoboken, NJ: Wiley.

Nelson, T. D. (Ed.). (2009). *Handbook of prejudice,* stereotyping, and discrimination. New York, NY: Psychology Press.

Book Chapters

Chan, F., Livneh, H., Pruett, S., Wang, C.-C., & Zheng, L. X. (2009). Societal attitudes toward disability: Concepts, measurements, and interventions. In F. Chan, E. da Silva Cordoso, & J. A. Chronister (Eds.), *Understanding psychosocial adjustment to chronic illness and disability: A handbook for evidence-based practitioners in rehabilitation* (pp. 333–367). New York, NY: Springer.

Funder, D. C., & Fast, L. A. (2010). Personality in social psychology. In S. T. Fiske, D. T. Gilbert, & G. Lindzey (Eds.), *Handbook of social psychology* (5th ed., Vol. 1, pp. 668–697). Hoboken, NJ: Wiley.

Materials from the Internet

American Psychological Association. (2016). *The road to resilience.* Retrieved from http://www.apa.org/helpcenter/road-resilience.aspx

World Health Organization. (2011). *World report on disability: Summary.* Retrieved from http://www.who.int/disabilities/world_report/2011/report/en/

Literature Reviews

Literature reviews are psychology term papers that summarize what is known about some psychology topic. The best review papers propose a particular point of view for examining the studies available on a topic. For example, it's likely that a paper comparing the incidence of depression in firstborn versus only children would be more focused and insightful than one comparing firstborn with only children in general. Specificity is a good rule to follow: More specific reviews say quite a bit about one topic, in contrast to broad reviews, which say little about many aspects of whatever is being considered.

Literature reviews typically also follow the basic outline of APA-style papers. However, because they do not usually contain original experiments by the author, they do not have a Method or a Results section. A quality student literature review has three main parts (Thaiss & Sanford, 2000, p. 88):

1. *A topic overview:* A clear explanation of the paper's theme and the purpose of the review.

2. *Main section of the paper:* A review of specific topics and issues drawn from a close reading of relevant studies. The main section can include subheadings to highlight key ideas.

3. *A closing section:* Identifies main conclusions to be drawn from the reviewed studies and suggests directions for future research.

Other Writing Formats

Although professors tend to have students write lab reports and literature reviews as a means of teaching the students how to write in psychology, they also assign other kinds of writing. What follows is a list of several of these types of writing assignments, with some pointers for writing effectively in those formats.

Posters. Your professor may ask you to convert a research project into a poster either in place of or in addition to a traditional research report. The **poster** should include the same kinds of headings that would appear in a paper, but the limitations of the format require you to summarize the key ideas and write concisely. Be sure that you use a font that is readable and use graphics to add some visual interest to your work. Include at least a partial list of the most important references (in APA format) for your work.

Grant proposals. Especially for those students who want to work in the nonprofit sector after graduation, learning how to write **grants** can be a useful talent. A **grant proposal** is a detailed request for funding to carry out a specific research project to solve a particular problem. At minimum, grant proposals include a list of the authors (called the *principal investigators* or *PIs*), a statement of the problem that needs funding, a brief literature review (with an APA reference list), specifications about how success will be measured, a timeline, and a clear and adequate budget to accomplish the aims of the grant proposal. Your campus may have an office that specializes in writing grant applications with experts who may be able to provide additional assistance.

Technical reports. Your professors may assign you to complete a project or technical report as part of their goal of preparing you for life after graduation. A **technical report** outlines the process, progress, or results of a technical or scientific research problem. For example, a class assignment might require that you serve as a consultant to a campus-based day care center by helping them work with toddlers. You might write a report recommending the use of particular play activities that promote active learning for toddlers. Your report should summarize the impact of your work. The writing in a technical report needs to be precise and objective. Your instructor will specify whether you need to include APA-style references.

Case notes. Some students may get internship placements that allow them to work directly with clients. In such cases, the agencies may require students to document their interactions in **case notes**, or client files. Although case notes do not require APA format or literature citations, case note writers do have to abide by some specific conventions. Clients may have access to their records so the notes need to be objective and free of bias or judgmental description. Unlike other, more public, forms of writing, case notes must be treated confidentially. Interns need to follow the policies of the organization in which they are working. Be sure to seek some feedback to ensure you are meeting the agency's expectations.

Journal entries. Certain classes may require you to create a record in which you reflect on your learning experiences in **journal entries**. Aside from following the rules of grammar and spelling, journal entries tend to have fewer constraints and no reference citations. Exercise discretion about disclosing too much personal information in this type of journal. Faculty members do have professional obligations to report certain criminal acts, such as child abuse.

Memoranda. Email has become a dominant medium for getting things done. However, writing the message in a formal business **memorandum** format, even if the memo is forwarded via email in an attachment, increases the professionalism of the communication. Using a conventional memo approach sets the communication apart from the deluge of messages most professionals must wade through each day. Put the following information at the top of a formal memo:

> To: Bruce Wayne, President, Batman Foundation
> From: Dick Grayson, lab assistant
> RE: Request for Batmobile renovation
> Date: March 15, 2016

If you use memos to conduct business about your coursework, be sure to provide enough context information to make clear the problem you are having, including noting which class you are taking. Be sure to indicate if you need an action taken by a specific deadline. You do not need to put your name at the end of the message.

If you send a request via email, the normal format of email will do some of the context-setting work for you, such as the date and some identifying information from the sender. But remember, your email name might not clearly communicate who you are to people who don't know you well (e.g., jwt29@ just won't help the reader know who is writing). Be sure to add your full name in the body or closing of the email, along with a good subject heading that orients the reader to what you need or want.

Stand and Deliver

Your work may not be over when you submit your paper. Many faculty members include a speaking component as part of the research and writing experience. Here are some tips to make the most of that opportunity:

1. *All good speakers started out NERVOUS.* With practice, you will be able to overcome your jitters.

2. *Even if people know who you are, introduce yourself and state the purpose of your presentation.* Good introductions give the audience an idea of the main points you plan to cover.

3. *Rehearse, rehearse, rehearse.* Don't wing it. Research studies especially have details that should be presented accurately. Rehearse so that you don't read from your index cards or PowerPoint and instead use a more conversational approach.

4. *Practice with technology.* You will lose precious minutes of your allotted time if you have to fuss with the volume controls or a recalcitrant video.

5. *Stay on topic.* Don't allow tangents to divert you from your main message.

6. *Look professional and act professionally.* Dress for the occasion in comfortable clothes that you won't be adjusting through the presentation. Don't fuss with your hair or pull your earlobe. Avoid using placeholders such as "um," "like," "you know," "literally," and "stuff like that."

7. *Engage your audience through creative language, examples, or involvement.* Maintain eye contact by sweeping your eyes across the room. Humor also helps presentations to be more memorable.

8. *Don't end abruptly.* Summarize the key ideas that you want your audience to remember long after you have stopped talking.

9. *Be thoughtful in response to questions.* If you are stumped, ask the questioner what his answer might have been. That response will give you more time to think through a better response. An honest "I don't know" is a better strategy than bluffing.

10. *Target your presentation to match the allotted time.* Talking too long indicates you aren't in control. Talking too little suggests you might not have done sufficient work.

We offer a final note, this one about your role as an audience member during your peers' presentations. Listen carefully to the presentations and try to formulate questions that will help elevate the experience for everyone. You will stand out as a critical thinker and get practice at being a good colleague.

Thought Questions

1. Do you have any other suggestions for ways to generate research or paper topic ideas?
2. Why are journal articles the preferred resources in psychology? Why should they be peer reviewed?
3. What are some challenges associated with using research from Internet sites?
4. If you had to write a research paper in psychology right now, what would your topic be? Why?
5. Why is it important to meet time or page limits in your communications assignments?
6. What situations would require you to write a memorandum? What problems might be more appropriate for a memo rather than an email?
7. Which presentation tip addresses a public-speaking weakness you might have witnessed? How will you address that problem?

8

Building Distinction Through High-Impact Practices

Don't say you don't have enough time. You have exactly the same number of hours per day that were given to Helen Keller, Pasteur, Michelangelo, Mother Teresa, Leonardo da Vinci, Thomas Jefferson, and Albert Einstein.

~H. Jackson Brown Jr., author of Life's Little Instruction Book

As Sam hoisted a big bag of mulch into the back of Jane's SUV, he described himself as being in a "holding pattern." Just graduated with an undergraduate degree in psychology, he was continuing to work as a stocker at a local lawn and garden business, a job he had begun while he was working on his degree. When Jane asked what he hoped to do with his degree now, Sam confessed that thought he had blown it. "I screwed up. I didn't take that **internship** course and now I won't be able to get a job in psychology. So I guess I'm just stuck here."

■ ■ ■

Conversations like these are challenging for students and professors alike. Sam's lack of vision and his limited hopes for the future following the completion of his degree were certainly disheartening, but buried in his confession were both a flawed conclusion and a painful reality. Sam was wrong about the damaging effects of missing out on an internship. Internships do provide a great context in which to apply what you have been learning in professional contexts, making you more valuable to a potential employer, but the obverse isn't accurate. The lack of an internship doesn't prevent you from getting a job; it simply makes proving that you "have the chops" harder. Unfortunately, Sam was right in that his holding pattern was a morass of his own making.

The painful reality inherent in Sam's current dilemma is that he recognized he didn't fully invest in the opportunities he had that would have made him a better job candidate after graduation. Sam is not alone. According to the National Center for Education Statistics (https://nces.ed.gov/programs/coe/pdf/Indicator_SSA/coe_ssa_2015_11.pdf), in 2013 approximately 40% of full-time students ages 16–24 worked while pursuing a degree. Just under 10% of full-time students worked a minimum of 35 hours a week. Unfortunately, between overbooked social lives, substantial work commitments, and a full academic load, students have little discretionary time available to pursue activities that will make them more valuable to the workplace after they graduate.

According to Pascarella and Terenzini (2005), the most successful undergraduates are good at blending academic, personal, and extracurricular pursuits. This involvement tends to translate to higher grades and to a higher likelihood of remaining in college. Kuh et al. (2010) suggested that students fare best in college when they have one high-impact practice (HIP) in their first year and another HIP in their senior year. High-impact practices are special opportunities that allow students to make a deeper connection to their chosen discipline, their faculty, and even their institutions or communities, such as being part of a professor's research team or helping in a food drive for the homeless. Some HIPs are embedded within courses; others involve extracurricular activities. Happily, psychology abounds with many HIP opportunities that enhance basic academic life.

The goal of this chapter is to explore the value added by participating in ways that create high-impact experiences for the undergraduate psychology major. We systematically review the more popular HIPs in psychology to make the case that investing your time will produce multiple positive opportunities in your life, potentially including:

- applying concepts and principles of psychology in assorted work projects;
- exercising leadership skills when completing projects;
- developing more personal relationships with people who might write letters of recommendation for you;
- expanding your portfolio with evidence of abilities and traits that will impress a future employer; and
- demonstrating your commitment to improving the lives of others.

In our experience, students who complete an exit interview upon graduation often express regrets that they didn't make time to take advantage of the enrichment activities that were available to them in college. In this chapter we ask you to consider carefully the decisions you are making regarding the

24 hours per day that you do have. First, we explore the importance of making thoughtful decisions about how to allocate your limited discretionary time and encourage you to review whether you might make some changes to the way you spend your time.

Making Strategic Decisions

You will have a variety of opportunities to enrich your learning and develop leadership skills that will help you stand out as a psychology student. Some will be easy to participate in because of their close connection to your major. For example, organizing and participating in study groups or working as an assistant in the department will give you a chance to gain valuable experiences that directly support your academic work. A term abroad can also be an excellent opportunity to build your self-efficacy as you master a new environment. Other activities, especially those that entail taking a formal leadership position, may require a considerable amount of your free time; being an officer in a psychology club or campus fraternity or sorority, serving in student government, or taking on significant community projects are all worthwhile but have a serious impact on how much time you can devote to your studies.

Choose your enrichment activities carefully. Consider this: Your number one priority in completing your degree is creating an academic record that will give you the best possibilities after you graduate. Don't allow yourself to be swept away by activities that you really don't have time to complete, no matter how exciting or ego boosting they might be.

Jeremy's story provides a good example. He enjoyed his psychology major but really loved being involved with student government. Eventually he had an opportunity to run for student body president but was concerned that the time demands of being president would be challenging. He chose the presidency and eventually fell behind in his studies. Although he did get exceptional leadership experience, it cost him. His GPA fell and he had to stay in school an extra year to finish his classes. In retrospect, his choice may not have been in his best interest. He gained leadership experience at the expense of a clean academic record that would have given him a wider range of options after graduation.

If you do decide to pursue a leadership position, recognize that a lot of effort goes into being a successful leader. See **Measuring Up: Do You Have What It Takes to Lead?** to assess the strengths you already show as a leader and to identify some areas where you could use some more experience.

We turn our attention now to some of the places in which you are likely to have experiences that will nicely augment the academic growth you are undergoing. We will start with an HIP that has a direct, positive impact on your academic success — establishing and leading study groups in psychology classes.

↑ 🛏 Measuring Up

Do You Have What It Takes to Lead?

College offers an array of leadership opportunities that can help you develop your skills and character, from organizing a study group, serving in student government, or presiding over Psi Chi. Look at the list below and identify the items that you think characterize your style as well as items you may still need to work on. Please place a check mark either in "mostly true of me" or in "area I need to work on" to capture your leadership profile.

This is mostly true of me.	Leadership Characteristics	*This is an area I need to work on.*
	Personal Attributes	
❏	I am more extroverted than introverted.	❏
❏	I am energetic.	❏
❏	I am self-disciplined.	❏
❏	I keep my promises.	❏
❏	I am punctual.	❏
❏	I am known for having integrity.	❏
❏	I speak with authority.	❏
❏	I can rebound from setbacks.	❏
❏	I am capable of being visionary.	❏
❏	I maintain a positive outlook.	❏
	Problem-Solving Skills	
❏	I notice when problems need to be fixed before others do.	❏
❏	I understand the situation thoroughly before taking action.	❏
❏	I am willing to do background research and planning.	❏
❏	I take immediate action once I've formulated a plan.	❏
❏	I predict consequences from the plans I'm implementing.	❏
❏	I enjoy change.	❏
❏	I can take calculated risks.	❏
❏	I show courage under pressure.	❏
❏	I take responsibility for errors and correct my mistakes.	❏

This is mostly true of me.	Leadership Characteristics	This is an area I need to work on.
	Team Skills	
❏	I'm oriented toward serving the needs of others.	❏
❏	I relate to and appreciate a wide variety of people.	❏
❏	I make a point to include others in my plans.	❏
❏	I can persuade others to take action.	❏
❏	I build and maintain effective collaborations.	❏
❏	I encourage team members to work from their strengths.	❏
❏	I can manage conflict.	❏
❏	I have strategies for working with difficult people.	❏
❏	I recognize and celebrate achievements.	❏
❏	I share the glory that follows an achievement.	❏

Organizing Study Groups

Consider organizing a study group for a class, particularly if the course is challenging. Campuses may provide some infrastructure for launching a study group; however, if you let your instructor know that you're interested in starting one, she or he can probably solicit interest from your classmates. Taking the initiative will establish your intentions to be successful and make you more memorable to your professor and classmates.

Discussing the course materials will reinforce your comfort with and recall of the content. The normal difficulties (e.g., using time efficiently and effectively) that result when students work together will provide a great opportunity to develop team skills and leadership. Improving your own performance and helping your peers with theirs through a study group may make it easier to figure out whether you would like to work as a teaching assistant in graduate school.

What's the best way to ensure your success? Weimer (2013) suggests that study groups often meander if they don't have a specific focus. She recommends several ideas to make the group experience a good one:

1. Each member identifies five things that are test-worthy, then the group constructs a master list of the concepts that were most frequently identified.

2. Each member writes a potential test question for a concept that is "fuzzy" or hard to understand. The group spends time answering each of these questions.

3. The group devotes a small amount of time to constructing one master summary sheet and uses the sheet to foster discussion.

Undergraduate Teaching Assistants

Some psychology faculty show special interest in students who express a desire to become teachers, especially college professors. In fact, some programs allow undergraduates to serve as teaching assistant (TAs) so that they can become familiar with aspects of being a teacher. Some undergraduate TA positions are paid; others are structured as a **directed**, or **independent**, **study**. If the latter, the supervising faculty member will likely assign the TA readings and perhaps some reflective writing to help the TA get the most from the experience.

Undergraduate TAs can have a variety of responsibilities, including grading low-stakes assignments, processing Scantron tests, coordinating and conducting study groups, meeting with students during office hours, and coming up with suggestions for active-learning activities. In some cases, undergraduate TAs might give a mini-lecture and get feedback from the professor as well as the students on the strengths and weaknesses of their lecture.

Even if there is no formal undergraduate TA program in your department, you can approach a professor about volunteering as a TA. If you perform well, your professor will be in a splendid position to write a strong letter of recommendation for graduate school, where you can pursue your dream of being a teacher.

Peer Advisors

Some programs offer students opportunities to practice counseling skills by joining a peer-advising team, usually as part of an independent study. Peer advisors provide practical advice to students about courses, professors, and program requirements. After they receive training to make sure their recommendations adhere to preferred departmental practices, they handle some of the more routine advising questions. They also can make referrals to special services on campus to help students whose needs are larger than just which courses to take.

Honors Program

Many campuses allow students who have proven their talent to enroll in an enriched program. Students may begin their college career in an **honors program** if their high school record qualifies them as scholastically talented; other students can earn their way into honors programs through exceptional grades in their first year. Typical honors programs provide some serious advantages for students, including smaller class sizes and being able to register for classes in advance. Honors programs tend to draw the most vibrant faculty, who thrive in working with small, highly motivated classes. Many honors programs also provide a social program in which students might find a comfortable place to develop what may become one of their most enduring friendships.

For all their advantages, honors efforts also require a great deal from participants. Being in small classes means that there is little chance a student can get away with not doing the work. Honors faculty design examinations and assessments to evaluate student knowledge at the highest levels of complexity. Honors programs are writing intensive and often require students to complete a thesis, which usually guarantees that honors students get to work one-on-one with a professor whose research interests them.

According to Astin (1999), honors programs produce multiple benefits. Students who successfully complete honors programs in college report high interpersonal and intellectual self-esteem and have greater sophistication in their appreciation of the arts. Honors students report more satisfaction with the quality of instruction they receive and with their relationships with faculty. They also demonstrate more persistence and are more inclined to pursue education in graduate or professional schools than students who are not enrolled in honors. Successful honors students can proudly add to their graduation regalia items such as honor cords to publicly display their achievements in their undergraduate major.

Psychology Learning Communities

Learning communities within majors are a relatively new form of HIP. Typically, these communities are designed to establish a strong *esprit de corps* among a limited number of first-year students who are all taking a common curriculum. The students are often housed together. The communities tend to attract exemplary faculty members who enrich their courses by inviting faculty guests and by incorporating field trips. Zhao and Kuh (2004) praised the potent results of being involved in these communities, including stronger persistence to graduation, higher GPAs, marked improvements in skills and competencies, significantly enhanced student involvement that is sustained through later years, and higher student satisfaction. Learning communities tend to be somewhat selective. Students routinely report that the intensity and scope of activities in the discipline-based learning community gives them a head start on knowing what they want to do professionally.

At James Madison University, students who participate in the Psychology Learning community can register earlier than other students for experimental methods classes and the department encourages informal interactions with learning community members so they can learn about the nature of research in the department (see http://www.jmu.edu/stories/orl/2014/05-08-rlc-caroline.shtml). At Rutgers, students in the Psychology House are ensured of being able to taking blocked courses with their peers. **Blocked classes** refers to having a cohort of students take a specified number of classes together. They can also participate in related social activities, a quiz competition, and a resource fair for summer funding (see http://rulc.rutgers.edu/content/psychology-discovery-house).

Psychology Study-Abroad Programs

If you have the financial wherewithal, consider studying abroad. Study-abroad programs can provide a particularly eye-opening experience and strengthen your background in psychology while you enjoy adapting to a new culture. Most people who have been in a study-abroad program say that it was transformative in part because their comfort zones were stripped away. Students must rely on what they have learned to help navigate the various daily challenges — language, social customs, novel foods — they hadn't even thought about before the trip. Unless they are part of a language-immersion curriculum, most study-abroad programs are conducted in English.

Students can secure an independent study arrangement through the variety of options hosted by specific psychology programs (Google "psychology study abroad" to see a dazzling array of options). However, it may be smartest to work with the international studies office on your own campus. That office may have preexisting agreements that will not only narrow down the wide range of choices but also can help students with the difficulties that can accompany international travel. There may also be some additional financial aid, including scholarships, available through your home campus.

Studying abroad can have a significant effect on personality development and leadership (Zimmerman & Neyer, 2013). Travelers must face and conquer ambiguous conditions, from those involved in making travel arrangements through the various adjustments to living in a new culture. Coupling travel vagaries with academic demands produces near-perfect conditions for developing confidence and problem-solving skills. Most travelers also report that they feel greater tolerance for and appreciation of people from different backgrounds as a result of the experience.

Many students report that studying abroad has an impact on how they think about politics, world conditions, additional educational goals, and career directions. Not surprisingly, studying abroad can influence personality development. The Big 5 personality framework (McCrae & Costa, 2003) that compares personality across five different dimensions predicts changes in three of the five dimensions from studying abroad. Experienced travelers show increased openness and agreeableness as well as decreased neuroticism).

Undergraduate Research

Dana got engaged with undergraduate research in his freshman year. He served as an undergraduate research assistant to a graduate student who was finishing a dissertation. Although his responsibilities were limited to data entry, it was a pretty heady experience to be mentioned in the footnote of a *Journal of Personality and Social Psychology* article. He was then able to secure a second research assistant position for a high-profile social psychologist. His tasks included recruiting student volunteers to participate in the study, scheduling data collection times, and collecting data. Not only did he learn a great deal about the rigor involved in social psychology experiments, he learned about the importance of having a strong work ethic. That experience served him well when it was time for him to design and execute his honors thesis, which he completed on short-term memory effects on voter decision-making.

Dana's experience is typical of students who understand the value of building a strong portfolio of experience in research. Lopatto (2010) praised involvement in undergraduate research for the improvements it brings about in the skill sets of scientists, including critical thinking; the ability to work with primary literature; communication; and teamwork. He also emphasized that overcoming the inevitable obstacles in undergraduate research builds self-confidence and improves independence. He recognized that successful experience seems to inspire students to want to pursue more complex research designs. Lopatto concluded that these benefits give people an advantage in any career path they choose.

Service Learning

Service learning is a popular means of having students apply what they are learning in the classroom to practical problems in the larger world. Because of its hands-on focus, service learning is often referred to as **experiential learning**. Students who give back to the community through volunteer work in psychology-related settings, or in organized service-learning or other forms of experiential learning settings, show their civic engagement. The caliber of the service-learning experience depends on the quality of supervision and the scope of the volunteer's responsibilities.

In psychology, especially for students with a clinical bent, volunteering in clinical settings may provide some advantages in developing employment planning. For example, students who volunteer at a local human services organization often begin to see that working with people with serious mental disorders requires enormous effort and patience. Seeing the nature of the work from close up can help students make better career choices, even if it means learning that a particular kind of occupation is not for them. Although volunteer work may be personally meaningful, supervised learning experiences provide more tailored feedback that reflects the use of psychology in the setting.

Service learning promotes the development of knowledge, attitudes, and skills in the context of specific classes (Bringle & Hatcher, 1995). Typically, service learning is project-based so that it can be adapted to the constraints of the academic term. Students take on a project, such as helping to build a house for an organization like Habitat for Humanity, but ground their experience in the relevant research literature. For example, they might look at the effects of income inequality or at what constitutes quality of life. "Service learning" can be the title of the course or it can be a special assignment embedded within a course. As an example of the latter, Jane's introductory psychology class consulted with a child abuse agency to make some recommendations for changes to the agency's parent-training curricula after they learned some basics about child development and principles of behavior modification in their course.

Internships

Internships are typically the most intense type of experiential learning. Psychology students move outside the traditional classroom structure and try out professional roles in settings that deal with psychological concerns. In the best internships, students receive feedback from both an on-site mentor and a faculty member with pedagogical expertise about activities at the site. Students might work in a politician's office, for example, solving problems for constituents. They can run leadership training sessions for the Girl Scouts. They may go to work as an extra pair of hands in a research laboratory. Because psychology relates to any enterprise that deals with data or people, the array of potential internships for psychology majors is fairly broad. Internships can be valuable for helping students decide which directions not to pursue before they get too far down the professional path. Not all undergraduate programs provide access to meaningful internships. In fact, a survey of recent graduates (McClendon, 2018) suggested that students place great value on internship experiences because they would lead to better preparation for the workforce. They expressed the desire for earlier introductions, and better access, to internships.

Psychology Interest Groups

Psychology students are often passionate about their major. It is not unusual to find psychology interest groups or clubs established on campus to help students spend more time in the discipline they are learning to love and to connect with other students and faculty who share their passion. Psychology clubs usually have a faculty sponsor who can provide light guidance about the kinds of activities that the club should undertake, including field trips, alumni visits, careers days, and service learning. See *A Major Success Story: Parlaying Student Leadership Into Professional Success* for an example of positive outcomes that can result from wise extracurricular choices.

Psychology Honorary Organizations

Many students find that becoming a member of an organization that honors strong academic work is helpful to their development. Begun in 1929, **Psi Chi** confers membership on students who have a particular GPA overall (top 35% of the class) and a minimum of 3.0 (on a 4-point scale) both overall and in the major (https://www.psichi.org/page/about#.XJ1LcOtKg_U). There are well over 1,000 chapters of Psi Chi around the world and the organization reports that it has 750,000 lifetime members. Members can apply for awards and grants, as Psi Chi gives away $400,000 annually to its membership. Psi Chi publishes *Eye on Psi Chi*, a magazine for members that features articles of interest to the psychology community. Psi Chi also sponsors special sessions at regional and national conferences. A career-enhancing advantage of being selected to Psi Chi is that members automatically meet a requirement for joining the civil service at the GS7 level. Visit the Psi Chi website at https://www.psichi.org.

Psi Beta, an honorary organization operating at the community college level, selects its members based on meeting similar high standards of scholarship. Many of the advantages that attach to Psi Chi membership are also available through Psi Beta. See the Psi Beta website at http://psibeta.org.

Other Extracurricular Activities

In becoming more well-rounded, you don't have to use all of your discretionary time in events that explicitly focus on psychology. Most campuses abound with opportunities to meet others who share your interests, even if your interests are rather esoteric. Are you a salsa dancer? A pickleball expert? A Harry Potter fan? An intramural sports fan? An amateur in improvisational theatre? Affiliating with others and planning events involving your hobby will develop your leadership skills while you deepen your leisure interests and expand your social network.

A Major Success Story ‹‹‹

FIGURE 8.1 John "Trey" McClendon amassed a significant number of high-impact experiences as a psychology major despite substantial physical limitations.

Eethany McClendon

Parlaying Student Leadership Into Professional Success

John "Trey" McClendon became involved in psychology-related HIPs when he began studying at a community college. He recalls that one of his first experiences was attending a guest lecture by a suicide survivor that pulled on his every heartstring and cemented his desire to become involved as a professional helper. His academic record qualified him to be inducted in Phi Theta Kappa, the national honorary for 2-year college programs. When he transitioned to a 4-year program, he affiliated with Psi Chi, and in his last year became the president of his organization's chapter. Under his leadership, the chapter grew both in number and vitality, and he spearheaded a variety of social events (board game night) and service projects (a campus cleanup called the Trash Dash). When he was ready to undertake a service-learning project—one of his academic requirements—he became involved with a group that developed survival backpacks for victims of human trafficking. Based on his consistently strong academic work and his enthusiasm, Trey was asked to be an undergraduate TA in his final semester. He was able to make a presentation at the American Psychological Association on a research project that we cite in this chapter (McClendon, 2018). He was designated the most outstanding psychology student on his home campus during his graduation year.

What made his involvement all the more impressive was Trey's physical condition. Before he started college, Trey was in a swimming pool accident that caused traumatic compression to his spinal cord and left him with quadriplegia, constraining his physical mobility. Although some people experiencing such a dramatic turn of events might have abandoned their goals, Trey was undaunted. He continually looked for opportunities that would enrich his learning and help others.

Upon finishing his bachelor's degree, Trey decided to go to graduate school in social work. As the result of his stellar undergraduate performance, he was offered a graduate assistantship that will offset many of the expenses he will incur while pursuing his master's degree. He believes the MSW will provide him immediate access to the workforce while allowing him to implement the social justice values he holds dear.

Best Advice? "Use your own energies to enrich your education. Make a strong connection with your professors outside of class. It's important to be proactive in advocating for the educational experiences not just for the goal you know but to support what you don't even know yet will be of value."

›››

On-Campus Employment

Recall that our chapter opening story about Sam's poor engagement choices suggested that he was working too much and exploring enrichment activities too little. Not all employment is a bad thing. In fact, faculty members expect that most (but not all) students can reasonably manage between 10 and 15 hours per week and still do well in their studies (Pena, 2010). If you need to work to cover your expenses and can handle the strain without compromising your academic success, we strongly recommend finding employment on campus and encourage you to work with the campus offices that streamline screening and selection.

Multiple advantages accrue to on-campus employment (Mayfield & Mayfield, 2012). Employers tend to be especially sensitive to the rhythm of the academic term and may allow you to work fewer hours during periods when academic demands (e.g., project completion, finals) increase. If a job has downtime, the employer may let you do your homework during the slow period.

On-campus jobs might also be part of a work-study program, which can have a positive impact on your financial aid. If you have been deemed eligible for work-study — which is based on financial need — you can apply for an on-campus job that is jointly subsidized by the school and the federal government. There are limits to the number of hours you can work and how much you can earn. Work-study money can help you pay for tuition and other college expenses and, most importantly, the money you earn does not count against the amount of financial aid you receive for future terms. The jobs available are often in the library, campus bookstore, cafeteria, the admissions office, or even in campus residence halls.

Psychology majors who end up working in psychology departments — a great way to learn more about the faculty and the discipline — must abide by confidentiality rules, particularly where handling course materials (including quizzes and exams) and student records are concerned. Students can use the experience of being a part-time student-employee to explore how a psychology department functions. Fulfilling this role can make it easier to figure out whether to apply to graduate school, as it provides a close-up look at what life in an academic department entails.

Professional Convention Participation

One of the powerhouse experiences Jane remembers was participating in the Midwestern Psychological Association (MPA) convention as an undergraduate. Everything about the trip was exciting. She got to see some famous psychologists and attend some stimulating presentations that whetted her appetite for graduate school. She was also impressed with the side features of conference life (great restaurants, access to museums, and networking) that made the prospect of attending regularly very appealing. She cites this event as contributing to her enduring status as "teaching-conference junkie."

Academic psychology sponsors a wide array of conventions and conferences, giving students ample opportunity to try out this aspect of professional life. Many faculty are active in the professional organizations that sponsor conferences. Consequently, those faculty may sponsor student travel groups to the conferences they would normally attend. They might also expect their advanced or top-performing students to participate in student-oriented poster sessions.

Conferences that are friendly to student participation, either undergraduate or graduate, happen at three levels: state, regional, and national. State psychology organizations tend to be more focused on concerns of clinical practice but still may have presentation or poster sections to showcase high-quality student work.

Many regional and national conferences hold special sessions to promote the submission of excellent student work. Regional psychology conferences (e.g., the Southeastern, Eastern, Midwestern, Western conferences) tend to be scheduled near the end of the spring term. In some cases, the conference traditionally takes place at one particular hotel, such as the MPA's Palmer House in Chicago. Most other regional conferences rotate among larger cities within the region.

National conferences also tend to dedicate specific parts of the program to students, but most tend to be geared to graduate students rather than undergraduates. The convention of the American Psychological Association (APA) draws thousands of psychologists and is typically scheduled in late summer and tends to rotate among the largest cities in North America (e.g., Toronto; Chicago; Los Angeles; Washington, DC). Both Psi Chi and Psi Beta offer programming designed to bring undergraduates together and help them make important decisions about their professional direction.

The convention for the Association for Psychological Science (APS), a newer national organization that focuses on research, takes place in late spring, over the Memorial Day weekend. With a slightly smaller number of participants, it moves among a variety of U.S. cities. See **Table 8.1** for a listing of regional and national conferences.

Well-organized undergraduate programs that facilitate student travel to conferences usually have orientation information for students so they know what to expect when they are away from campus. Preparation for going to a conference often involves holding fundraising events — such as bake sales or carwashes — to supplement departmental funds and make it financially easier for students to attend. Student fees for participation in these conferences tend to be fairly modest. If faculty from a particular school are involved in the leadership of the conference, their students may be able to work at the registration table and thus reduce their cost of attending the conference. If you are planning on attending a conference and wish to cut costs, try contacting the director of programming to see if you can work at the conference in exchange for the registration fee.

Student Convention Presentations

Regional conferences dedicated to showcasing student work represent another place for students to sample conference life. These conferences accept presentations by students at all levels whose papers meet the published criteria. If students have been

TABLE 8.1

Regional and National Psychology Convention Venues

National Conventions	Southeastern Psychological Association
American Psychological Association (APA)	www.sepaonline.com/
https://apa.org/	April 1–4, 2020, New Orleans
August 6–9, 2020, Washington, DC	Mar 17–20, 2021, Orlando, FL
August 12–15, 2021, San Diego, CA	**Rocky Mountain Psychological Association**
August 4–7, 2022, Minneapolis, MN	www.rockymountainpsych.com/
August 3–6, 2023, Washington, DC	April 16–18, 2020, Denver, CO
August 8–11, 2024, Seattle, WA	April 7–11, 2021 Albuquerque, NM
Association for Psychological Science (APS)	**Western Psychological Association**
https://www.psychologicalscience.org/	https://westernpsych.org/
May 21–24, 2020, Chicago, IL	April 30–May 3, 2020, San Francisco, CA
Regional Conventions	**Midwestern Psychological Association**
New England Psychological Association	midwesternpsych.org/
http://www.newenglandpsychological.org/	Apr 23–25, 2020
	Apr 22–24, 2021
	Apr 21–23, 2022
	Apr 20–23, 2023
Eastern Psychological Association	**Southwestern Psychological Association**
https://www.easternpsychological.org/	www.swpsych.org
March 12–14, 2020, Boston, MA	April 3–5, 2020, Frisco, TX
March 4–6, 2021, Philadelphia, PA	April 9–11, 2021, San Antonio, TX
March 3–5, 2022, New York, NY	

part of a research team that produced the paper, faculty may ask them to participate in the paper presentation. Research papers are often presented in shared sessions. An increasingly popular format for displaying student work is poster sessions. In some cases, faculty may assign projects with the intention that good student work can be presented in the student research sessions at conferences. **Table 8.2** summarizes some undergraduate research conferences that were held in 2014.

Student conferences provide great venues for practicing professional communication skills. **Table 8.3** shows a feedback sheet for poster sessions that addresses effective communication and research skills.

In addition, conferences routinely feature stimulating keynote speakers who are engaging to both students and professionals. Conferences typically include career-advising sessions to help students prepare for the steps after graduation. If you have the opportunity to present, step up! You may be surprised at how much interest you stir and how much fun you have.

TABLE 8.2

A Sample Of Student Research Conferences*

General Conference

National Council on Undergraduate Research (NCUR)

https://www.cur.org/what/events/students/ncur/

Psychology Conferences

Georgia Undergraduate Research in Psychology Conference

https://www.gcsu.edu/gurc

Great Plains Students' Psychology Convention

https://www.greatplainsconvention.com/

Hudson Valley Undergraduate Psychology Conference

https://www.dc.edu/academic-divisions/division-social-sciences/psychology/
   psychology-conference/

Mid-America Undergraduate Psychology Research Conference

https://www.mauprc.org/

Minnesota Undergraduate Psychology Conference

https://apps.carleton.edu/mupc2018/

L. Starling Reid Undergraduate Psychology Conference

http://psychology.as.virginia.edu/reid-undergraduate-psychology-conference

Stanford Undergraduate Psychology Conference

www.stanfordconference.org

* Websites may reflect a site during a specific year. Search under the name of the conference if the link no longer works.

Mentor Relationships

Consider finding a mentor from among students who have experience in the path you plan to follow. Seeking advice from seasoned students can help you avoid classes that are deadly. Such connections may also lead to your being able to join a research team as early as possible in your college career. When you consider adopting a mentor from among more seasoned students, make sure you recruit someone who has been successful and is recognized within the psychology program.

Faculty can also serve as mentors. Undergraduates may be particularly drawn to the nature of the work being done by a specific faculty member in the department. Especially in this digital age, when so much communication takes place over the Internet, faculty welcome in-person visits from students, particularly those who show enthusiasm for their work. If the connection is a strong one, the relationship can become one of the most important that collegiate life has to offer, as your mentor will tailor advice to you about your plans for after graduation and will be receptive to your requests to write strong letters of reference on your behalf.

TABLE 8.3

Sample Rubric for Undergraduate Posters

IUP Undergraduate Scholars Forum
Poster Session Evaluation Rubric

Poster Number: _____   Judge: _____

The following judging rubric lists and explains the 7 elements used to evaluate the poster. The total number of points possible is 35 (7 elements × 5 pts).

	1–2 Points	3–4 Points	5 Points	Total
Organization of Content (5 pts)	Poster lacks a clear organization. Components and content are difficult to identify and find.	Most components and content can be found, but they are not clearly identified and/or not logically organized.	Components and content are easy to identify/find and follow. Appropriate, logical organization.	
Scholarly Presentation (5 pts)	Presentation may be informational or educational, and may be creative or appealing, but it does not reflect a scholarly presentation.	Poster contains some elements of a scholarly presentation, but does not consistently reflect a scholarly approach to presenting content throughout.	Reflects a scholarly presentation, includes components common to scholarly presentations in the discipline (i.e., abstract, research question, review of the literature, methods, results, etc.).	
Scholarly Knowledge (5 pts)	Content may report information but includes little or no scholarly knowledge (theory and/or research); includes no original research by the students.	Content reflects scholarly knowledge (theory and/or research), but no original research conducted by the student(s).	Content includes scholarly knowledge (theory and/or research), and reports on original research conducted by the student(s).	
Clarity of Information Presented (5 pts)	Fails to convey key ideas and/or information; or information does not clearly convey the pragmatics of the topic/project.	Some lack of clarity. Some connections may be unclear. Some information not presented concisely (e.g., presents raw data or output rather than summarizing results succinctly).	Information is presented clearly and concisely (e.g., effectively synthesizes scholarly knowledge and summarizes results of the research project). Provides a clear picture of the pragmatics of the topic/project.	

Continued

Accuracy of Information (5 pts)	Poster contains substantial inaccuracies. Three or more errors in grammar and/or spelling.	Poster reflects minor inaccuracies. One or two minor grammatical or spelling errors.	Poster contains no discernable inaccuracies. No grammatical or spelling errors.	
References (5 pts)	No citations in text and/or no list of references, or cited references missing from reference list.	Only one or two errors in citing references (failures to cite sources or include a reference in list of references).	All references are cited in the text and included in a list of references.	
Aesthetics (5 pts)	Presentation is neither neat nor professional looking. Colors may not coordinate or may distract from content. Title and/or font in text are too small. Font types and/or margins are not uniform.	Presentation is neat in appearance but lacks professional polish. Colors may coordinate, but still distract. Fonts may not all match. Title not quite large enough and/or text slightly too large or too small.	Presentation is neat and professional in appearance. Colors coordinate. Fonts are uniform. Title is large and easy to read; font of text is easy to read.	
	Total Points Possible: 35		**Total Points:**	

Comments:

Summer Opportunities

Especially if you are not taking summer classes, use your summertime wisely to gain more psychology-related experience and potentially enhance your leadership skills. Your campus may provide a service to help you locate work that will allow you to apply psychology principles, exercise your leadership skills, and earn money to support you in your next academic year.

Conclusion

The variety of ways that psychology majors can become more engaged is impressive. Students who are headed to graduate or professional school may see the greatest gains through becoming involved in research, but virtually any outside activity can have a huge effect on developing leadership and building a strong portfolio. However, students should be mindful about the choices they make, as these activities should enhance and support rather than interfere with academic work.

In *Reality Check: High-Impact Enrichment: Make It Happen* we ask you realistically to think about how you might build in at least one high-impact experience to

Reality Check

High-Impact Enrichment: Make It Happen

You spent time in this chapter exploring strategies that would help you stand out in positive ways from your peers. Examine the inventory below and identify any HIP (high-impact practice) that you have already completed and think about how the HIP may have benefitted your knowledge, skills, or attitude. For those that you have not yet participated in, rank their appeal from 1 (no appeal) to 5 (maximum appeal). In a final step, strategize about how you can actually accomplish those that have maximum appeal by devising an action plan and timeline.

High-impact practice	Indicate which you have completed in this column and what you gained	Rate the HIPs you haven't participated in from 1 (no appeal) to 5 (max appeal)	What should you do to be able to participate in those HIPs that most appeal to you?
Study group organizer			
Undergraduate teaching asssistant			
Peer advisor			
Honors program			
Learning community			
Study abroad			
Undergraduate research assistant			
Service learning			
Internship or field experience			
Psychology club			
Psychology honorary (Psi Beta, Psi Chi)			
Other extracurricular activity			
On-campus employment			
Convention attendance			
Conference presentation			
Formal mentoring experience			
Off-campus employment			

enhance your distinctiveness as a student. Identify the HIPs that have already been part of your development, but assign priority to those you have not participated in so you can come up with a realistic plan to make your mark. In keeping with the time-management concerns emphasized by our opening quotation from H. Jackson Brown, recognize that you may have to forgo something you are currently engaged in to make room for a new worthwhile quest.

Thought Questions

1. What kinds of high-impact practices appeal most to you?
2. What are the advantages and disadvantages of studying abroad?
3. How motivated might you be to participate in a study-abroad program while you are an undergraduate?
4. Where and when have you been able to exercise your leadership skills?
5. What would you need to do in general to make a study group effective?
6. What would be your ideal on-campus job?
7. What kind of research team would be most attractive to you? What kind of research team would you want to avoid?
8. How would you manage the cost of attending a student research conference?
9. What style of mentor would best suit your needs for planning for your future?

What Career Options Exist for Students With a Bachelor's or an Associate's Degree in Psychology?

Find out what you like doing best
and get someone to pay you for doing it.

—Katherine Whitehorn, British Journalist

Wouldn't it be fantastic if finding your career pathway were as simple as Katherine Whitehorn suggested? Getting a great job in psychology isn't really a mysterious process, although the connection between a background in psychology and meaningful employment in the workforce is seriously misunderstood. Our focus in this chapter is to help you learn how identify a meaningful occupation that fits your skills, interests, and degree.

■ ■ ■

First, we will examine why psychology majors have such a bad reputation for landing a job. We look at how expectations differ from college to the workforce. Then we will explore the range of possibilities for which a liberal arts or science degree qualifies you. We describe strategies that can help you target the jobs that are a good match for your skills and interests. We conclude the chapter with some great profiles of students who successfully navigated the job-search process with associate and baccalaureate degrees.

"Will You Have Fries With That?"

A few years ago Jeb Bush, an aspiring presidential candidate, caused quite a stir on the campaign trail when he suggested a dire employment fate for liberal arts graduates, particularly those who study psychology and philosophy; he predicted that they would end up "working at Chick-fil-A" (Mills, 2015). His outrageous statement inspired a social media campaign on Twitter to illustrate how wrong Bush was in his dismissal of psychology's job prospects; students and professionals across the country shared what they were doing with their "worthless" psychology degrees (see **Figure 9.1**) (Langley, 2015).

Langley offered a cogent response to Bush's attack on psychology-major employ-ability. He shared that he worked for 2 months at a fast-food restaurant after he grad-uated before he found another position — a job as a child-abuse investigator and case manager — that was better suited to his psychology background. He criticized Bush's warning that psychology majors were doomed to the dire outcome of work-ing in food service because he found that the work provided valuable experience in working with the public.

FIGURE 9.1 Presidential candidate Jeb Bush touches off a Twitter war from outraged psych majors who felt demeaned by his prediction that those with psychology degrees end up working in the fast-food industry.

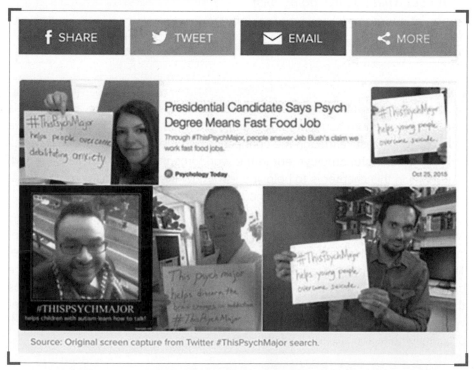

Source: Original screen capture from Twitter #ThisPsychMajor search.

In addition, Bush's attack implied that food service is dead-end work. As Langley's story demonstrated, paying the bills by taking a customer-service position need not be a dead end. Entry-level jobs often can be stepping stones to higher levels of responsibility and pay (e.g., you can work your way up to become the manager of the Chick-fil-A). Or you can build your resume by explaining how such experience makes you even more suited to the next position you seek. From his humble beginnings in food service, Langley eventually became a professor and author.

We hope this chapter will sufficiently arm you to deal with this popular unemployability misconception when you encounter it from friends and relatives who speak with ill-informed authority about how limited your prospects will be when you have a psychology degree. In fact, the world is full of psychology-related jobs that involve working with people or with data — and most likely both! The secret is knowing how to translate your experience and values into the profile that prospective employers will find appealing. To start that process, let's take a look at the different kinds of degrees that prepare you for a psychology-related career. But first, see **Reality Check: Defending Your Major Decision** to help you properly defend your major.

⊘ Reality Check

Defending Your Major Decision

It is as predictable as the sunrise. At any family gathering you are likely to face an onslaught of questioning about your status in college. One of your relatives is bound to imply — or state outright — that majoring in psychology is a bad idea. That relative knows for certain that you can't get a job without going to graduate school; how will you ever pay for your student loans? Given the bad rap psychology has with the public, it is understandable that your relative's concern for your future might become an unwelcome centerpiece of the gathering.

Forewarned is forearmed. Use the following cues to develop your best response. Craft a one-line statement for each of the bullets below that contribute to a strong defense of your major.

- ☐ Types of jobs available:
- ☐ Enthusiasm for working with people:
- ☐ Expertise in managing data:
- ☐ Entry salaries and living wage:
- ☐ Entry salaries as a starting point:
- ☐ Willingness to go to graduate school:
- ☐ Importance of values other than economic:
- ☐ Opportunity to make creative contributions:

Upon completion, select the top two arguments that you find most appealing. Convert those two elements into an "elevator speech" that will serve you the next time someone tries to give you unsolicited and negative advice about your major choice.

Defining Degrees: The BA/BS and AA/AS Degrees

There are essentially four degrees that undergraduate students — including psychology majors — can earn: a bachelor of arts or bachelor of science degree, and an associate of arts or associate of science degree. All four degrees prepare students to take on viable positions in the workforce.

The bachelor of arts degree. A **bachelor of arts (BA) degree** is usually awarded to students who complete 4 years of undergraduate study in the humanities or the social sciences. On many campuses, psychology departments organizationally are grouped with the humanities or social sciences but they can also be found allied with natural sciences or education, depending on the traditions of the campus).

The design of the psychology BA major varies. In addition to the psychology requirements, BA psychology majors typically complete a series of courses in the liberal arts — classes from the humanities (English, history, philosophy) and the social sciences (political science, sociology) — as well as in mathematics and statistics, and one or more in the natural sciences (biology, chemistry, physics). Most BA degrees also allow students to take a number of electives; that is, classes the student freely chooses out of interest or to pursue a minor or a second major, or even to do a combination of these. Sometimes students earning a BA are obligated to complete more credits in foreign language and perhaps spend less time on research-focused classes.

The bachelor of science degree. The **bachelor of science (BS) degree** is awarded to students who finish 4 years of undergraduate courses that emphasize the sciences. On some campuses, psychology is housed with the natural science departments and seen more naturally as being part of the STEM (science, technology, engineering, and mathematics) disciplines.

In some schools students can also opt to receive a BS in lieu of a BA degree in psychology by taking more math and lab-oriented science classes than are usually required to fulfill general education requirements. Students who choose the BS can also take electives; however, the additional math and science classes often reduce the number of slots available for electives. With some planning, most BS degree candidates can still complete a minor or even a second major.

In 2017, around 3.5 million people in the United States had a BA or a BS in psychology. For 57% of them, psychology was their highest degree, while the other 43% obtained a graduate degree (13% did so in psychology; the remaining 30% earned a graduate degree in another field; APA, 2018).

Should you pursue a BA, a BS, or an AA/AS? That depends on your career goals, your time, and your resources. For many students, a bachelor's degree in psychology can be either a terminal liberal arts degree or it can be the basis for pre-professional or workforce employment. In other words, the liberal arts degree provides students with a wide array of skills enabling them to pursue a variety of careers. As a pre-professional degree, the BA or BS prepares students well for a graduate degree in psychology (see Chapters 11 and 12) or some other field. Compared to an AA/AS degree, a bachelor's degree provides more career flexibility, more potential for mobility, and greater career earnings. On the other hand, an AA/AS degree is a solid choice for someone who is looking for marketable employment in a particular area.

The associate degree. An associate degree, either the **associate of arts (AA)** or the **associate of science (AS)**, is an undergraduate degree earned at a community college, a junior college, a technical school, or a 4-year college or university. Students opt for an AA degree either as stepping-stone to a 4-year program or as a valuable end in itself to provide more targeted preparation for specific jobs in the workforce.

Generally, AA/AS degrees are equivalent to the first 2 years of coursework in a bachelor's degree. The degree may not officially designate a major or concentration in psychology or, more broadly, the behavioral sciences. However, getting a solid background in general education still allows for some specialized attention to psychology courses and fosters an identification with the discipline of psychology. Typical choices beyond the introductory course that may be available in a 2-year program include courses in developmental psychology, social psychology, human adjustment, and other classes that have practical worth for getting ready for the workforce.

For some jobs, a person only needs an AA/AS degree and not a bachelor's degree. Many lab technicians, paralegals, drafters, early childhood education teachers, people who work in some computer and data-processing positions, and machinists, for example, often have only an AA or an AS degree. People with an AA/AS often work in human or social services agencies, in mental health agencies (e.g., clinics, crisis intervention centers), and in drug and alcohol rehabilitation counseling centers (not necessarily as counselors but as aides to the counseling staff or case managers).

Of course, employers can offer many of these jobs to candidates who have no college background, but we would argue that 2 years of college provides a knowledge base, skill set, and perspective that will help you stand out among your peers. That advantage can accelerate promotions or facilitate access to other kinds of opportunities even in entry-level positions.

Career Matters for Bachelor's Degrees in Psychology

Psychology majors can pursue an impressive array of employment opportunities. A study published in 2016 found that 27% of recent graduates with a bachelor's degree in psychology work in jobs that can be described as closely related to their major (American Psychological Association, 2016). Another 35% said that their work was "somewhat related" to their psychology major, and 38% indicated their job was "not related" to psychology. So, close to 62% of former psychology majors have careers that deal directly with or are somehow related to psychology.

On the other hand, those judgments may be a matter of perception. In our experience, many students categorize their successful occupational path as "not related

to psychology" if it doesn't involve graduate school. Sadly, many psychology professors contribute to this false impression by marking a clean boundary between jobs
"in psychology" (requiring graduate school) and jobs that may not have the word
psychology in the job description. In contrast, we speculate that it is hard to find a job
that isn't psychology-related. Even lighthouse managers have to work with data and
people at some point in their workweek. We prefer the distinctions of "professional
psychology" for positions that require graduate school versus "psychology related" or
"workforce psychology" positions. We encourage you to adopt this practice, too.

Figure 9.2 illustrates the results of a second survey, one published in a 2015 issue
of the APA *Monitor on Psychology* on the range of directions a psychology major can
pursue and the relative popularity of those jobs. Graduates work in STEM fields
such as computer and social sciences; in the STEM-related health-care fields; and in
a variety of non-STEM occupations, such as social services, management, business,
and education. Although the range of options underscores psychology's flexibility,
job hunters may feel frustration because the pathways into specific options are sometimes not very clear. In this section, we discuss employer expectations and places
where those with psychology degrees work.

What Do Employers Want From New Hires?

One of the most reasonable questions psychology majors ask is, what do potential
employers look for in job applicants? Generally, employers who hire bachelor's-level
students want to employ those who earned good grades in college and who, while
there, learned how to learn. They want to hire people who are enthusiastic and

FIGURE 9.2 In What Contexts Do BA/BS Graduates Work? Originally published in
Christidis, P., Stamm, K., & Lin, L. (2015, May). How many psychology bachelor's-degree
holders work in STEM occupations? *Monitor on Psychology, 46*(5). Retrieved from
https://www.apa.org/monitor/2015/05/datapoint. Copyright © 2015 American
Psychological Association. Reproduced with permission.

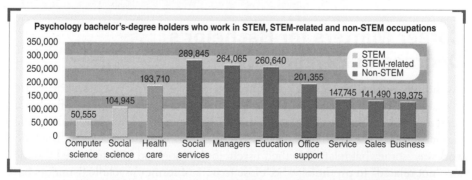

Note: STEM is science, technology, engineering, and math. Occupations with less than 5% of psychology
bachelor's degree holders were not included in the figure. These occupations include engineering, mathematics, statistics, life science, architecture, legal, arts, entertainment, construction, production, and agriculture.
Data source: U.S. Census Bureau, American Community Survey. (2012). Retrieved from http://www.census.gov
/dataviz/visualizations/stem/stem-html.

committed to doing high-quality work. Most employers are willing to teach or train their employees to perform the kinds of work necessary to their success, but they want the people they hire to arrive possessing some skills already.

In a prior chapter we already reviewed the APA (2013) *Guidelines for the Undergraduate Psychology Major 2.0*, which highlight skills linked to psychology's knowledge base, scientific inquiry and critical thinking, ethical and social responsibility, communication, and professional development. When those goals and outcomes were developed, the task force adapted the guidelines to include student learning outcomes that should be expected after students have finished their first 2 years. **Table 9.1** from the *Guidelines* illustrates how these expectations play out regarding career-seeking skills at both the foundational (AA/AS) and baccalaureate (BA/BS) levels.

Beyond good grades and psychology-related skills, what are employers looking for? *Measuring Up: Developing A Digital Profile* lists a variety of skills

TABLE 9.1

Targeting Professional Directions at the Associate and Baccalaureate Levels

APA's *Guidelines for the Undergraduate Major*

	At the AA/AS Level	At the BA/BS Level
	Foundational	**Baccalaureate**
5.5 Develop meaningful professional direction for life after graduation	5.5a Describe the types of academic experiences and advanced course choices that will best shape career readiness	5.5A Formulate career plan contingencies based on accurate self-assessment of abilities, achievement, motivation, and work habits
	5.5b Articulate the skill sets desired by employers who hire or select people with psychology backgrounds	5.5B Develop evidence of attaining skill sets desired by psychology-related employers
	5.5c Describe settings in which people with backgrounds in psychology typically work	5.5C Evaluate the characteristics of potential work settings or graduate school programs to optimize career direction and satisfaction
	5.5d Recognize the importance of having a mentor	5.5D Actively seek and collaborate with a mentor
	5.5e Describe how a curriculum vitae or résumé is used to document the skills expected by employers	5.5E Create and continuously update a curriculum vitae or resume
	5.5f Recognize how rapid social change influences behavior and affects one's value in the workplace	5.5F Develop strategies to enhance resilience and maintain skills in response to rapid social change and related changes in the job market

⬆ 📏 Measuring Up

Developing a Digital Profile

As you assemble the information you need to make a persuasive case for employment, consider the value of designing a digital portfolio that captures your history, achievements, and unique spirit. A digital portfolio represents a great way to illustrate your grasp of communicating with an audience in a professional and engaging manner (Bubb et al., 2018). Many capstone courses in psychology now require that students complete a digital portfolio to make them more competitive in the job market. Some website services (e.g., Wix, Weebly, Squarespace) provide useful templates as a starting point to build an impressive visual display.

What elements should be present in a digital portfolio? It should demonstrate your ability to express yourself eloquently, your skill at using proper language conventions, and your capacity to manage technology. The most successful projects will address the following questions:

■ *What is your current occupational objective?* Be specific about your career plan and consider articulating both your preferred plan and a backup plan as well.

■ *What achievements provide support for the goals you have in mind?* Clearly identify academic achievements, honors and awards, any recognitions, and volunteer experiences that set you apart from other applicants.

■ *What classroom experiences have contributed to your aspirations?* Harvest your academic experiences that underscore your fitness as a candidate. Select specific learning experiences and write about their positive effects with enthusiasm. Be prepared to modify your portfolio by highlighting different experiences for different purposes.

■ *What would you consider to be your strengths as well as areas that you plan to develop further?* Rather than admit to a weakness, indicate your interest in aspects of your work profile that might be improved with additional experience.

■ *Who can vouch for your character?* Pick your references wisely. People who have gotten to know you in an academic, professional, or volunteer capacity will create more persuasive references than will family or friends.

To kick-start your reflection on experiences that will make your portfolio strong, consider the following skills that employers take into account when deciding which candidate to offer a job.

Workplace Skill	Example From College Experience
Solid work ethic	
Computer/digital technology skills	
Honesty/integrity	
Ability to function well on a team	
Oral and written communication skills	
Analytical/research skills	
Self-direction/initiative	
Interpersonal/social skills	
Adaptability/flexibility	
Self-confidence	
Professionalism	
Listening ability	
Problem-solving skills	
Willingness to learn new things	
Client/customer focus	
Quantitative skills	
Multicultural awareness and sensitivity	
Planning/organizing skills	
Time management skills	
Leadership skills	

Information from: Landrum & Harrold (2003); Appleby (2000); Hansen & Hansen (2014).

and character qualities that many employers say they want from those they hire. The entries here are all positive qualities that are self-explanatory and can be developed and refined during college. Most are qualities that students demonstrate in class, on writing assignments, when engaged in group projects, and by taking part in extracurricular clubs and organizations. To complete this exercise, think about what evidence you could provide to an employer to indicate you have these sorts of skills and character traits. Whenever possible, point to specific behaviors or incidents that support your claims. Consider using your list to create a working document for your professional portfolio of the skills and experiences you gained during your college years. This can help you capture aspects of your history that might be useful in the workplace.

TABLE 9.2

Some Perceived Distinctions Between the College Campus and Workplace Cultures

College Campus	Workplace
Professors	Managers or supervisors
Individual effort and performance	Team effort and performance
Frequent and concrete feedback on performance	Infrequent feedback on performance, often not specific
More freedom and control to set schedule	Less freedom or even control over schedule
Frequent breaks, time off, vacations	Limited time off. Vacation days are often limited until after you have been there a while.
Structured courses and curricula	Less structure, fewer directions
Few changes in routine	Constant and unexpected changes
Academic or intellectual challenges	Organizational, coworker, and client challenges
Environment of personal support	Usually less personal support
Correct answers are usually available	Few "right" answers

Information from: The Senior Year Experience (p. 102), by J. N. Gardner, G. Van der Veer, & Associates, 1997, John Wiley & Sons; permission conveyed through the Copyright Clearance Center, Inc.

Work life is distinct in many ways from college life. You may be surprised to learn that responsibilities in most workplaces are actually less structured than those in school. Having a career means that you must be a consistent self-starter who is punctual, prepared, and able to accomplish job-related tasks in a timely manner. The transition from the campus to the office or other work setting will likely not be a struggle if you know what to expect. **Table 9.2** lists some of the perceived distinctions that former students identify as making their work life different from the life they enjoyed on campus. Review Table 9.2 to develop a sense of what to expect in the future, and plan to use your energy and efforts accordingly. As Hettich (2004) noted, starting a new job out of college is like being a freshman again—you have to learn the written and unwritten folkways of a new culture.

What Jobs Attract Psychology Graduates?

People with a bachelor's degree in psychology get hired in a wide range of jobs, including as sales agents, educators, health-care providers, researchers and consultants. Quite a few former psychology majors find careers as human resource managers and personnel specialists, as probation officers, employment counselors, and even as writers. **Table 9.3** includes a list of jobs that have attracted former students with a bachelor's degree in psychology. The entries have been grouped

TABLE 9.3

Selected Workforce Occupations for People With a Psychology Bachelor's Degree

Related to Children
Assistant youth coordinator
Behavior analyst
Career counselor
Career planning and placement advisor
Child-care worker
Child-protection worker
Day care–center supervisor
Foster home parent
Residential youth counselor
Youth minister

Related to Clinical Populations
Activity director
Alcohol/drug abuse counselor
Case-management aide
Caseworker
Community outreach worker
Community support worker
Counselor aide
Family services worker
Gerontology aide
Group home coordinator
Life skill counselor
Mental health technician
Rehabilitation advisor
Residential counselor
Social services assistant
Social work assistant
Vocational rehabilitation counselor

Related to College Students
Academic advisor
College admissions officer
Director of alumni relations
Housing/student life coordinator

Related to Communications/Writing
Film researcher/copywriter
Historical research assistant
Media buyer
Newspaper reporter
Public affairs coordinator
Public information officer
Public relations specialist
Radio/TV research assistant
Technical writer

Related to Government/Public Service
Congressional aide
Intelligence officer
Lobbying organizer
Political campaign worker

Related to Management
Director of volunteer services
Fast-food restaurant manager
Hotel management
Intellectual disability unit manager
Nursing home administrator
Program manager

Related to Data Management/Research
Energy researcher
Director of fundraising
Financial researcher
Laboratory assistant
Property management
Publications researcher
Research assistant
Statistical reports compiler
Statistical assistant
Urban planning research assistant

Continued

Related to the Military

Veterans' advisor

Related to Criminal Populations

Corrections officer

Crime-prevention coordinator

Juvenile probation officer

Law enforcement officer

Parole officer

Probation officer

Security officer

Related to Human Services

Camp staff director

Community organizer

Community recreation worker

Community relations officer

Neighborhood outreach worker

Parks and recreation director

Task force coordinator

Volunteer coordinator

Work activity program director

Related to Education

Driving instructor

Educational coordinator

Private tutor

Secondary school teacher

Teacher

Related to Animals

Animal trainer

Veterinary assistant

Zoo specialist

Related to Business Contexts

Administrative assistant

Advertising agent

Advertising trainee

Events coordinator

Management trainee

Marketing representative

Marketing researcher

Office manager

Small business owner

Store manager

Warehouse manager

Related to Human Resources

Affirmative action representative

Employee counselor

Employee relations assistant

Human resources director

Human resources recruiter

Job analyst

Occupational analyst

Personnel worker/administrator

Staff trainer and developer

Related to Customer Service

Airline reservations clerk

Bank manager

Claims specialist

Customer relations agent

Customer service representative

Hospital patient service representative

Insurance agent

Insurance claims/underwriter

Loan officer

Sales representative

Adapted from R. Eric Landrum (2001).

in categories; we clustered the jobs according to a defining characteristic, such as an interest in working in human services or in wanting to combine psychology with jobs that involve politics or communication. This list is representative but not exhaustive and there are many jobs that at first glance may not seem in the realm of possibility for psychology majors but turn out to be a good fit. Use this list as a starting point to help you identify some possibilities that may not have occurred to you before. You may discover still other career options as you begin your job search.

To illustrate just some of the occupational directions available to students with bachelor's and associates degrees, we conclude this chapter by expanding the number of our "Major Success" stories. Each profile represents a different success story with people who found employment at the associate or baccalaureate level and concludes with specific advice to inspire you to think about what you like doing best so you can find someone to pay for it.

A **Major** Success Story ‹‹‹

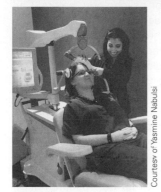

Courtesy of Yasmine Nabulsi

Yasmine Nabulsi
BA, MA, in Applied Experimental Psychology

FIGURE 9.3 Yasmine Nabulsi demonstrates how a transcranial magnetic device can be used in mental health interventions.

Building a Mental Health–Focused Career

When Yasmine Nabulsi spent her adolescent years in Jordan, she learned that her pursuit of a career in psychology was in conflict with the traditions of her culture. In Arab cultures, mental health disorders or psychiatric illnesses tend to be attributed to flawed individual character or lack of direction or faith. However, moving back to the United States at age 17 opened up new opportunities for Yasmine to pursue her passion about understanding human behavior and helping those in trouble.

Yasmine's drive for experience was insatiable. She pursued every opportunity — big or small — to prepare for a mental health career. Although the prospects were initially terrifying, she volunteered at both a rape crisis center and a suicide hotline, which she described as significant in developing her interpersonal skills and confidence. She sought opportunities to talk informally with multiple professors in her undergraduate program to try out her ability to generate researchable hypotheses and to get feedback on her professional direction.

After graduation, Yasmine became a psychology technician at a clinic doing interesting work in the area of transcranial magnetic stimulation (TMS). Her current job with the clinic involves duties that include psychometric testing of children, research coordination, and technician responsibilities for TMS research. She has also earned multiple certifications that add value to her undergraduate degree. She credits her family's support of her goals as instrumental to keeping her dreams on track.

Best Advice? "Do not wait around for your bachelor's to lead you somewhere. Let yourself be known. If you are always in your comfort zone, growth will not occur. Reading and memorizing will not get you to your goal. It is the application of your own unique ideas and your passion that employers will see and will value. This is a very unique field with tremendous job opportunities."

‹›››

Los Angeles County Department of Public Health

Carl Bolano

AA in Behavioral Science, BA in
Psychology

**FIGURE 9.4 As a CDC public
health associate, Carl Bolano
had the opportunity to work
at Los Angeles County Department of Public Health's Veterinary Public Health program
(VPH). During LA's public health
week, they provided free vac-
cinations and services to dogs
and cats, and Carl used the
opportunity to educate children
on bite prevention while doing
some creative face-painting.**

The Advantage of Data-Management Skills

Born in the Philippines, Carl Bolano emigrated to the United States after graduating from high school. A year later she entered a community college to pursue an AA. When she transferred to a 4-year school, she completed a psychology BA with a minor in statistics. She subsequently entered the workforce, where she found an array of opportunities to use her research and statistical skills.

An advocate for psychology majors, Carl was hired after graduation as an instructor to staff a course to help students successfully pursue research careers. She points out that realistically, psychology majors are not likely to make as much money as some other majors, such as engineering and business, but she has no regrets. She stated, "I am the kind of person who values passion, experiences, and connections over monetary rewards. There is a different kind of fulfillment and satisfaction in helping and serving others."

She is confident that her research background in psychology has made a substantial contribution to every job she has had. To date, those have included serving as a behavior interventionist, an instructor, a program manager, a public health associate, a cancer survivorship researcher, and a public health researcher.

When Carl worked as a behavior interventionist, she applied behavior analysis (ABA) therapy with children and teenagers diagnosed with autism spectrum disorder in home settings. She had learned about behavior modification techniques, such as positive and negative reinforcement, from her psychology courses and field work. Her objective was to improve her clients' communication, social, and adaptive skills.

She later applied her data-management skills in work at the Centers for Disease Control and Prevention (CDC). In this job, Carl worked on program development, program evaluations, and surveillance projects. She also facilitated health promotion and education events where she honed her oral presentation skills by presenting to diverse audiences.

Best Advice? "Expect the unexpected. Be open. Be flexible. Be adaptable. Utilize your uniqueness in creating your own path."

⟩⟩⟩

A **Major** Success Story   ‹‹‹

Courtesy of Amy Salada

Amy Salada
BA in Psychology,
Addictions Counselor

FIGURE 9.5 Amy Salado has enjoyed a successful career in addictions counseling with a bachelor's degree background.

A Camp Prediction Comes True

When Amy Salada was a young girl attending camp, her tentmate ran into some an unanticipated problem. She got her period for the first time, but because it was unexpected, it was not just upsetting; it felt tragic. Amy empathized, reached out, and helped her cope. Her camp counselor complimented her intervention and added, "You will make a great counselor someday." Amy completed her bachelor's degree in psychology to support her professional goals, but she credits her camp experience as the event that launched her professional interest in helping others cope with the trauma that comes our way.

She describes trauma as "the lemons life throws at everyone." In both individual and group therapy formats, her interventions focus on how to cope with life events that cause stress. She notes that people don't always want to take time to heal after psychological injury, which she attributes to a society driven by seeking immediate gratification. She believes schools could do a better job of teaching essential life skills, including empathy, coping, and listening, adding that most of the time these skills will be even more valuable than knowing algebra or iambic pentameter.

Her 20-year career in addictions counseling has been very satisfying. Many clients in need of support to help kick an addiction don't really want professional help; some flat-out refuse to attend scheduled sessions or don't participate actively when they do come. However, she has confidence that her work helps to plant some seeds that may someday sprout and bloom. She still receives calls and messages from prior clients who continue to reach out to process their life. "Being called an angel never gets old," she admits.

One drawback she describes about the field is that society does not place great value on addictions work. The field is very difficult; therapists hear horrid stories about human experience but salaries in addiction recovery don't reflect the intensity of the work. For example, when Amy had more than 15 years of experience in addictions, she was being offered positions that paid as low as an "insulting" $28,000 per year. She maintains that our contemporary problems in heroin addiction and other opioid abuse suggest that good drug and alcohol therapists clearly deserve a better salary than they currently receive. For those considering a career in addiction recovery, Amy stresses the important of self-care.

Best Advice? "Do not underestimate vicarious trauma and compassion fatigue. Know how to de-escalate your own emotions and cope with your own feelings. Know your personal boundaries and limitations and stick with them. Analyze the Serenity Prayer for yourself and know how to keep your emotions safe."

›››

Tyler Secor
BS, MS, in Educational
Psychology; Family Counselor

**FIGURE 9.6 Tyler turned
his enthusiasm for video
gaming into a meaningful
intervention plan for working
with troubled adolescents.**

From Batman Fan to Counseling Superhero

Something about *Batman: The Dark Knight* unlocked a powerful curiosity in Tyler Secor to understand human nature. Taking an introduction to psychology course sealed the deal. Tyler embraced the idea that psychology could offer him a fulfilling career. Although his family valued his pursuit of higher education in general, they were a bit more skeptical about the value of a psychology degree, which they perceived as something akin to pseudoscience. Tyler's eventual career success has shifted their enthusiasm for his choice in a positive direction and encouraged newfound respect for his chosen field.

Learning about research was surprisingly exhilarating once he discovered topics that stirred his passion. He was thrilled to recognize that psychology and research were not just abstract ideas taught in a classroom but real-life adventures in science that could help people create better futures. He credits exceptional professors who helped him find an intellectual home in psychology while remaining authentic as essential to his professional success.

After he graduated, Tyler worked in a variety of child-care settings focusing on mental health interventions and supervised family visits. Earning an MS in education psychology stimulated him to theorize about how people use art, especially video games, to process and manage emotions. He used video games as a therapeutic vehicle to help adolescents work through complex emotions, such as anxiety or grief. He hopes eventually to earn a doctorate to continue to combine his research curiosity and his clinical service.

Best Advice? "Developing relationships is the foundation of success and its importance can't be overstated. The other cornerstone of success is to get involved. Contact local nonprofits and volunteer! Every moment you spend in the field, whether observing or doing the work yourself, will enrich your classroom experience and provide context for what you're learning. This is also another great way to build relationships!"

A **Major** Success Story ⋘

Jarred Honora

Jarred Honora
BA in Psychology

FIGURE 9.7 Hurricane Katrina motivated Jarred Honora to major in psychology and pursue his passion for helping people.

Katrina's Surprising Positive Impact

Natural disasters usually have horrific consequences, but they can also engender some unexpected positive outcomes. In Jarred Honora's case, Hurricane Katrina devastated his beloved city of New Orleans in 2005 and upended his senior year in high school. However, the turmoil motivated him to pursue the passion that he had developed for helping people and to declare psychology as the perfect route to achieve that goal. He stated, "I started college in a city that I loved and was born and raised in, that I couldn't even recognize. I had to drive through the streets of my destroyed city and help rebuild what, I thought, could never be broken. I survived because of my major."

Raised by a single mother, Jarred discovered that he had to step up and serve as a role model for his sister. He recalls that it was a struggle to find time just to be a kid. By the time he entered college he knew he wanted to find ways to help people and to make a positive impact on society. He credits his talented professors with inspiring him to be a lifelong learner who digs deep, challenges assumptions, and actively pursues multiple perspectives. He dedicated himself to his major because of the potential for healing that psychology offered.

Jarred currently serves as the director of admissions for a high school in New Orleans. Before this, he was an admissions counselor at the college where he earned his degree. His background in psychology helps him work effectively with students to develop unique communication styles that emphasize creating goals, monitoring progress, and preparing for a future filled with creative opportunities. He describes himself as providing "a road map and a verbal compass" to help students navigate their journey.

Best Advice? "Do not be quick to declare one area of psychology as your only focus. Psychology offers a very large umbrella with several sides to view. Enjoy the journey through the major. On my journey to my college degree, I learned about myself through my studies and was able to heal parts of me that inspired my curiosity in the major."

Thought Questions

1. Are you prepared to deal with negative feedback about your choice of major?
2. What degree are you seeking? Why?
3. Do you have any idea what sort of work appeals to you?
4. What would your ideal workplace be like?
5. What population has the greatest appeal for you?
6. What would you say are your current skills? What other skills would you like to develop before seeking employment?
7. Is it possible to develop a satisfying career without going to graduate school?

10

How to Land a Job With Your Degree in Psychology

Don't worry. There are always good jobs available for good students.
~John Patrick Crecine, Late President of the
Georgia Institute of Technology

Austin is a senior psychology major. He enjoys his coursework but has decided that graduate school in psychology is not in his future. He wants to apply what he has learned about behavior into some business setting, perhaps doing marketing or sales. When he graduates in 6 months, he will have a BA in psychology. Austin knows he should start looking for a job sooner rather than later, so he makes an appointment at his university's career center to learn about job opportunities, job search strategies, and résumé writing. He is pleased to find out that there are many jobs out there that appeal to his interests and abilities and use the skills he has developed in his psychology major. Austin plans to spend the months before graduation trying to narrow down his interests and to apply to as many entry-level positions as he can.

■ ■ ■

Austin's plans may be similar to yours. Like Austin, you probably need to know how to find meaningful work that fits your skills and interests. In this chapter we offer suggestions for doing a job search, writing a résumé and cover letter, requesting letters of recommendation, and asking someone to be a reference, and we review behaviors that help interviewees do well in interviews. We close the chapter by considering what to do if you don't get a job after an interview.

Searching for Jobs: Where to Begin

Effective job searches rely on using a wide variety of resources. Most of these resources will be convenient and accessible to you.

Campus career center. If your college or university is like most, it has an on-campus office dedicated to helping students explore their career interests and options. This career services center or office can often help students identify possible careers through vocational tests and inventories. Many career offices bring recruiters to campus and arrange for senior students to sign up for information sessions, mock (practice) interviews, and actual job interviews. They typically offer help with résumé writing (an important matter discussed in detail below) as well. Make a visit to the career services office on your campus to learn what resources are available and to talk with the director about your interests. Don't forget: It's very likely that you can continue to rely on the services of your campus career center after you graduate.

Alumni networks. Your school may maintain a very valuable resource: an alumni network that allows current students to seek job advice and career guidance from graduates. Alumni who sign up to help in this way are delighted to share their experiences, insights, expertise, and even potential job leads with students who are graduating from their alma mater.

Internships. Doing an internship in a community or a business setting can provide you with invaluable insights into whether a line of work or a workplace setting fits your skills and interests. Your college may run an internship office that keeps a list of local sites. Some students do internships for course credit during the regular academic year, while others do them during the summer months. Although many internships are volunteer experiences, others include some remuneration. Having an internship on your résumé can be an asset as you enter the job market — and many times a successful internship leads the site to extend the student intern an offer for a permanent job after graduation.

Job shadowing. Some career services offices offer students the opportunity to **job shadow** — to spend a few hours or even a day following a professional as he or she "lives" a typical workday. This shadowing affords students a chance to discover whether a given career and its routine responsibilities appeal to them. Check with your campus career center to find out whether any job-shadowing program is available. Alternatively, if you know someone whose career is of interest to you, ask if you can be his or her shadow for a day — what have you got to lose?

The Occupational Information Network. The Occupational Information Network (O*NET, at https://www.onetonline.org/) is an online center dedicated to providing information about a wide variety of occupations. For each job, the site lists details about the knowledge, skills, and abilities required, as well as a description of the work context, salary information, and other important details. The website is very user-friendly and provides specific information on more than 1,000 occupations.

TABLE 10.1

Other Resources for the Job Search

Books	Websites
Kuther, T. L., & Morgan, R. D. (2020). *Careers in psychology: Opportunities in a changing world* (5th ed.). Thousand Oaks, CA: Sage Publications.	**General job searches**
	www.Indeed.com
	www.CareerRookie.com
Landrum, R. E. and Davis, S. (2014). *The Psychology Major: Career Options and Strategies for Success*, (5th ed.) New York: Pearson.	https://www.collegegrad.com/
	https://www.monster.com/
Sternberg, R. J. (2017). *Career paths in psychology* (3rd ed.). Washington, DC: American Psychological Association.	**Government employment**
	https://www.governmentjobs.com/
	https://www.usa.gov/job-search
	https://www.usajobs.gov/
	Median salaries for various occupations
	https://www.salary.com/

Informal networks. Do not overlook your personal connections when you are look-ing for job and career opportunities. Ask your family, friends, and coworkers about the work they do, why they do it, and whether they know of any job leads. The peo-ple in your informal networks will often want to help and may be able to provide helpful suggestions about the job search.

Other resources. Table 10.1 lists some other resources you should use to locate infor-mation on jobs for psychology majors. The top of the table lists three specific books that discuss careers in psychology — including the profiles of many professionals — in depth. The bottom of the table lists some helpful websites for general job searches, jobs in the government, and includes a website that offers salary data about various positions.

Writing a Résumé

A good résumé is your entry to an interview and a possible career. A résumé is a brief written account of your personal, educational, and professional qualifications. As such, it must be thoughtfully conceived, well written, polished, and focused. You should have both a hard copy and an electronic version available, as many websites want applicants to upload a copy. Be prepared to edit or modify the contents of each résumé you send out as necessary to fit the requirements of particular jobs. Here are the basic requirements for a good résumé:

■ Set the text on high-quality, standard 8.5 × 11 inch white, ivory, or light-beige paper (the electronic version should be on a white page). Print on only one side of a page.

■ Do not write in complete sentences and avoid using the word *I*.

Instead, begin each entry with an action-oriented word that highlights an achievement or a goal you met ("Reduced staff attrition" or "Supervised peer tutors").

■ Personal information that is unrelated to the job you are seeking, such as hobbies, should not appear in your résumé. At best, it looks like filler; at worst, it creates a negative impression of you in the mind of the reader.

■ The résumé should be brief — one page is the rule for college students and recent graduates. Never go beyond two pages. If an employer specifies a required length, do not exceed it.

■ Proofread carefully to catch spelling or grammatical errors. Have someone from career services, your academic advisor, and someone you know to be an excellent writer proofread a draft of the document. Having multiple reviewers increases the likelihood of catching errors, correcting phrasing and spelling, shortening sentences, and of having a clearer résumé.

■ Do not use elaborate or outsized fonts — stick with a basic font; for instance, Times New Roman in a 12-point size.

■ Never fold or staple your résumé, even for mailing purposes (send it in a large, flat mailing envelope).

The basic parts of a résumé include:

Heading. Center your name at the top of the page. Put your address and contact information below your name using a format that makes the heading easy to read. Don't use a wildly oversized font, as it distracts readers' attention from the résumé's content.

Objective or skills summary. The objective is a concise and precise statement regarding the sort of position you desire for employment. The objective should be revised or edited for different positions, which means you will be creating different versions of your résumé.

Some professionals suggest using a skills summary in place of the objective statement. A skills summary is a list of six bullet points that highlight the range of your most impressive achievements or abilities. Like the objective, it appears at the top of the résumé. The advantage of the summary is that potential employers can scan résumés with an applicant-tracking system to identify résumés that contain particular skills they are seeking. Here's a list of six skills that could comprise a skills summary:

■ Time management
■ Data analysis
■ Self-motivated
■ Accounting
■ Foreign languages
■ Teamwork

In *Measuring Up: Write a Skills Summary*, you will carefully consider the skills you might have to offer an employer who is interested in your psychology background.

⬆ 📏 Measuring Up

Write a Skills Summary

Earlier in this section of the chapter you read and learned about adding a skills summary to your résumé. Although you may not yet need to draft a résumé, it's never too early to identify and reflect on the skills you have that you could share with prospective employers.

Step 1: Write down a list of as many of your skills that you can think of (remember the advice in the *Measuring Up: Brainstorming Your Way to Research Topics* on page 113 in Chapter 7. Don't censor yourself; jot down whatever skills come to mind).

Step 2: Review the list you generated in step 1. Now you can be more critical. Select the six skills you believe will best represent your abilities on a résumé. Be rigorous with yourself: If you say you are skilled in a foreign language, for example, are you fluent enough to carry on a simple conversation with a native speaker? If you believe you work well in groups, can you point to concrete instances from your past where your work in a group (on a class project or in an actual workplace) really paid off?

Step 3: For each of the six skills on your list, describe one or more concrete examples of behaviors or situations (including current or past jobs, of course) in which you have displayed that skill. Think about how you could explain each skill to a potential employer during an interview. Keep your skill summary so that you can use it when you do write a résumé.

Education. List the degree or degrees you have earned, the school from which you received your degree, and your college major. Academic honors and awards can also be briefly noted here. Once you have a college degree, you no longer need to note that you have a high school diploma.

Experience. This section usually has a chronological list of your previous work experiences (from most to least recent). Each entry should include the dates of employment as well as your work responsibilities and any noteworthy accomplishments. Bulleted lists of these are fine. Avoid listing mundane duties.

Activities. List any key extracurricular activities, including internships and volunteer or community work, in this section. Avoid listing too many things or you will give the impression that you are padding your résumé.

Awards. If you have been honored for an important contribution or achievement, by all means mention it briefly.

References. Indicate at the end of the résumé that the contact information for your references is available upon request. If you are asked for specific contact information for your references, then list each person's name, title, academic or work affiliation, mailing address, phone number, and email address. Always ask your references for permission to list their names and contact information on your résumé in advance — don't assume they will be willing to do so.

A sample résumé appears in **Table 10.2**. As you can see, the formatting is simple and straightforward and the information is easy to follow. Clarity is important, as an

---

TABLE 10.2

A Sample Résumé for a Student With a Bachelor's Degree in Psychology

---

SUSAN L. WHITMAN

Current and Permanent Address:

27 Beverly Avenue

Foxbridge, MA 02175

(555) 875-9901

slwhit@gomail.com

OBJECTIVE

Seeking employment in marketing and sales where I can use my knowledge of human behavior.

EDUCATION

Bachelor of Arts in Psychology, cum laude, May 2019

Moravian College, Bethlehem, PA

GPA 3.5/3.75 in major

EMPLOYMENT

Intern. Creative Marketing Solutions, Allentown, PA (1/5/19–5/1/19). Designed marketing campaign for orthodontic group; researched local competition; worked with firm's principal to prepare for client meetings.

Sales Associate. Your Line Apparel, Norton, MA (5/8/18–8/25/18; 5/10/17–8/20/17). Greeted customers, showed new stock, and managed register; restocked shelves; arranged clothing displays; managed web closeout sales.

Waitress. Hometown Diner, Wexley, MA (5/15/15–8/20/15; 5/17/16–8/22/16). Took and delivered customer orders, bused tables, and prepped for food service.

ACTIVITIES

Campus Marketing Club. President, 9/1/16–4/20/17; member of executive board, 9/1/15–4/19/16; member since 9/5/15. Updated bylaws; invited local CEOs and advertising executives to speak at bimonthly speakers series; recruited new members.

Sigma Iota Tau Sorority. Chaired membership and recruitment drive; doubled sorority membership in one year; member since 11/5/15.

AWARDS

Dean's List

"Best Student Poster" in Campus Research Symposium, 2018

REFERENCES

Available upon request

evaluator will only spend between a few seconds and a couple of minutes reviewing a given résumé — that's it. If your résumé is odd, confusing, or too busy, chances are it will be passed over in favor of one that is easier to read.

Now that you have developed some expertise in what impression good résumés should make, see *Reality Check: Would You Hire This Woman?* to help you see what improvements you might make to your own résumé.

 Reality Check

Would You Hire This Person?

Take a look at the résumé below and see if you can come up with at least five suggestions to improve it in such a way that would help it make a persuasive case for hiring this person and would enhance her chances of getting an interview. Assume you might be in charge of screening applicants for an entry-level human resources position.

ELIZABETH ANN GORDEN
(Call Me Lizzie!)

email: hotbabe49@massnet.com

social security no: 555-62-1234

address: I'm moving and will let you know when I get my leased signed

Long-Term Employment Goals: To become a clinical psychologist

Education: Hard Knocks Universtiy

    Majored In: Anatomy, Home Econmics, Logistics, and Psychology

    Grade Point Overall: 2.2 (It could have been higher but I had a lot of family troubles that meant I couldn't always make it to class).

Hobbies: Knife collection, salsa dancing, travel

Skills: People say I'm really good with people. So if this job has anything to do with people, I can probably do it pretty good. I really like working with people. I'm also a quik learner.

Work Experience: exotic dancer

    Tool sharpener

    Video game developer

Awards: None.

References: You can ask me for these if you give me an interview.

So would Lizzie get serious consideration based on how she presented herself on paper? The answer is obviously no. How many errors did you find in her approach?

Key:

- ☐ The heading is jarring and too informal.
- ☐ Her email is not appropriate for a professional context.
- ☐ To protect your identity, you should not include your social security number on public documents.
- ☐ The coy way she wrote her address information gives two bad impressions — that she can't provide a straight answer and that her home life may be unstable.
- ☐ Describing a long-term professional goal that has nothing to do with the immediate job encourages the screener to think this résumé might be generically prepared and used for lots of applications without being tailored to the specific needs of the company.
- ☐ Multiple misspellings suggest either chronic spelling challenges or lack of attention to detail, because the proofreading of the résumé was ineffective.
- ☐ It is not a requirement to list a GPA and you probably should not do so unless it is strong and makes a good impression.
- ☐ Offering an explanation for poor performance isn't required and may hint that your attendance would be a problem if you were hired.
- ☐ Listing four majors suggests you could have a commitment problem.
- ☐ Unless the hobbies have a direct bearing on the job requirements, they should not be listed.
- ☐ The work experiences listed provide no real details that relate to the job being pursued and many of them may detract from your purpose.
- ☐ The skills list description is problematic because it meanders and is not persuasive. It also uses complete sentences, when the current standards tend to focus on bullet points that can be easier to read.
- ☐ If you have no awards, you should just skip the category.
- ☐ The manner in which the references is listed implies a threat.
- ☐ The order of the entries is not particularly logical.

Writing a Cover Letter

A **cover letter** must accompany your résumé. Like the résumé, it is tailored and brief, usually one page or less in length. Most cover letters will have three parts that translate into three paragraphs. The first paragraph explains the reason for your letter, identifies the position you are applying for, and indicates how you heard about the opening. The second paragraph describes your background and why you believe you would be a good fit for the position. You might, for example, briefly explain how your skills match the needs of the organization or how your experiences match the needs of the position. The third and final paragraph highlights your interest in the job and invites the reader to contact you.

Table 10.3 shows a typical cover letter, which, like the résumé, should be on white, ivory, or light-beige paper. The letter should look formal, not friendly. Keep an electronic copy that you can upload with a copy of your résumé and edit or update for other positions.

TABLE 10.3

A Sample Cover Letter

June 25, 2019

Mr. John Harcourt
Human Resources Department
Alliance Pharmaceuticals
427 Ridge Ave.
Pleasant Vale, NJ 07022

Dear Mr. Harcourt:

Please allow this letter and my attached résumé to serve as my application for the assistant marketing manager opening in the sales division of Alliance Pharmaceuticals. I learned of this position when I visited the job listings on the company's website.

My education and work background fit the description for the assistant marketing position, as I have a liberal arts degree and have completed several courses in accounting, marketing, finance, and economics. My internship with Creative Marketing Solutions in spring 2019 allowed me to work on a marketing and sales campaign for an orthodontics group. Working with the firm's principal partner, I met weekly with the clients, drafted agendas, researched competitors, and outlined a radio commercial script that was eventually produced as part of the campaign. I believe my experience in marketing dental health care can serve as a solid bridge to marketing pharmaceutical products.

I enjoy working with others on teams and I am quite willing to relocate to New Jersey. I would be delighted to speak with you further regarding the job opening. I may be reached at (555) 875-9901 or via email at slwhit@gomail.com. My mailing address may be found on my résumé. I look forward to hearing from you.

Sincerely,

Susan L. Whitman

Enclosure

Interviewing Skills

If your résumé, cover letter, and references pass muster, then you will be invited for an interview, a formal part of the personnel-selection process. Traditional interviews are done in a face-to-face manner, where you meet the interviewer in person. Increasingly, however, many employers will interview candidates online using Skype or some other web interface that allows the interviewer and interviewee to see and interact with one another using their computers' cameras. If you have an online interview, it is a good idea to do a dry run with some friends to ensure that you know how to connect technologically as well as how to position the camera for the best camera angle. It doesn't tend to impress favorably if during the entire interview the only thing visible is the top of your head!

Organizations often interview several people for one opening, so understand that you are likely to be competing with others for the job. When you have a face-to-face interview, there may be other candidates in the waiting area who are competing for the job you want. Additionally, it is not at all unusual to be interviewed more than once for the same position (one of our friends was eventually hired after four separate and lengthy interviews spread across several weeks).

Before you embark on the interview, make certain that you have learned all you can about the company or organization by reviewing any materials available on the web. You want to appear both knowledgeable and very interested in the position — this is not the time to play hard to get. Indeed, your goal is to convince the interviewer(s) that you are the right person for the job, someone who will fit in and contribute to the organization's enterprise. As you do that, the interviewer(s) will be looking for any weaknesses — aspects of your behavior or character that make you a risky choice. It is sometimes an easier process for interviewers to use data from these interactions to rule out prospects rather than to a declare a winner or identify the most qualified person.

Interviewers will ask you a variety of questions about your educational and work background. They want to get to know you and learn what skills you could bring to the work setting. **Table 10.4** shows examples of two types of interview questions. Trained interviewers — especially those whose sole role is hiring — often rely on **structured interview questions**, which are a company's standard questions that all prospective employees are asked. Untrained interviewers tend to use **unstructured interview questions**, which have an informal and unplanned quality to them. You should be prepared for both types of questions because you likely will not know much about the person who will be interviewing you.

TABLE 10.4

Examples of Structured and Unstructured Interview Questions

Structured Questions

Describe a work incident in which you had to come up with a creative solution to solve a problem.

Tell me how you handled working with a difficult person. Be specific.

Provide a specific example of an instance in which you demonstrated leadership in your last job.

Give me some specific examples showing how you worked effectively with coworkers on a team.

Unstructured Questions

Why do you want this job?

What are your strengths? What are your weaknesses?

Tell me something about yourself that I cannot learn from your résumé.

What would your former supervisor say are your greatest accomplishments in the workplace?

Presenting Yourself Well

Your ability to answer questions, to provide concrete examples of your work skills, and to discuss your career goals is only half of the interview strategy. The other half involves how you present yourself to others. You want to make a very favorable and lasting positive impression. Here are some suggestions for doing so:

Appearance. How you look matters, as first impressions are often lasting impressions. One way to make a good first impression is to learn how current employees at your prospective employer dress, and come to the interview appearing just a little more formal than that. For many positions, you should be dressed in conservative business attire. Your appearance, from your hair to your shoes, should be neat, not flashy. Give yourself a once-over to make sure you are stain-free. (Jane recalls with some mortification that she gave a job talk during an interview, looked down, and realized she was wearing one blue and one black shoe. She got the job despite her uncoordinated attire. Her fashion-conscious colleagues later confirmed that they had indeed noticed the fashion faux pas but offered her the job anyway, demonstrating that minor interview flubs may not prove to be fatal).

It may be a useful exercise to create a business-casual fashion day to check out your own sensibilities about what looks will impress future employers. You can conduct a full-blown fashion show, complete with a runway down the middle of a classroom, that will allow you to receive feedback about your clothing choices from the class. If your course is online, consider taking and sharing a selfie to solicit feedback on whether your interview outfit is appropriate.

Poise and eye contact. Although you may be nervous, you should look relaxed and attentive. However, you should not look too comfortable — don't sit back and lounge in a chair, for example. But don't be rigid, either. Sit up straight with a slight lean toward the interviewer. Smile. Make and maintain comfortable and friendly eye contact. Avoid displaying nervous tics, such as playing with your hair or biting your nails. When the interviewer speaks, watch closely and listen carefully — don't look around the room. Also, silence your cell phone; if it rings, quickly turn it off, apologize, and turn your attention back to the interviewer. Under no circumstances should you check your phone during the interview, as it signals that you may inappropriately do so on the job as well.

Questions to ask — and not ask. At some point, you will be given the chance to ask questions. Be certain you have at least three or four in case one or more of your questions is answered in the course of the interview. "I don't have any questions" does not convey sincere interest in the job.

Examples of some standard questions you could ask include the following:

- How long have you worked for the company?
- What do you like best about working for this company?
- How has the company been faring in this economic climate?
- What kinds of projects do you like working on?

Asking if there is a timeline for making the hire is a reasonable question as long as you don't press the matter. Asking about the salary or the salary range is *not* a good idea — it's presumptuous. Wait until (and if) the employer extends a job offer to you; at that time, he or she will also present you with a salary figure. Asking how many vacation days you would have in the first year is also not a good idea. That, too, will be explained by the employer at a later date, if there is a later date. Focus on questions about the job and what it's like to work there — people usually enjoy talking about where they work and the interviewer is unlikely to be an exception. You will be able to tell a lot about the workplace's culture from the interviewer's response.

Initiate, don't just answer! Besides the questions you prepared prior to the interview, it is absolutely reasonable — and it conveys your genuine interest — to ask questions that naturally emerge from the flow of the interview. Once you have answered a question, for example, it's fine to say, "May I ask you a question? As I was talking about the leadership I showed in my last job, I remembered I was curious if each work team here has a designated leader?" You don't want to fire back a question after each interview question, but asking a few during an interview makes the setting more like a friendly conversation, allows the interviewer to get to know how you think, and lets you present yourself a bit more.

Send a thank-you note. Once the interview is over, you should follow up with a thank-you note to the person who met with you. In the note, acknowledge that you enjoyed the interview, that you remain very interested in the position, and that you would be pleased to answer any additional questions. Mailing a thank-you note is fine as long as it gets there within 3 or so days. Emailing a note is fine, too. Just do so the next day, indicating you took some time to reflect on the interview. Emailing a note immediately after the interview looks a little needy. Whether written or digital, keep the note professional and brief. If you handwrite the note, be sure your writing is legible before you drop it in the mail.

Be prepared to wait. You may not hear for a while whether you received the job. Be patient and understand that there may be other interviewees, for example, and that the task of hiring someone involves steps internal to the organization. In the meantime, be hopeful but continue looking for other jobs.

If you don't hear back, should you follow up with the interviewer? Unless the interviewer told you a probable date when you could expect to hear back about the position, you can send a friendly follow-up inquiry a week or so after the interview. Doing so can illustrate your interest in the job. Don't inquire more than once, however. You may also be able to get this information by talking with office support people rather than speaking directly with the interviewer.

In this chapter's success profile, we give you a glimpse of a psych major who went on to specialize in helping companies make good selections from among job candidates. See **A *Major Success*: Helping Companies Invest in Their People.**

Sadie O'Neill/reConnect HR

FIGURE 10.1 Sadie O'Neill provides expert consultation for companies wanting to choose the best candidates for employment.

Helping Companies Invest in Their People

Sadie O'Neill didn't wait long after earning a PhD in industrial-organizational psychology to launch her own consulting business. Becoming an entrepreneur suited her positive energy and her desire to use psychology to make a difference. One side benefit for her is that her consultation work is never boring. She says, "I could talk forever about all the numerous, unexpected, and wonderful hats you get to wear."

Her company, reConnect HR, helps businesses to make human capital decisions based on data and statistics rather than on hunches and history. She transforms data into specific steps that companies can take to improve their environment by conducting their own in-house research and describing how to use the data to make better people decisions in the future. For example, if a company has challenges related to the diversity of their employees, her company can analyze the demographics "from pre-hire to post-fire" and help the client discover and correct inequities with proven best practices. Her company follows up with an analysis to demonstrate whether or not an intervention has been effective.

The employment outlook in human resource (HR) consultation is especially bright because of the growth of tech start-ups. Since people typically account for a third of a company's investment, bad hires are costly. This reality makes it especially important for HR departments to be strategic and to learn how to make smart decisions by recruiting, hiring, and retaining talented people who are the best fit for the company.

Sadie reports that she uses almost everything she learned in graduate school in some shape or form. She is grateful for all the weeks that she spent begrudgingly reading research articles because she now can digest research on the fly during a meeting and then provide informed advice about the topic. Although statistics can be a painful class, being comfortable with data about people gives her a competitive advantage since most people seem to be "allergic to numbers."

Best Advice? "Look at job descriptions and postings first so you know what skills to obtain to get to your end goal. Many HR jobs don't require higher education, just that you have gained relevant skills and experience along the way. But, if grad school fits with the skills you need to acquire, then best of luck!"

After the Interview: What's Next?

Once the interview is over, what happens next? Well, there are two possibilities.

You Don't Get the Job

What happens if you follow the advice in this chapter but don't get the job? Unfortunately, this may happen — you may not get the first job you interview for, or even the second one. Try not to be too discouraged if a job you want does not pan out. There are many different reasons why a person may not get a particular job offer, even when all the signals seemed to be positive ones. There are often multiple variables in play, many of them beyond your control. These include:

- the qualifications of the other applicants;
- the possibility that an internal candidate has the inside track for the job;
- the number of applicants in the hiring pool;
- the impact of factors that actually influence hiring decisions in the organization (such as budget constraints or sudden hiring freezes — factors that you would not be privy to).

Instead of second-guessing the hiring process and ruminating about the variables involved, focus on what you can control. Reflect on the interview and ask yourself if there were things you might have done differently. If there were, then make those changes for your next interview. If there weren't, then assume you did what you were supposed to do and that you did it well. Continue your job search and look ahead to the next interview. Be persistent. Ideally, you are looking for an employer who will be as enthused about hiring you as you are in working for them.

Here's another suggestion to consider: Are there any skills you might hone or any additional training you might get while you are in the interview stage of looking for a position? Acquiring more skills while you are searching can make you a better candidate for future interviews.

You Get the Job

Congratulations! Let's assume you decide to accept the position. What's next? Your work is just beginning because now you need to focus on doing well in the job. In a way, getting an offer is actually the easy part; now you need to succeed and keep the job. You will not be surprised to learn that many new employees end up losing their jobs for rather predictable reasons (Gardner, 2007), including:

- not meeting required deadlines;
- being late for work;
- acting in unethical ways;
- showing little or poor motivation;
- failing to follow directives.

Note that these same behaviors should be avoided during your undergraduate years; indeed, these are precisely the sorts of actions that lead to bad grades and negative impressions. Thus, while an instructor's deadline for a paper or project, for example, can seem arbitrary, keep in mind that meeting deadlines is a requirement out in the so-called real world. It is never too soon to develop professional habits.

Avoid making these sorts of mistakes on the job by having a positive attitude, taking initiative, setting priorities, seeking regular feedback on your performance, and being committed to the job and the people in your workplace. Being a well-regarded employee is similar to being a good student — you must work consistently and concentrate your efforts effectively.

Thought Questions

1. What degree are you seeking? Why?
2. Do you have any idea about the kind of work that appeals to you? What would your ideal workplace be like?
3. Have you considered doing an internship? If you have, what sort would you want to pursue?
4. What would you say are your current skills? What other skills would you like to develop before you look for work?
5. What experiences have you already had that you can put on a résumé?
6. What questions would you ask a prospective employer?
7. What look will you strive to have for a face-to-face interview?

11

What Can You Do With an Advanced Degree in Psychology?

If it is both terrifying and amazing,
then you should probably pursue it.

~Erada

Graduate study in psychology is very popular, but it is not for everyone. Approximately one out of every four undergraduate majors bolsters the necessary courage, orchestrates the funding, and commits the time necessary to pursue an advanced psychology degree. Psychology doctoral degrees increased by 25% from 2008 to 2017. During this same time period, master's degrees in psychology increased by 28% (K. Stamm, personal communication, April 13, 2019). Interestingly, 45.3% of psychology majors obtain some sort of graduate degree; overall, only 35.1% of all college graduates earn a graduate degree (APA *Monitor on Psychology*, 2016). It is not just a simple matter of deciding to go, though. But let's first explore the factors that might influence whether graduate school is right for you.

■ ■ ■

In this chapter, we develop a good approximation of what it means to be employed with an advanced degree in psychology. First, we look at the kinds of degrees that qualify graduates for professional psychology employment, starting with specific opportunities at the master's level. Next, we turn our attention to doctoral-level training, examining the settings in which psychologists are employed. We describe the occupations that psychologists can pursue and explore the job outlook for psychologists over the next decade. We offer some advice about mounting a successful job search. Finally, we provide an array of success profiles to illustrate the diverse occupational paths that are possible with an advanced degree in psychology.

What Does This Decision Mean?

Making the commitment to graduate school is a huge step. Graduate education is costly and will probably end up adding to your student debt. It requires diversion of your attention from family and friends. It may require you to relocate. And you probably need to develop a taste for macaroni and cheese or ramen noodles for the duration of your graduate study because you won't be flush with cash. As you will learn in the next chapter, applying to graduate school can be extremely time consuming; getting into a graduate program is intensely competitive. Many prospective psychologists don't get accepted to graduate school the first time they apply. However, completing a graduate degree opens an amazing number of professional pathways. The majority of people who hold advanced degrees in psychology work in one of these areas: professional service (47%), research (18%), teaching (16%), management (14%), and sales and marketing (3%) (Lin, Stamm, & Christidis, 2018).

Let's take a look at the different kinds of graduate degrees you might pursue after your bachelor's degree.

Master's-Level Training

Students may choose to pursue a master's degree for several reasons. First, they know they want to work in a psychology-related context but may not have settled on a specific career goal. If they stop when they complete their master's degree, the degree is described as **terminal**. On the other hand, the master's degree may also be a stepping-stone to additional training at the doctoral level. Students who enter a PhD program directly after they finish their master's degree may execute a master's project as a proof of fitness to enter the PhD program.

Master's degrees also come in two flavors (comparable to bachelor's degrees). The Master of Arts (MA) reflects that the degree has a strong liberal arts orientation. The Master of Science (MS) conveys more of an emphasis on science and research. The majority of psychology master's programs also tend to have identified concentrations in these areas: experimental, clinical/counseling, or industrial-organizational.

Master's training provides a solid means of developing expertise in psychology without the long-term obligations that go with doctoral training. In fact, for many occupations, a master's degree is just the right level of education, whereas a doctorate may be overkill.

Graduates with master's-level degrees do get to work in the discipline they love but their autonomy depends on the context in which they work as well as the type of psychology they practice. In business contexts, the master's degree supports independent function. In clinical contexts, a graduate with a master's degree can have an independent practice but in some contexts they may need to work under the supervision of those with doctoral-level training. Despite that constraint, people with master's degrees can work in fulfilling jobs in a number of settings. See **Table 11.1** for some suggestions for master's employment.

TABLE 11.1

What Can You Be With a Master's Degree?

In higher education	**In government-sponsored human services**
Community college teacher	Vocational rehabilitation specialist
Four-year college adjunct teacher	Substance abuse counselor
Academic adviser or academic recruiter	Human resource manager
Career counselor	Parole officer
	Rehabilitation counselor
In clinical contexts	
Behavioral counselor	**In business contexts**
Health-care coordinator	Human resource manager
Mental health technician (someone who implements elements of a treatment plan)	Employee developer
	Advertising and marketing specialist
Mental health therapist	Public relations specialist
Rehabilitation specialist	Project manager
Group home supervisor	Sales representative
Child-protection specialist	Store manager
Child-care program manager	

⟂ Measuring Up

Reflecting on Possible Degrees and Jobs in Psychology

You may still be finishing your bachelor's degree and unsure as to whether graduate school is in your future. Still, it may be worth to take a few minutes to narrow down some possibilities by answering these questions.

1. If you do go to graduate school, would you seek a master's degree or a doctorate? Why?
2. If you decide on a master's degree, which career(s) in Table 11.1 appeal(s) to you? Why?
3. If you decide on a doctorate, which type — a PhD, a PsyD, or an EdD — would you like to pursue? Why?
4. Which, if any, of the psychology subfields presented interests you? Why?

Doctoral Degree Options

The term **psychologist** is usually reserved for people who have doctoral training in psychology. Let's explore all the ways a person can earn the title of doctor in psychology. But first, let's look at where psychologists, prepared at the doctoral level, do their work. As shown in **Figure 11.1**, the vast majority of psychologists are employed in university (26%) and health-care settings (25%) (APA, 2014). Both clinical and research-oriented psychologists tend to predominate in these hires. Government and Veterans Administration (VA) medical centers constitute the third-largest employer, at 16.3%. At 10.4%, business and nonprofit settings represent the fourth-largest employer and tend to hire psychologists with an applied orientation rather than those with a research or clinical background. Educational settings (8.1%), medical settings (6.3%), and private practice (5.7%) each employ fewer than 10% of psychologists.

The Doctor of Philosophy Degree

Most people think, with good reason, of psychologists as holding a doctorate degree. It is recognized as the most prestigious degree that can be conferred. A **doctor of philosophy (PhD)** degree provides optimal independence for those with psychology backgrounds and prepares students for careers in academia and in clinical and business settings through an emphasis on research. The PhD typically concludes with a research dissertation — an original research effort, often experimental in nature, that

FIGURE 11.1 Where Do Psychologists Work?

Data from: D. Michalski, J. Kohout, M. Wicherski, & B. Hart (2011), *2009 Doctorate Employment Survey.*
Note: This chart, from the APA Career website, represents employment settings for those with recent doctorates in psychology. Totals amount to 97.7% due to rounding and exclusion of 17 "not specified" responses.

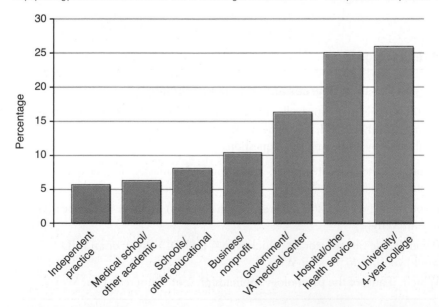

occupies the last year or so of graduate education. The PhD degree usually takes about 7 years to complete, and those who pursue one finish about 8.3 years on average after completing a bachelor's degree (Lin, Green, Stamm, & Christidis, 2017). Clinical PhDs take a little longer to finish because most clinicians complete an internship in a mental health setting that adds another year beyond the dissertation. Under ideal conditions, a clinical PhD may be possible to complete in 4 to 5 years, but that assumes the candidate encounters no major obstacles along the way. The PhD is the doctoral path that provides the most latitude for careers that have the fewest constraints.

The Doctor of Psychology Degree

The **doctor of psychology**, or **PsyD**, degree represents another, newer option for those interested in clinical psychology. The PsyD degree prepares clinicians by providing a wide range of clinical exposure and reducing the emphasis on research. Experts estimate that the PsyD degree takes a comparable amount of time to the PhD degree, typically between 4 and 7 years (Cherry, 2019). PsyD programs should be considered only when the applicant knows he or she plans to work in a clinical context and is less interested in conducting research. PsyD degrees tend to be less competitive than PhD's in academic and medical settings.

What are some other factors that might help applicants decide which route to go between the PhD and PsyD options (Norcross & Castle, 2002)?

- *Acceptance rates.* It is easier to get into a PsyD program (acceptance of 4 out of 10 applications) than a PhD program (acceptance of 1 to 1.5 out of 10 applications).
- *Program size.* PsyD programs admit 16 students on average, whereas PhD programs average 9 admissions.
- *Financial support.* PhD programs have a better track record of providing support through grants and assistantships. Recent estimates suggest that PsyD graduates tend to carry significantly more student debt (a median of $160,000) than those carrying debt from a research PhD (a median of $72,500) (Doran, Kraha, Reid Marks, Ameen, & El-Ghoroury, 2016). Students enrolled in a graduate program reported a median debt of $80,000; those who also carried a debt load from their undergraduate education reported a median debt of $120,000 (Doran et al., 2016).
- *Theoretical orientation.* PsyD faculty tend to be drawn from more diverse orientations, including psychodynamic, cognitive-behavioral, and family systems. The dominant orientation of PhD clinical faculty is cognitive-behavioral.

Figure 11.2 shows acceptance rates by subfield of psychology and degree level (master's or doctorate) for the 2013–2014 academic year (Stamm, Michalski, Cope, Fowler, Christidis, & Lin, 2016). More than 110,000 applications were submitted to graduate psychology programs in the United States and Canada, and about 26,000 applicants

FIGURE 11.2 Acceptance Rates for Graduate Psychology Programs by Subfield and Degree Level, 2013–2014

Originally published in K. Stamm, D. Michalski, C. Cope, G. Fowler, P. Christidis, & L. Lin, (2016, February). What are the acceptance rates for graduate psychology programs? *Monitor on Psychology, 47*(2). Retrieved from https://www.apa.org/monitor/2016/02/datapoint. Copyright © 2016 American Psychological Association. Reproduced with permission.
Note: "Applied other" includes applied behavior analysis, educational, community, forensic, sport, quantitative, and behavioral psychology programs. Data source: American Psychological Association. (2016). *Graduate Study in Psychology.* Washington, DC: Author.

Acceptance rates by subfield and degree level, 2013–14

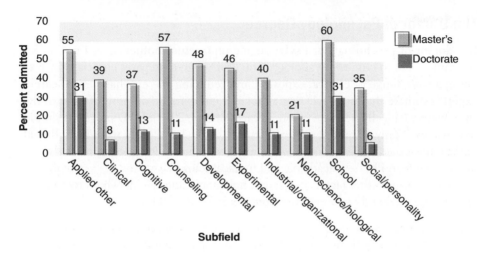

were admitted (an acceptance rate of 24%). As shown in Figure 11.2, however, acceptance rates vary substantially depending on the subfield and degree level in question. A low acceptance rate should not keep you from applying to a particular field, of course, but it is important to be aware of the competitive nature of applying to graduate school.

The Doctor of Education Degree

The **EdD**, or **doctor of education**, is an option for those who are interested in more clinically oriented activity but want to focus on more mild rather than severe forms of dysfunction. Typically, EdD programs tend to accept people who already have a master's degree, so it takes from 3 to 5 years to complete the EdD. The area concentration of the EdD tends to be counseling, developmental psychology, or school psychology, and includes an emphasis on research but typically is not perceived as being as rigorous in terms of research as the PhD. EdDs are offered in departments of education rather than psychology. Those who earn the EdD usually work in educational settings, such as secondary schools and colleges and universities. As therapists, they sometimes receive lower reimbursement rates from insurance companies who are reluctant to place the same value on therapy from EdD's that they do on that from other doctoral-level clinicians.

Job Possibilities Across Different Subfields

What follows is just a sampling from the American Psychological Association (APA) of the vocations most commonly held by psychologists (APA, 2014).

- **Clinical psychologists** work in mental health–care settings to alleviate the challenges of emotional or behavioral disorders. They conduct psychological tests and design therapy programs for individuals, groups, and families.

- **Cognitive psychologists** focus on how people think, remember, reason, and make decisions. They work in research contexts and also help create treatment plans for people with cognitive impairment.

- **Community psychologists** work in larger social systems to improve the lives of those who live in the community. They may provide assistance after trauma or may concentrate on prevention programs to improve the mental health of the community.

- **Counseling psychologists** focus on problems of everyday adjustment and can be found in schools, hospitals, and businesses. They tend to work with clients whose problems aren't as severe or disruptive as the problems of the clients with whom clinical psychologists work.

- **Developmental psychologists** concentrate on behavior across the life span. Originally focused on childhood and adolescence, developmental psychologists are increasingly choosing to work with aging populations.

- **Educational psychologists** explore issues that help or hinder learning. They can design effectiveness studies in classrooms or consult with individual teachers on interventions to improve learning performance.

- **Engineering (human factors) psychologists** work in the area where machines and humans intersect. They assist in the design of efficient and adaptive devices.

- **Environmental psychologists** examine the impact of environments on behavior and can serve as consultants. For example, environmental psychologists may advise architects on the potential effectiveness of producing specific effects on behavior from their designs. They can also help develop ideas for improving adherence to practices that reduce pollution and waste.

- **Experimental psychologists** apply their knowledge of good experimental design to advance science in academic settings as well as in manufacturing and engineering. Many academic psychologists publish their work in competitive journals in experimental psychology.

- **Forensic psychologists** support the judicial system by, among other things, providing expert testimony, conducting research on jury selection, or providing evaluations regarding child custody.

- **Health psychologists** consult in health-care systems to develop interventions that address the psychological reasons why patients may not comply with doctor's orders. They also conduct research on the large-scale health challenges in the culture (e.g., obesity, smoking, high-risk behaviors).

- **Industrial-organizational psychologists** attempt to make the workplace better through improving systems of production, providing HR training, and consulting about personnel processes such as hiring and firing. They can serve as agents for change within organizations.

- **Military psychologists** focus on the unique psychological needs of those who are or have been in the armed services and their families. They work on deployment concerns as well as reentry problems, including the high rates of suicide and substance abuse among military personnel.

- **Neuropsychologists** examine brain function and may be critical team members working with people who have had traumatic brain injury. They study both normal and abnormal (disease, injury) brain processes.

- **Personality psychologists** examine individual differences in the patterns of people's thoughts, feelings, and behaviors. Personality psychologists often develop assessment tools that identify people's characteristic and stable responses to stimuli, including situations and other people.

- **Quantitative psychologists** combine expertise in psychology research design with mathematics to assist in high-quality data analysis. They may propose mathematical modeling for complex behaviors and can quantitatively determine the quality of test instruments.

- **Rehabilitation psychologists** provide direct service to patients with stroke, disability, or developmental delays. They help clients adapt to situations and overcome problems, often working in teams with other health-care professionals. They can also be called on for expert testimony in legal cases related to rehabilitation and disability.

- **School psychologists** provide a wide range of services to children and families in education settings, including counseling, testing, and designing interventions to improve school performance.

- **Social psychologists** are in great demand for their expertise on how people form and change their attitudes. They can consult with businesses to shape advertising and marketing strategies. They also can provide coaching on ways to enhance group performance.

- **Sports psychologists** help athletes achieve their goals by reducing their fears and improving their motivation to prevail in competition.

Additional Facts About Professional Helpers

Psychologists who provide therapy for a living must complete some additional steps to become licensed to practice. The prospective clinician must pass a comprehensive content and ethics examination and work for 2 years under clinical supervision. The laws that govern professional psychology vary by state. Each state is responsible for addressing public concerns and complaints and has the power to take away a psychologist's license in response to such concerns. The Association of State and Provincial Psychology Boards oversees this process (see https://www.asppb.net/).

Similar constraints exist for those who want to practice at the master's level. For example, in Florida, master's program graduates can sit for a state licensing examination. They are then qualified to serve in an internship to earn practice hours. After 1,500 hours of supervised practice, they can earn their license. Be advised that states' requirements for becoming licensed vary. If you intend to reside in a particular state after graduate school, you should consider this as you begin your application process.

We would be remiss if we didn't point out another popular option to become professional helpers that doesn't involve the intense focus on science and math required in psychology. Many psychology majors opt to go to graduate school in social work, particularly if statistics and psychological research do not appeal to them. Those with a master's in social work (MSW) degree and appropriate supervision can work in private practice and in mental health agencies. A psychology major provides a great foundation for pursuing an MSW.

Job Outlook for Psychologists

The news on this front is promising! According to the *Occupational Outlook Handbook* (Bureau of Labor Statistics, 2014), for psychologists, the growth rate in employment from 2016 to 2026 is expected to be 14%, which is faster than the expected average growth of all other occupations, at 7%.

Psychology Salary Projections

Although BA/BS psychology salaries are among the lowest of the liberal arts, salaries improve dramatically with each level of degree. Probably the highest-paid job in a field related to psychology belongs to Phil McGraw ("Dr. Phil"), a media psychologist whose annual income has been estimated to be about $80 million (https://www.celebritynetworth.com/richest-celebrities/actors/dr-phil-net-worth/), but unfortunately, that job is taken. Salaries tend to be the highest for psychologists who combine their disciplinary expertise with management responsibilities (e.g., CEOs, university presidents) or with other enterprises that are more scientific and technological (engineering psychology, neuropsychology, or forensic psychology). Salaries tend to be lower for psychologists working in the community or nonprofit sector. See **Table 11.2** for estimates of current salaries by category.

TABLE 11.2

Estimated Salaries in Psychology by Category

Doctoral-level training

Industrial/organizational psychologist	$109,030*
University administrator	$94,340*
Neuropsychologist	$86,000
Forensic psychologist	$85,000
College faculty	$78,470*
Clinical psychologist	$76,990*

Master's-level training

Advertising manager	$132,620*
Sales manager	$124,220*
Public relations	$114,800*
Human resource manager	$113,300*
Training and development manager	$107,770
Personal financial advisor	$99,920
Educational administrator	$95,390*
Management analyst	$89,990
Social worker	$74,700
Social service manager	$65,750
Claims adjuster	$65,670*
Vocational counselor	$56,160
Sports psychologist	$55,000
Health educator	$53,800
School counselor	$56,310*
Child-care manager	$52,010
Marriage therapist	$50,090*
Mental health counselor	$43,700
Substance abuse counselor	$41,090

Data from: Bureau of Labor Statistics (2013).; * Data from Bureau of Labor Statistics (2018).

Note: *Careful scrutiny of this chart reveals that some occupations at the master's level of training have higher salaries than do those at the doctoral level. The salary discrepancy usually is accounted for by larger salaries generally being connected to business contexts or administrative responsibilities.*

FIGURE 11.3 Average Salaries of Psychologists by State
Data from: Bureau of Labor Statistics (2018).

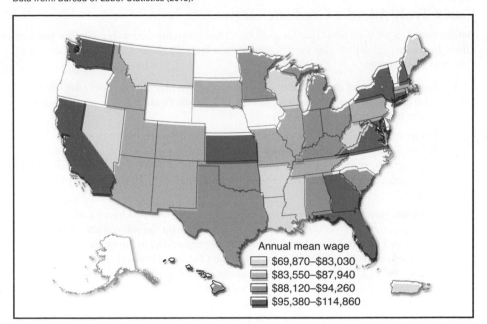

Annual mean wage
- $69,870–$83,030
- $83,550–$87,940
- $88,120–$94,260
- $95,380–$114,860

Salaries also vary by region, affected by cost of living and availability of people to do the work. The Occupational Employment and Wages data from the Bureau of Labor Statistics provide a mean of psychologists' salaries by state in 2018. The bureau distinguishes between clinical, industrial, and other kinds of psychology. The distribution of the "other" category is shown in **Figure 11.3**. The most lucrative jobs for these kinds of psychologists appear to be in Florida, California, Connecticut, Georgia, Kansas, Maryland, New Hampshire, New York, Virginia, Washington DC, and Washington.

Calculating Debt Load

Whether you choose to pursue a master's or a doctoral degree, you need to have your eyes open about the financial cost. You will be forgoing a potentially substantial amount of income while you are in graduate school. As well, you may need financial aid to get you through school — in some cases, a great deal of financial aid. You need to do some careful math to determine whether you can afford to start your professional life in such a big hole. See *Reality Check: Can I Truly Afford a Graduate Degree?* to make some realistic calculations about your **debt load**.

Reality Check

Can I Truly Afford a Graduate Degree?

Before you sign on the dotted line for graduate school, carefully consider whether you can afford to pursue the degree you want. Calculate the following to determine whether it is in your best interest to go.

1. **Estimate the total cost of the degree.** Each program may feature a net cost calculator on the university admission's website to help you figure out how much money you will need to complete your degree.

2. **Project the total income you can count on during your graduate study.** For example, many programs may provide teaching or research-based assistantships; grants; or even help you find part-time work within the field that will help with your expenses. This income should offset some of the cost of your degree.

3. **Estimate your post-degree first-year salary.** Using websites that have salary estimates, such as Glassdoor.com or Salary.com, look up the job you are interested in and pick a conservative figure (below the average salary) to project how much you might earn. Also look at the *Occupational Outlook Handbook* (Bureau of Labor Statistics, 2014) to get a good sense about whether the level of training you are aiming for will be in demand. This will give you some confidence that you might find a job after you finish your degree.

4. **If the combination of your undergraduate and graduate debt will exceed the estimate of your first-year salary, don't go.** The sacrifice will simply be too great. Currently the average debt load for just an undergraduate degree is approximately $30,000 (Forbes, 2018). Taking on additional debt may create an insurmountable obstacle for your future financial stability. Determine whether or not you will have enough money after your living expenses to pay back your student loans within 10 years. If you won't, your quality of life, even if you do land your dream job, may suffer.

5. **Calculate the lifetime impact of the potential income generated by the degree.** Determine how many income-generating years you can expect to have between the time you finish your degree and your retirement. Although your salary is likely to increase over time, be conservative in your estimates. Don't forget that every year you spend in graduate school deprives you of income you could have earned with just a bachelor's degree.

6. **Recognize that your estimate doesn't come with guarantees.** You may struggle to land that first job. On the other hand, you might find a job with a high salary. You could also lose the high-flying job should we have another serious economic downturn. Consider the knowns carefully, but prepare for the unknowns.

Information from: Shin (2014).

Getting Ready for the Job Market

Just as you would before receiving a bachelor's degree, prepare for employment with a graduate degree long before the university president hands you your diploma and places your hood over your head. Chief among your considerations should be the following:

What income will support the lifestyle you have in mind? As the Bureau of Labor Statistics has shown, salaries for occupations requiring advanced degrees can be remarkably lucrative, particularly for people whose talents run to management or whose interests include science and technology. On the other hand, people with a bachelor's degree in business can easily outearn those with a graduate degree who are in social services. Thus it's important to understand your values, including your work ethic, as you begin planning for your ideal job. An anonymous source offers some sound advice: "Choose a job you love and you will never have to work a day in your life." This wisdom points to the importance of having passion for what you do that can sustain you, regardless of the size of your paycheck.

Psychologists can subsidize their full-time salaries with various types of part-time work. This includes consulting, adjunct teaching, and writing. For example, both Dana and Jane have served as consultants to the College Board as Advanced Placement (AP) readers. In that part-time gig, they commit to a stretch of 10 days in which they read and score AP Psychology exams taken by high school students. Although this particular job is reserved for educators who teach introductory psychology, it demonstrates that psychological expertise can be used to increase one's income. Both Dana and Jane take on paid writing assignments, although they complete the bulk of their scholarly research in conjunction with their responsibilities as professors.

What kind of work–life balance will be most satisfying? Quality-of-life issues are a major focus of research for organizational psychologists; recent data suggest that employees are less willing to work long hours to get ahead; they would rather have a better balance between work and other aspects of life (Korkki, 2010). Professionals can usually expect to work more than 40 hours a week. However, some positions in psychology require more sacrifice of private time than others. For example, launching a private practice in clinical psychology is very time consuming. Factors that can contribute to work–life balance satisfaction include having flexible work hours, being able to work from multiple sites (including home), spending less time commuting, and having access to compatible colleagues. Carefully consider positions that might rob you of time with your family and friends.

How much independence will you require to be fulfilled? Generally speaking, the more education you attain, the more power and autonomy you have in your professional life. In the case of an advanced degree in psychology, that power differential is quite explicit. Only those at the doctoral level can technically be called psychologists. In addition, some master's-level psychotherapists, especially those in clinical contexts, may work under the direct supervision of others with more experience and education. The drive for personal and professional autonomy can motivate those with a master's degree to return to school in part to be in greater control of their professional decisions.

Will there be jobs in the part of the country where you want to live? You may envision an idyllic pastoral lifestyle in the country or the dynamism of living in an urban center; however, psychology jobs may not be plentiful in the area where you wish to reside. You will increase your employability by being flexible about where you are willing to live. That adventurousness means you can apply to any position that gives you the salary that facilitates the kind of lifestyle to which you aspire. It may be possible to use your degree in work outside the country as well.

Can you develop a network that will help you land the job you want? By joining professional organizations (e.g., APA, APS), attending psychology conferences, and making connections at gatherings of local professionals, you can build a collective of people whom you can ask to help you identify any emerging opportunities that suit your skills and interests. Most psychologists are talented as mentors; they see helping new psychologists get properly launched as a great way to give back.

Can you monitor job availability comprehensively? Think broadly about where to look for employment. Listings for psychology positions don't necessarily lead with "Psychologist wanted." Consider looking at overall categories (human services, research, health care) to see if any descriptions match your desires and skill sets. Job and career fairs sponsored by universities can be a source of inspiration. Job listings in professional organizations (e.g., APA, APS, *Chronicle of Higher Education*) can also be useful. The Internet hosts multiple sites that list job openings. Being familiar with these will help when the time comes to launch your search.

Can you be flexible about moving on? Life throws some curves. That ideal job that seemed to meet all your needs may come with a soul-sucking boss or a toxic work environment. The commute you thought you could tolerate may test your goodwill toward humanity. Fortunately, having a background in psychology gives you flexibility and portability that make it easier to find a new job that may provide you with a more satisfying life. In addition, psychologists are well prepared for new and emerging types of jobs that require strong problem-solving and people skills — skills for which psychologists are known.

Is It Worth It?

As psychology professors, we believe we have the best jobs in the world and would follow the same path if we had to do it over again. The value of the job was confirmed by *Money* magazine's annual publication of the top 50 best jobs in America, in which both "college professor" (ranked #2) and "psychologist" (ranked #10) fared very well (Kalwarski, Mosher, Paskin, & Rosato, 2014). Psychology scores well in terms of flexibility, creativity, and career advancement. Unfortunately, the job market right now is intensely competitive but, according to Psychology Career Center

(2014), the job market for psychology professors is likely to grow more than 30% in the next decade as baby-boomer professors retire. If you genuinely like your experience as a student, consider using your advanced degree to teach or mentor others who are interested in psychology. See A *Major Success Story: Choosing Academic Life*, especially if you are thinking about an academic career. We also include other profiles to illustrate the many careers that people with a graduate degree can pursue. Although their stories are diverse, what those profiled have in common is that they were able to face what was terrifying and make the investment to enable them to live amazing lives.

A **Major** Success Story ⟨⟨⟨

John Blackie/University of West Florida

Darren Bernal

PhD, Counseling Psychology
Professor

FIGURE 11.4 Darren Bernal combines his interest in social justice and counseling in working with students as a professor in a regional comprehensive university.

Used with permission from University of North Carolina, Ashville. Retrieved from https://psychology.unca.edu/faces/darren-bernal-phd.

Choosing Academic Life

Born in Jamaica, Darren aspired to be an archaeologist until about age 12, when his curiosity about dreaming made him rethink his goal. He began to read psychology texts (Freud, Jung, and others) to understand dreaming better and ended up committed to studying psychology. He became convinced that the mind is the next great unexplored frontier and could picture himself becoming a psychology researcher to indulge his curiosity. Opportunities were better in the United States for completing an advanced degree. Darren's interests went beyond pathology to include health, well-being, and social functioning. He completed a PhD in counseling psychology and embarked on an academic career stateside, where he has shown great promise of becoming an outstanding educator.

Darren describes college teaching as an ideal career for him because it provides a direct impact on many more people than he would have through individual counseling. He also is able to explore new ideas every day and to excite passion in others. He especially enjoys working with students for whom academic success doesn't come easily. He likes to think that his passion for learning will inspire and nurture new generations of psychologists, therapists, and social workers. Because the work is so satisfying, he concludes that none of what he does on a daily basis seems like work.

Best advice? "Follow your passion. When you pursue a promising direction, all kinds of avenues open up to promote personal growth. Going on that passion-driven journey is a great way to find not just a home for your interests but to discover yourself in the process. Trust that good things will happen when your passion provides the energy."

⟩⟩⟩

A **Major** Success Story ⟨⟨⟨

Sandy Huffaker/Getty Images

FIGURE 11.5 Getting internship experience caring for dolphins was one of several factors that persuaded Summer Brooks to pursue professional roles related to animal behavior.

Summer Brooks, MS, in Interdisciplinary Studies, With an Emphasis on Animal Behavior (Sea)Lions and Dolphins and Chimps...Oh My!

When you grow up in San Diego, it's not hard to fall in love with animals. The San Diego Zoo and SeaWorld inspired Summer Brooks to want to work with animals professionally. In high school she became a veterinary assistant but wasn't so crazy about the "blood and guts" side of the job. On the other hand, she loved being able to help veterinarians and pet owners with pets' behavioral troubles.

Although originally she thought she would have to pursue a biology major to do what she wanted to do, she recognized that psychology offered her the information she needed to be able to make a difference. Learning and cognition classes were especially helpful in developing interventions with animals, but she found her entire major was very satisfying. She says, "Studying psychology just makes you a better human."

She earned her first college credits at a community college before transferring to a 4-year school to complete her bachelor's degree. Summer pursued several internships that further clarified her decision. She worked as an animal trainer intern with dolphins and sea lions at the U.S. Navy Marine Mammal Program. She also conducted some observational research with killer whales at Hubbs-SeaWorld Research Institute. Her internship at a Los Angeles sanctuary for chimps focused on whether chimpanzee demonstrated memory for American Sign Language. She subsequently received an MS in interdisciplinary studies, with an emphasis on animal behavior. She currently teaches an online course that explores animal behavior and works as a registered veterinary technician.

Best Advice? "Volunteer or intern anywhere you can. Do it, and see if you like it. You will see what the work day is like, whether you will enjoy the work, and connect with other people who like to do the same things you do. It's also a great way to find out what you don't want to do."

⟩⟩⟩

A Major Success Story   <<<

Jacob Entinger
MS, Research Specialist

FIGURE 11.6 Jake Entinger parlayed his general interest in psychology to a career in solving behavior-related challenges in the Navy.

Psychology Solves Navy Challenges

A casual conversation with a graduate student led to a major life decision for Jacob Entinger. Like many people who begin a psychology major, Jake thought he would pursue a career "on the clinical side" with an interest in helping those who were less fortunate. But the more he spoke with a wide range of professionals in psychology, the more that he learned how big his options were. When he was talking with the graduate student, Jacob reports, he had a "this is it moment" that settled his focus on industrial-organizational psychology and helped him dig deep as an undergraduate.

Although his family was supportive, Jake points out that support and understanding are not the same thing. Even now as a professional and after what feels like "the millionth time" he has explained what he does in psychology, his family still asks if he is going to brainwash them or they offer themselves up as a personal case study.

As he was completing his internship for his master's degree, a unique job opportunity presented itself to join a team of research psychologists working with the U.S. Navy. The work mostly entails developing and evaluating training systems and tends to be split between actual research and project management. As a newer member of the team, he performs legwork on conducting literature reviews, writing proposals, and creating presentations. He has already headed up his own research project and expects that his opportunities will become more diverse the longer he is a member of the team.

Best Advice? "If you've chosen to pursue psychology, I encourage you to really take a step back and ask yourself why you are there. If you know why you have chosen psychology you can begin to formulate where you want it to take you because honestly, if done right, psychology can take you more places than you would imagine. Also, take the time to form relationships with the faculty and graduate students. They're an excellent source of wisdom and inspiration that can help you find your place in the great big world of psychology."

A **Major** Success Story ‹‹‹

David Klein

MS, HR Manager

FIGURE 11.7 David Klein focuses on organizational change as an HR specialist, building an HR department of a national cruise line.

Human Resourcefulness

One occupational direction that many psychology majors pursue is human resources (HR). An HR specialist serves both the employer and the employees by offering guidance regarding benefits, feedback on the rules of the job, and interventions to keep employers on track. Effective HR people foster positive feelings among employees toward their employers and generally earn among the highest salaries of those with a bachelor's degrees right out of college. (Those with a master's degree earn even more.)

David serves as a good example. He decided to major in psychology because he found the content of the classes fascinating. He was initially drawn to forensics but after he took additional psychology classes, he thought more about the idea of working in business settings, so he decided to minor in business. He went into a master's program in industrial-organizational (I/O) psychology, and found himself more drawn to the "O" side (consulting with people) than the "I" side (working with statistics). He captured a plum internship at QVC as part of his program. Within 3 years he was a human resources (HR) director for QVC. He developed his niche in helping organizations cope with change.

After 8 years, David decided that he wanted a job that was closer to his home state of Florida. In that job he began building an HR department in the commercial division of a prominent cruise line where he worked with marketing, guest services, and fleet deployment, including figuring out new ports of call. Describing his undergraduate degree as "very purposeful," David states that he uses his undergraduate degree every day.

Best Advice? "Think about the "sweet spot" where experience and level of education will support the kind of work you might find most interesting. Although pursuing a doctoral degree was tempting, for me, the master's degree was a great passport into a satisfying professional choice and lifestyle."

Karima Modjadidi
PhD, Forensic Psychologist

FIGURE 11.8 Karima Modjadidi has been dedicated to using psychology to free those who have been wrongly convicted of crimes.

Using Psychology to Right Legal Wrongs

Karima Mohadidi remembers distinctly when she became interested in forensic concerns, tracing it back to an encounter she had in middle school with a criminal. She described walking past a stranger in the hallway who greeted her and she smiled and said hello. Five minutes later the school was evacuated because a bank robber was reported to be on campus. Once she informed her teacher that she had seen a stranger in the hall, Karima found herself being interviewed by the police. She was disappointed and perplexed by the fact that all she could remember was "white man, medium height," which was not at all what she expected eyewitness testimony to be like from watching TV crime dramas. Her curiosity about the discrepancy between the dramatic treatments and the reality of poor eyewitness recall fueled her pursuit of a degree that combined psychology and criminal justice matters.

Karima completed a PhD that allowed her to develop expertise in eyewitness (mis)identification as well as in how jury members are selected and how they make decisions, with the goal of making positive changes in the judicial system. Her psychology background allows her to explore interesting questions using solid experimental methods. She feels gratified that the results of these studies promote strategies that reduce inaccurate identification and wrongful convictions. For example, one of her current research questions involves looking at differential driver's license-suspension practices that appear to show disproportionate sentencing of African Americans.

Her most satisfying work to date has been with the Innocence Project, an organization that strives to free innocent people who have been wrongly convicted of a crime. She notes that such activities reminded her of the wisdom her father had shared with her when she was growing up: "I'd rather ten guilty people go free than one innocent person be in jail."

Best Advice? "Do not worry about choosing a major or a job early. Take time to explore what interests you and don't let other people decide what you should do. Work hard, be persistent, and ask for help!"

›››

A **Major** Success Story <<<

Marissa Frangione
MS, Performance Coach

FIGURE 11.9 Marissa Frangione spends most of her training day in the field and sometimes in planes to teach leadership and resilience skills in the military.

A Master of Resilience

Marissa Frangione decided a psychology major would be her destiny when she took an Advanced Placement course in psychology from a talented high school teacher. When her teacher performed a demonstration of how the brain ignores redundant information and explained why it does so, she was intrigued to learn more about how the brain interprets experience. She became fascinated by psychological theory and, as a dance enthusiast and soccer player, was curious about how psychology might support athletes to perform better. She set her sights on becoming a sports psychology consultant and enrolled in a master's program.

"Grad school is not for everyone," she says. "You have to be passionate about what you are learning and want to put in the time and effort it takes to get through the courses." Graduate school is financially challenging. Marissa had to take out loans to cover the costs, but also managed to work each semester. She recommended trying to secure a teaching or graduate assistantship, which sometimes includes tuition remission.

Her current job is "Master Resilience Trainer-Performance Expert" on a government contract. She provides classes and one-on-one training with army personnel to build psychology-related skills, such as leadership, team building, goal setting, and energy management, along with academic skills such as memorizing, time management, and even note taking. She enjoys traveling as she rotates among different Army bases. Most of the time she is out in the field with soldiers rather than behind a desk.

Best Advice: "There are so many routes this major can take you. You do not have to become a psychologist or psychiatrist (although both are great choices). But psychology is the study of people. You will be better able to understand yourself and others that you interact with, no matter what career you find yourself in. All it takes is asking questions and reaching out to people in the field that you want to be in and ask what they did to get there."

Thought Questions

1. Why would average starting salaries for psychologists differ so widely between states? Is there a state where you especially want to live?
2. What subspecialties in doctoral-level training are the most appealing you?
3. Which occupations tend to provide the highest and lowest salaries?
4. What does a master's degree in psychology qualify you to do?
5. What are some strategies you should use during graduate school to prepare yourself for a future job search?
6. How much economic risk are you willing to take to secure an advanced degree in psychology?
7. What do you think the best part of being a college teacher would be? What would make being a professor a challenging career?
8. If graduate school is in your future, when do you plan to enroll? How long will it take you to finish your degree?

12

How Do You Get Into Graduate Programs in Psychology?

If you are serious about going to graduate school,
you better have a fire in your belly.

~J. William Hepler, former psychology department chair

That was some pretty tough advice Jane received when she first floated the idea about getting a letter of recommendation from her advisor, who was one of her favorite teachers. Going to graduate school doesn't represent simply adding another year to your education. It signifies that you have a strong intellectual curiosity that you want to invest in a specialized area. It means you are willing to work strategically in advance of graduate program admissions deadlines regarding where you want to apply. Going to graduate school may entail moving away from a comfortable environment, and you will most likely have to learn to survive on very little money. While your college friends are getting themselves established in careers, your life will be "on hold." Making such sacrifices over years of additional schooling does indeed require a passionate commitment—a fire in the belly—to sustain your efforts and help you persist until you have your degree.

■ ■ ■

Cavan had known she wanted to become a psychologist since she was in high school. She loved what she learned in her high school psychology class and, once she began college, she looked for opportunities to volunteer in her school's psychology department. During her 4 years there, she worked with a professor on his research, served as a teaching assistant and tutor, and in her senior year, did a year-long honors project. All throughout college, Cavan studied hard to get the best grades she could, as she had heard that admissions to top graduate programs were very competitive. Once her senior year began, Cavan felt confident that she had prepared as best she could—all she had to do was to submit her applications and then wait for a verdict. In her case, things worked out. Cavan is probably a bit unusual as a student: She knew after one class in psychology that she wanted to be a psychologist and that she was willing to make the sacrifices her goals would entail. She had the fire.

However, even with a strong motivation and appropriate background, there is no guarantee that you will get into graduate school just by applying. Successful campaigns require strategy and hard work. At this point in your academic career, you may be wondering whether graduate school is right for you. This decision is not a simple one.

Should You Go to Graduate School in Psychology?

Graduate school in psychology requires energy, enthusiasm, and a major time commitment, minimally 4, and very often more, years. But the most important issue to address is why you want to go. See *Measuring Up: Do You Have the Fire?* to sort out your motives for applying to graduate school.

 ## Measuring Up

Do You Have the Fire?

Undergraduates have a mix of motives for going into a graduate program in psychology. Decide whether each reason below is part of why you want to go. Which of the following are true of your quest?

1. I would like to become a scientific researcher or a professional in the discipline.
2. I earned good grades in psychology during college so I probably should become a psychologist.
3. I hope to contribute to the discipline through research, practice, or a combination of both.
4. I don't really want a "real" job.
5. I want to educate people about basic and applied psychological science.
6. I want to be addressed as "doctor" or "professor."
7. I want to dedicate myself to promoting psychological well-being and to ameliorating distress.
8. I don't know what else to do now that I have my undergraduate degree.

9. I enjoy research, writing, publishing, and giving professional talks.
10. I don't want a 12-month job — I want to be a college professor and have my summers off.
11. I am deeply curious about the human condition.
12. I've always been a student and I'm pretty good at it — why stop now?

Interpretation

If you checked off any of the odd-numbered rationales, your motives are consistent with those who are likely to be in graduate school for the right reasons. Adopting one or more of these entails making a serious commitment to your education, doing hard and often solitary work (studying, engaging in critical thinking, writing, research), and entering a very competitive job market.

If you checked off even-numbered items, then you may want to reconsider. These rationales tend to be more shallow and your commitment will be hard to sustain during the rigor of graduate school.

You must be realistic about your genuine motivation to attend graduate school. If your reasons are sound, then you should begin to prepare sooner rather than later.

Preparing for Graduate School During College

Preparing to apply for graduate school is not something that can be done quickly. The decision to apply is a mature response, one that should motivate you to assess your strengths and weaknesses as a student (and we all have both), to engage in a series of systematic steps during college that can help to ensure your success, and to formulate a plan for submitting applications. You should begin to develop a comprehensive application strategy as soon as you start to think about potentially going to graduate school in psychology. Ideally, at the start of your junior year in college, you should begin to think about and carry out some of the steps suggested in this chapter. Once you enter your senior year, you will not have a lot of time to pull together materials. Many applications are due in late fall — by November or early December, sometimes sooner. Thus, the summer between your junior and senior years should be invested in research that will help you make the most appropriate and strategic decisions about your application process.

Of course, preparing for graduate school is in large part about your coursework and what you do with it. Not surprisingly, grades matter for admission; the higher your **grade point average (GPA)** the better your chances of getting in to graduate school. Keep in mind that you will be competing with students who have worked hard during college, perhaps even harder than you, to develop an academic record that reflects sincere interest in graduate study in psychology — getting into many graduate programs is much more difficult than getting into undergraduate programs, for example. Anecdotal evidence suggests that getting into some specializations in psychology (e.g., clinical and neuroscience) is actually more difficult than getting into medical school.

As a result, when you are looking for the graduate programs that fit your needs, you will need to evaluate the level of selectivity that is right for you. Rigorous programs admit only a handful of students each year. Other programs recruit larger numbers of students. There is a variety of published lists of nationally ranked graduate programs in psychology, including lists that focus on particular subfields (e.g., clinical psychology, social psychology). Naturally, programs at the top of such lists tend to be the most selective and have the most intense competition. Don't limit your search just to these lists, however. Speak to your instructors about which graduate programs they know, where their graduates have been able to apply and succeed, their perception of the quality of those programs, and whether one of them might be a place for you to consider applying.

In addition to examining the likelihood of you being admitted to the program of your choice, consider some other factors about graduate school, such as:

- *Cost.* Some graduate programs support their students with fellowships, teaching assistantships, or sources of funding; others don't. You may have to decide if you want to take out loans to cover tuition and living expenses, for example. Programs that are selective often provide very good student funding, which is part of the reason why competition for admission to those programs is so fierce. Although it may be easier to get into less selective programs, that access may come with a much higher student debt load upon graduation.

- *Research mentor.* Who will you work with? In other words, is there a faculty member in each graduate program you are considering who does research that interests you? Many high-quality graduate programs rely on a system in which admitted students are assigned to a research advisor whose work is aligned with their interests. Such compatibility can be beneficial during the application process.

- *Location.* Are you willing to move to another state or even across the country to attend graduate school? Would a university in the Midwest or South work for you? Or must you be in the Northeast or California? Would you prefer to live in the city or in a more rural setting? Are there reasons you must stay close to home?

- *Placement.* How well do the graduates of the programs you are considering do in the job market? Do they tend to pursue teaching, research, or other sorts of careers? How well do their choices match with your plans for the future?

To apply to psychology graduate school, you should have taken an array of courses in psychology. A well-designed undergraduate psychology major requires you to complete introductory psychology, at least one research methods course and one statistics course, as well as one course in each of the four core areas of the field: neuroscience, developmental, cognition, and sociocultural (comprised of courses such as social psychology, personality, and clinical psychology) (Dunn et al., 2010). Taking at least one applied course like health psychology, industrial-organizational psychology, or environmental psychology is also recommended. Finally, some capstone course — an advanced seminar, for example — that ties together the skills you learned across the psychology major is an ideal way to wrap up your undergraduate schooling and get some perspective on the major.

Some psychology curricula have nine or so course requirements — this is likely the minimum number of courses for a psychology major. Other curricula include many more psychology classes. Take advantage of every opportunity you have to demonstrate your rigor as a student. Avoid taking filler classes; choose instead classes that will help you build the best foundation for graduate study.

It is not the number of courses per se but the skills you acquire along the way that will have the most impact on your candidacy. Can you design (and ideally execute) experiments and then collect and analyze the resulting data? Can you navigate the psychological literature to find studies pertaining to issues of interest? Can you write a standard lab report or theoretical review using APA conventions? These and other skills, as well as the varied content of the courses, give evidence of breadth in your disciplinary learning. But what about depth?

Depth: Choosing an Area of Interest

An important part of applying to graduate school in psychology is identifying and pursuing a specific area of interest. Generally, student interest is linked with course work. Perhaps you took a course in cognition and found the abundant research on memory to be fascinating. Or you became interested in how people differ from one another, so you were drawn to the study of personality. A lab-based experience in neuroscience might have wakened your interest in the biology and chemistry of the brain, and so on. Although you should take the recommended set of core courses, you certainly can take one or more courses in the subfield of psychology that interest you most (recall the list of APA divisions that correspond to interest areas — see Table 2.1 on page 18).

As you learn more about psychology across the life span, for example, you may decide to become a developmental psychologist. Thus, when considering where to apply for graduate school, you will want to identify those universities with good developmental psychology programs. By channeling your professional interests in a particular direction, you may target research areas or topics within the field that speak to you. You can then focus on graduate programs that specialize in those research areas — someone interested in gerontology development, for example, would look for developmental programs emphasizing that focus instead of those programs that focus on child development, and so on.

How do you find out this sort of information? Naturally, the Internet makes gathering information about graduate programs in psychology easy to do: Just type in "graduate programs in adult development" and you will get a number of websites. This approach to searching is not very selective, however. In addition, websites are designed idiosyncratically so that desired information that you find on the pages of one graduate program may not be described similarly or located in the same place on other websites. Another way to gather information is to speak to your academic advisor about graduate programs they know by reputation, rank, or experience. Speaking to a faculty member who specializes in or teaches developmental psychology (or whatever area you are interested in) is also a good place to begin. Your advisor may also know which schools may be especially open to applications from their graduates.

A time-sensitive way to find good programs is to look at the most recent edition of the APA's *Graduate Study in Psychology* (**GSIP**), which is published yearly (e.g., American Psychological Association, 2019) and is also available on the APA website. In brief, the *GSIP* provides detailed information on the approximately 600 or so graduate programs in the United States and Canada. Each entry contains contact and department information (mailing address, phone, fax, email addresses, program website), a listing of the programs and degrees offered, APA accreditation status (for programs in clinical, counseling, and school psychology, and for joint professional-scientific degrees), number of applicants, admissions statistics (including information on required GRE scores, GPAs, and other admissions criteria; how many people applied, were admitted, and eventually enrolled in the previous year; and the anticipated number of openings for the next year), financial aid/assistance policies, and employment outcomes among recent graduates. The *GSIP* has two useful indexes. The first lists programs by the area of study (e.g., biological psychology, clinical psychology, community psychology, personality psychology) and degree(s) offered (e.g., MA, MS, PsyD, PhD), allowing users to quickly locate the schools that offer study in their area of interest. The second index is an alphabetical list of all the programs.

What information does the *GSIP* identify as generally mattering the most for gaining admission to graduate school in psychology? Most graduate programs report that letters of recommendation, college GPA, and applicants' statement of goals are among the most important criteria for admission. Research experience and GRE scores follow close behind. Extracurricular activities are the least important criterion for admission to graduate programs. As should be clear, the *GSIP* is a very helpful and portable publication. Your department might have a copy; if it doesn't, check the reference section of your school's library or career center or consider investing in a copy for yourself. You can also visit APA's Graduate Study Online database, which can be found at https://www.apa.org/pubs/databases/gradstudy/?tab=2. View a sample of a graduate school program at this website: https://www.apa.org/pubs/databases/gradstudy/sample-record.pdf.

Research Experience

Traditional PhD graduate programs in psychology are dedicated to producing scientific research in psychology. As an applicant, you will need to demonstrate to the admissions committee that you are capable of doing research. More important for yourself, you need to want to do research — really, you need to enjoy doing it. If you don't, graduate school will not be a pleasant experience and you will be guiding yourself toward a career that you will probably not like very much. We believe it is a very good idea for students to obtain research experience before applying to graduate school in psychology. Not only does this tend to make an application more competitive (recall that the *GSIP* indicates that having research experience is almost as important as having good grades), but it also helps you figure out whether a worklife doing research appeals to you. If it doesn't, better to know sooner than later so that you can choose a different type of graduate education in psychology rather than the PhD.

There are distinct advantages to doing research as an undergraduate (e.g., Landrum, 2002), including:

- learning about different approaches to doing research, including diverse methodologies;
- gaining hands-on experience doing psychology outside the classroom;
- improving teamwork skills by working with faculty members and other students on interesting questions;
- developing writing and speaking skills by learning to summarize research results; and
- potentially contributing to the psychological literature through being a team member or a coauthor on a conference presentation, journal publication, or the like.

How can you gain research experience? The best way is to become involved in research being conducted by faculty members in your undergraduate psychology department by being a **research assistant**. Do so as early in your schooling as a psychology major as you can; that way you are likely to see the results of your labor in the form of some professional product, such as conference presentations or a journal publication that can be listed on your résumé. Many faculty members will actively seek out good students to help them with their research projects. Some will advertise openings in their labs, for example. It may be easiest to approach individual faculty to find out if they are conducting research and if they welcome undergraduate assistance with it. Obviously, if you know you are interested in cognition, then you should try to work with a faculty member who conducts research in cognitive psychology. Even if no one is currently doing research in your area of interest, research experience in any area is important, so try to get a placement in a lab — remember, although research topics may differ greatly from one another, the research process is similar across subfields of psychology.

What do research assistants do? Here is a short list:

- perform library and database searches to locate existing research on given topics;
- participate in lab meetings to review current research and to plan future investigations;

- work as part of a research team;
- run data-collection sessions with research participants;
- enter data into spreadsheets and perform statistical analyses using software (e.g., SPSS); and
- write research summaries for conference proposals.

A second way for you to conduct research is to do a senior thesis. On many campuses, students with sufficiently high GPAs or those in capstone courses have the option to do a research-intensive project during their senior year. For psychology majors, this may entail writing an in-depth literature review or proposing and conducting an experiment or other research project from start to finish. At the end of the academic year, you would produce a thesis, which is usually a written work that is much more advanced than the sort of paper you would write for a lower-level course. Thesis work requires high levels of initiative, organization, independence, effort, and tenacity, which makes the experience good preparation for graduate school.

In addition to writing the thesis, you might also have to give an oral presentation (sometimes called a *defense*) to psychology faculty, fellow thesis students, and interested members of your college's community. In some contexts, the oral presentation may take the form of presenting results using a poster. This facilitates exposure to a wide range of student projects.

If the option to write a senior thesis is not available, you may be able to do an independent or directed study on a topic of your choosing. An independent study is a solo project — usually one semester in length and thus much smaller than a thesis — that is supervised by a faculty member. You might want to learn a lot about a topic that interests you (e.g., animal sleep patterns) but which your school doesn't offer a course about. An independent study enables you to become reasonably expert on that topic. You would likely create a specialized reading list to help you prepare to write some sort of term paper. You might meet weekly with a faculty member to report on your progress. Since it is possible to do an experiment or other research investigation as part of an independent study, such a study can be a reasonable substitute for the senior thesis.

Collaborating on faculty research and doing a senior thesis (or an independent study) are both great ways to learn about research, develop relevant skills, and add weight to your graduate applications. Consider being a teaching assistant (TA) in addition to these other activities. When Dana was an undergraduate, for example, he was a TA in a course on cognitive psychology. He ran a weekly recitation section where a small group of students (12 or so) came to discuss the week's lecture material, do brief in-section exercises, and ask for help with any concepts they did not understand from the three lecture sessions. This sort of opportunity can prepare you for more formal teaching during graduate school, where working as a TA or eventually as a course instructor is a source of income.

A final way to gain research experience is through summer programs that offer concentrated undergraduate research. Some universities provide financial support to their most promising students who become part of an existing research team, and there are some competitive national summer research opportunities that provide both funds and experience. Check with your advisor about which options might make the most sense for your applications.

Sometimes students become enamored of the idea of being in graduate school but show less real excitement about the nature of the work (primarily research rather than coursework) a graduate program entails. Perhaps they are afraid of not being successful in forging a career in the workforce and see graduate pursuits as somehow less risky. Or they just assume graduate school is the next step and that a career plan will naturally materialize as a by-product of pursuing a graduate degree. In **Reality Check: How Are Your Research Chops?**, we provide some questions that should help you clarify whether generating research will provide the excitement you will need to sustain your interests through that graduate program. How fluid is your ability to think in variables?

Reality Check

How Are Your Research Chops?

Most graduate programs focus on research skills and assume that you will be enthusiastic about being able to exercise your curiosity and problem-solving skills in a graduate context. Work your way through the following questions to assess how much interest you can generate about this important feature of graduate work.

1. What is your favorite research study published by a psychologist? Why is it your favorite?
2. What was the hypothesis of the study?
3. Did the results confirm the hypothesis?
4. Were there any special ethical concerns about the study?
5. Describe one other variable that you think might be related to the phenomenon being researched.
6. Speculate about a hypothesis that could extend the study you admire by predicting how that variable could influence the phenomenon.

Reflect on how easy or difficult it was for you to generate new research idea. If you have developed the capacity to think about behavior in terms of variables and their effects, you are well on your way to being the kind of graduate student whose skills will be sought by graduate faculty.

Presenting Research at a Conference

Let's imagine you work with a faculty member on his or her research or do some research on you own. What's next? An important part of the research process — some would say its *essential* aspect — is to share what you learned with other people. Admittedly, writing a senior thesis or other paper achieves this goal, but it is also true that few people beyond your research advisor will read it. A very good alternative that will enhance your potential as a graduate student is to present research at a psychology conference. Some conferences are explicitly for undergraduates to share their work with other students (recall Table 8.3 on page 146), while many regional, national, and even international conferences for professionals have sessions in which undergraduates can present (recall Table 8.1 on page 144).

Most conferences are sponsored by an organization (APA, for example). Thus, if you want to submit a conference proposal (which must be reviewed and then accepted), you will be required to join as a student affiliate before you can present. Membership costs for students tend to be reasonable. Your research supervisor will probably need to be a full member of the organization to qualify you to present. Specific information regarding these and related issues can be found at the organization and conference websites.

Undergraduate psychology conferences tend to be offered by an individual college or university or sometimes a consortia (in which more than one institution sponsors an annual undergraduate conference that moves from school to school). Your own school may host an annual "Scholars' Day" or student research symposium where you can present (these events are held annually on both Jane and Dana's home campuses).

Generally, there are two modes of conference presentations: poster sessions and oral presentations. A poster is a highly visual summary of a research project that more or less follows APA style (i.e., introduction, Method, Results, Discussion) but does so with little text and with an emphasis on tables and graphs. The poster is hung in a conference room or large hall with other posters. Interested attendees (including peers) stop by, read the poster, and then ask the researcher questions about the work. The situation is generally a lower-stress one that involves having a quick 2-minute summary to share with the people who drop by (for information about creating a poster, recall the poster rubric shown in Table 8.2 on page 145; see also Dunn, 2013; Wilson & Schwartz, 2015).

In contrast, an oral presentation is a talk where the speaker stands in front of an audience to present his or her research, usually for 15 or 20 minutes. Most oral presentations rely on PowerPoint slides or some other digital graphics package like Keynote or Prezi. Like posters, oral presentations are also brief. If you are giving the presentation, you won't have a lot of time so you will need to focus on the hypothesis, the methods used to test it, what was found, and what it means. In addition, you will need to reserve some time, usually 5 minutes, to allow audience members to ask you questions about what you did or found, why, and so on. Oral presentations are a little more stressful than posters but learning to do them is a valuable skill, one that will pay dividends in graduate school (where you give lots of talks in and outside of classes or lab meetings) and in the workplace (where you will lead discussions in meetings, present reports, and the like). For suggestions on giving talks, see Dunn (2013) or Wilson and Schwartz (2015), as well as the points on good public speaking practices provided in Chapter 7 on page 129.

Applying to Graduate Schools: Planning and Process

What is involved in applying to graduate school? What do you need to know to plan for and complete the process? Try this self-assessment to get started.

Self-Assessment: Know Yourself and Apply Strategically

When you are deciding where to apply to graduate school, perform an honest and clear-headed appraisal of your chances of being admitted. Carefully review the admissions information about the programs that interest you in the GSIP and on each program's website; again, fit matters. Take the admissions data seriously, no matter how sobering it may be. If your GPA or GRE scores are below the average for a particular program, don't ignore that; it's a potential problem. This is different than the process of applying to undergraduate schools, where students are often told to apply to at least one "reach" school. Unlike undergraduate schools, graduate programs are looking for specific skills and abilities that students must possess before they begin graduate-level training. However, if your application is somewhat balanced by excellence in other areas — sustained research with a faculty member, conference presentations, a senior thesis, excellent letters of recommendation, and so on — then taking one or two application risks might be worthwhile. But do not raise your hopes unrealistically. It is best to concentrate on applying to those programs where you have a reasonable chance of being accepted.

In addition to searching for programs that match your interests, you might also look for a specific faculty member in each program whose research appeals to you and with whom you would like to work, because most graduate programs rely on an apprenticeship model. Some applicants report success in contacting the researcher directly to express interest in his or her research. Sending a polite and professionally worded email is fine. In it, describe your background and explain why you would like to work with him or her. You may learn that the faculty member is not currently taking on any new graduate students; if you are lucky and have presented your case effectively, you may be able to stimulate the person's interest in you. Only make such contacts, however, if you are genuinely interested in the person, have read at least some of the person's research, and have a sincere interest in that particular program.

Do be prepared for rejection. Even with a strong undergraduate performance record, when Jane applied for clinical programs the first time she only made it onto the wait lists of some of the schools to which she applied. She invested the following year in working at a research-oriented job and applied again to a new set of schools whose entrance standards more closely matched her profile; that second year, she was accepted into several programs. Many professionals we know and work with applied to graduate school several years running before they were admitted. There is no shame in this; admissions to competitive programs are just that — competitive. You should only apply to those programs where you have a good chance of being accepted. There is no guarantee that even when you "fit" a program's profile you will be admitted, just as there is no way to accurately assess the competition in a given year's applicant pool.

Applying to Doctoral or Master's Programs—or Both

Should you seek a doctorate or a master's degree, or get a master's first and then go for the doctorate? Generally, pursuing the doctorate from the start is the wiser course, particularly because so many professional opportunities in the discipline, such as full-time tenure-track teaching in a 4-year college or university or being a practicing psychologist, require a doctorate (recall Chapter 11). On the other hand, many people only want master's-level training, which can be a fine option if it matches their particular applied career goals. Our point is that you should make a decision about what you want to do well in advance of the application deadlines. When you read entries in the *GSIP* or look at program websites, be sure to find out what type of degree candidates (master's or doctoral) a given program is accepting. In some programs, students can earn a master's degree as they work toward their doctorate; however, these programs only admit those seeking a doctorate; they do not offer a terminal master's degree. In effect, this type of master's degree is a proving ground for fitness to pursue the doctorate rather than a goal in itself.

One strategy that some students take is to apply simultaneously to doctoral and master's programs. Their logic is simple: If they are not admitted to any doctoral program on their first (or even second) try, they may be able to attend a master's program to prove their graduate school capability. Once they have an MA or an MS, they can reapply to doctoral programs with their master's degree in hand. Presumably, if they work hard in the master's program, their application will be stronger, as they will have completed a number of graduate courses, conducted research, written a thesis or the equivalent, and should have strong letters of recommendation from faculty in the master's program, and so on. We both have friends and colleagues who followed this route; it worked for them, but we do want to point out that it can potentially involve an extended time commitment as well as extra expenses.

As we end this section, we are mindful of the commitment graduate education requires and how long it can take to complete a degree. One study of graduate education found that the 10-year doctoral completion rate in psychology was only 65% (Council of Graduate Schools Ph.D. Completion Project, 2008). In other words, 35% of the original doctoral students did not complete a degree after being in graduate school for 10 years (and this *after* 4 or so years of undergraduate school). No doubt many of these students left their graduate program to do something else, but some were still hanging on and pursuing their degree after a decade. Some training programs have imposed limits so that if students aren't finished within a certain amount of time (typically 10 years), they are bounced from the program, probably with a pile of debt and no degree to show for their investment. Remember that going to graduate school is a serious decision. Make it with your eyes — and mind — wide open.

Stay mindful of these important factors when you are applying to graduate school:

■ Only apply to programs you would honestly consider attending.

■ You will be in graduate school for several years, so keep in mind the school's location when you are applying to and deciding on a school.

■ Consider how much debt you can reasonably carry. You will likely need to take out loans and find other forms of financial aid for graduate school.

A Few Words on Applying to Doctoral-Level Clinical Psychology Programs

Admissions for PhD programs in clinical psychology can be extremely competitive. One reason for the competition is that many students associate psychology more or less exclusively with clinical or counseling psychology (recall Chapter 2), so they apply to such programs because they know less about other options. Because of the sheer number of applicants, graduate programs in these areas typically demand that applicants have higher GPAs and GRE scores and rely on other application criteria, such as volunteer work in mental health contexts, than do programs in most other psychology subfields, thereby making the competition fierce. We offer this information not to dissuade you from applying to clinical programs. Rather, we encourage you to develop a backup plan to strengthen your application if you intend to pursue a clinical PhD and are not admitted the first time you apply.

An alternative to a traditional PhD program in clinical psychology is the PsyD (doctorate of psychology) degree (Murray, 2000). PhD programs in clinical psychology concentrate on conducting clinical research according to what is referred to in the discipline as the *Boulder Scientist–Practitioner Model*, which came out of a series of conferences in Boulder, Colorado, in the 1940s and was adapted as the APA's model in 1949. PsyD programs, which are based on a model developed in Vail, Colorado, in 1973, emphasize clinical practice over producing clinical research. This degree provided new options for those wishing to complete doctoral-level clinical training. See ***A Major Success Story: From BA to PsyD to Rehab Psychologist*** for a description of how a PsyD psychologist found just the right occupation.

Many PsyD programs are in university settings. Applicants are likely to find such programs to be highly competitive. However, over the last few decades, for-profit PsyD programs, which accept larger classes, have been established. These programs tend not to be as selective and can also generate substantial debt load for students by the time they graduate.

Two additional points to consider in choosing which schools to apply to are the school's accreditation status and its internship placement records, both of which are indices of program quality. Rigorous PhD and PsyD programs maintain their accreditation through the APA, which evaluates program quality, faculty qualifications, and curriculum structure before accrediting the clinical program. Occasionally programs lose their status if accreditors determine that they have significant deficiencies.

◄◄◄

A **Major** Success Story

From BA to PsyD to Rehab Psychologist

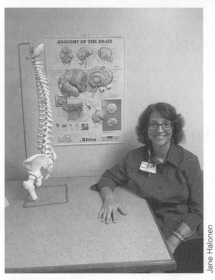

Jane Halonen

Joann Massey
PsyD, Rehabilitation Psychologist

FIGURE 12.1 Joann Massey helps individuals recover from trauma and stroke in her role as a rehabilitation psychologist.

Joann knew before the end of her undergraduate education that a traditional clinical pathway in which she would complete a PhD was just not for her. She knew her clinical instincts were solid, based on her volunteer experiences in mental health settings. However, she found the research required by PhD programs simply didn't fit with her strengths. She considers herself extremely lucky that the alternative of a practice-focused PsyD degree emerged at just the right time for her to enroll in a relatively new and rigorous PsyD program, in which she ended up thriving.

During her clinical training, she gained a lot of experience with populations of all kinds. She found herself especially drawn to people whose life circumstances produced massive physical challenges. She became a rehabilitation psychologist, working in an inpatient clinic affiliated with a major urban hospital. She collaborates with a multidisciplinary team in helping people recover from trauma, including accidents and strokes. She admires the resilience she routinely encounters as she works with her patients. Although her work is physically and emotionally challenging, she can't imagine feeling more satisfied with another professional direction.

Best Advice? "Learn how to connect and network with individuals in other departments, such as social work. Consider taking electives in subjects that complement psychology. Don't be afraid to reach out to psychologists and therapists who are established in the community as well as grads from doctoral programs if you plan to apply. The art of networking should not be limited to students in business and communication programs."

An emerging problem over the last few years, which is being compounded by recent higher numbers of PsyD-trained internship candidates from for-profit programs, has been ensuring that students in clinical PhD and PsyD programs have access to appropriate internships (Clay, 2012). The APA has been dedicating additional resources to increasing the number of quality internships for students. However, clinical programs should be able to say how successful their students are in getting placements in appropriate internships at the end of the formal internship-selection process that students participate in after they have finished the academic part of their training. Think twice about applying to programs that have poor internship-match percentages. Doing an internship at an unaccredited placement will limit your professional credibility and job options in the future.

How Many Applications?

How many graduate school applications should you submit? There is no magic number, really. You need to consider the cost involved in applying; virtually all graduate schools charge an application fee (however, most will waive that fee if you provide evidence that you have a limited income). We advise you to apply to more than one program, but beyond that the number is up to you. Some students become fixated on being admitted to their dream graduate program or to work with a particular researcher in his or her lab or research group. Such desires are understandable but must be tempered by a realistic appraisal of the chances of being admitted into that particular program.

Grades Matter — and So Do Test Scores

The grades you earn in your undergraduate courses matter for admission to selective graduate programs. You should strive do as well as you can in all of your college courses from your freshman year forward. This is critical because graduate schools do not just look at grades in psychology courses; they also examine students' GPAs in classes outside their major. What GPAs do programs look for? The minimum starting cutoff is probably 3.0 — and we intentionally use the word *minimum* here. Competitive programs can and do require higher GPAs, if only in the major courses. The best guideline is to consult the GPA requirements listed on program websites and in the *GSIP*.

What about standardized test scores? Most graduate programs in psychology require students to submit their scores on the Graduate Record Exam (GRE), which contains questions that help assess verbal reasoning, quantitative reasoning, and analytical writing, and on the GRE Psychology Subject Test. The latter is comprised of 205 multiple-choice questions covering the experimental and natural science sides of psychology (e.g., learning, cognition, memory, perception), the social science side (e.g., clinical, abnormal, social, and personality psychology), and general questions covering the history of psychology, statistics, research methods, and applied psychology, among other issues.

Official testing centers sponsored by the **Educational Testing Service (ETS)** administer the tests by computer throughout the year around the country. Once you finish the test, you are instantly given your unofficial scores, so you leave the testing session knowing how you did.

Like the grades on your college transcript, scores on the GRE and the GRE Psychology Subject Test do carry weight with programs that include test scores as a factor in their admissions decisions — the higher the scores you earn on both tests, the greater your chance of being admitted to competitive graduate programs. If your score falls below the GRE cutoff score of a graduate program, you will likely be wasting your time applying to that program. However, admissions officials may make some exceptions to the cutoff scores if there are substantial extenuating circumstances that justify admission. For example, students who have been particularly successful in undergraduate research demonstrate that they can perform at the level that will be expected in graduate school. In such cases, the publication record and exceptionally strong letters of reference may offset a disappointing GRE score. Look carefully at the application requirements; some programs may not require the GRE but might instead specify the Miller Analogies Test.

We strongly encourage you to prepare for both the general (verbal and quantitative) and disciplinary (psychology) tests. Helpful information about the nature and type of questions, scoring and score ranges, as well as tips on test taking can be found on the ETS websites for each test. A variety of books with practice questions are available and, of course, there are also formal preparatory courses that you can take weeks or months before you take the test. These books and courses can be very helpful, especially if you do not feel confident about your performance on standardized tests. On the other hand, each requires money and time. Only you can decide whether such additional investment is a good idea.

If you get disappointing scores, you should consider retaking the exam. However, without additional preparation and practice, chances are very good your scores will fall in the same range as they did the first time. You can decide which scores to forward to your target schools, so there is little risk in retaking the tests.

Requesting Letters of Recommendations

Chances are good that at some point you will want to request letters of recommendation from your instructors — perhaps your academic advisor and professors who know you well — and possibly your former supervisors or employers. Such letters are routinely used in applications for graduate school, but you may also be asked to supply a recommendation letter or two for a job opening. The appropriate etiquette for asking for letters of recommendation is discussed in Chapter 6.

Whether you ask people for letters of recommendation or to serve as references, be sure to provide them with the following:

■ a list of addresses and due dates for letters of recommendations, or for references, a list of the employers who may be calling;

■ a copy of your curriculum vitae (CV — see page 225); for job applications, a copy of your résumé (see Chapter 10, page 171);

■ a copy of your personal statement if you are applying to graduate school; or for jobs, a few paragraphs that describe your career interests and objectives;

■ a list of courses and the semester they were taken, grades earned, and meaningful or significant interactions you had with the faculty member you are asking to write your letter;

■ an unofficial copy of your undergraduate transcript;

■ a copy of your GRE and Psychology Subject Test scores (and the results of any other standardized tests) if you are applying to graduate school;

- any required recommendation forms; and
- a preaddressed envelope for each recommendation form or letter, with a stamp if your letter writer is mailing the materials directly.

Many letters of recommendation are now uploaded to university websites by the recommenders themselves. You must provide their contact information to the graduate schools you are applying to — remember, you must ask your potential recommenders in advance if they would be willing to write a letter on your behalf. Once they agree and you submit their contact information, they will receive an email from each graduate program containing instructions about how to submit your recommendation information.

The one issue remaining is unique to the graduate school application process — whether to waive your right to see a confidential letter of recommendation. Most recommendation forms contain a statement in which you indicate whether you waive (give up) or do not waive your right to see what a recommender wrote about you. If you waive this right, you can never ask the graduate school (whether you are admitted or not) to see what your recommenders said in their letters. If you don't sign the waiver, in theory, you could ask to see the letters once an admissions decision is made.

Which choice should you make? We believe that it is in your best interest to waive your right. Many faculty members will give you a copy of the letter they write on your behalf even if you waive your right. However, if a recommender doesn't offer you a copy and you don't waive your right, you run the risk that your recommender may be less likely to write an honest recommendation on your behalf. Instead, he or she may craft a neutral letter that will not say much that would make a persuasive case for your admission. Some recommenders may refuse to write a letter for you unless you waive your right to see it. This is one of the reasons why we have stated clearly that it is in your interest to ask potential recommenders if they can write strong letters on your behalf — if they demur or say they cannot do so, then you should find someone else to serve as a reference. When a recommender indicates he or she can write a strong letter for you, then you should not need to worry about the content — nor do you need to see the letter. In summary, we encourage you to waive this right so that graduate programs will receive candid assessments of your abilities and character.

One final strategy is worth mentioning. Follow up with the programs you are applying to in advance of your deadlines to make sure all of your recommenders have sent in their letters. If any are missing at that point, you still have time to gently remind the person who promised the letter but may have not yet written it to send it in. You don't want your application thrown out because a letter is missing.

Writing a Personal Statement

Most of the materials in graduate applications are a matter of record (grades, test scores) or the opinion of others (letters of recommendation). In contrast, the **personal statement** is your opportunity to present yourself and to describe your interests, skills, experiences, and career goals. Some programs refer to these as applicant or candidate statements, autobiographical statements, or letters of intent. Whatever they are called, short of a face-to-face interview, they are the one personal aspect of the application. Your statement allows you to do a few things:

- introduce yourself;
- explain your particular interest in psychology;
- share valuable background information about yourself (the aspects are most relevant to your decision to pursue advanced work); and
- provide a sample of your writing skills.

Issues and areas you should try to cover in your personal statement include (Keith-Spiegel & Wiederman, 2000):

- your academic interest areas in psychology;
- your academic background and achievements;
- why you are applying to this program and what attracted you to it;
- specific research experiences in psychology or related disciplines;
- teaching experiences relevant to psychology;
- relevant internship or volunteer experiences (e.g., youth counseling, work in clinical settings);
- objectives for graduate school and career plans (What do you hope to accomplish? Where do you see yourself in the future?);
- one or two faculty in the graduate program with whom you might want to work because of similar research interests;
- particular skills you possess (e.g., math, statistics, programming, foreign languages); and
- any personal material you think the admissions committee should know (but be judicious in what you share).

Depending on what you are asked to write about as well as any length constraints on the essay, it's unlikely that you can comment on each item on this list. Whatever you do, be sure to provide answers to the questions on the application and stay within the allotted length. Be concise. One effective strategy for writing a personal statement is to avoid discussing information (GPA, GRE scores) included elsewhere in the application — you don't want to waste space or be redundant. Still, some topics — your research experiences — can be described in greater detail here than in other places in the application.

Once you have a draft of your personal statement, share it with several allies who can help you make it very polished and persuasive. For example, get feedback from your academic advisor, the faculty member with whom you have done research, and someone you know to be excellent with grammar. Consider asking for help from someone who knows little about psychology; this last reader can identify any part of the statement that is hard to follow for a general reader — you are trying to make your personal statement be clear, not to demonstrate that you know psychology jargon. Listen to the comments from these readers and revise, revise, revise, until you are certain the statement reads well and conveys what you wanted to share about your enthusiasm for psychology and your future in the discipline.

After you have written your general personal statement, be prepared to modify it for each individual application. Some programs provide very detailed directions about what they expect applicants to discuss in this personal essay, along with length requirements (often in terms of some number of words, say, 500). Other programs use a more open-ended format. Be certain to read each program's essay requirements and tailor each statement accordingly. You want to make a persuasive case that there is a strong match between you and the program. You can be equally enthused about all your potential options but each argument you make about a high-quality match is necessarily going to be slightly different from the others.

We have one final suggestion regarding the personal statement for students who are applying to clinical programs. Avoid using the personal statement as an opportunity for an extended discussion about your own mental health struggles. Protracted disclosure of such details tends to send up red flags about your motives and may weaken your attractiveness as a candidate. If your own mental health history plays an essential role in your decision to apply, your discussion of these matters should be brief and to the point and should emphasize positive outcomes of the struggle.

Creating Your First Curriculum Vitae (CV)

In Chapter 10 we provided suggestions for crafting a résumé to send to potential employers. In this chapter, we discuss the academic version known as the **curriculum vitae**, or **CV**. A CV summarizes your academic life, particularly any scholarly accomplishments or experiences you have had. We introduce the CV here because if you go to graduate school, you will certainly write one, particularly as you get closer to the end of graduate school. So why not start one now, as you apply to graduate school?

Although CVs are somewhat like résumés, they are also different from them. CVs provide personal information (address, contact information), educational background (institutions, degrees), and any honors or awards, but they specifically focus on materials and experiences related to the person's academic discipline — in this case, psychology. CVs often contain:

- professional experiences, including jobs, that are related to psychology;
- research interests, including current projects;
- teaching interests;
- any professional publications (usually listed chronologically and in APA style);
- conference presentations and other talks (usually listed chronologically and in APA style); and
- references (names, addresses, email addresses for three or four professionals who know you and your work, or an indication that you will provide such information upon request).

As a college student or a recent graduate, your CV will probably be brief, but it will grow as you move through graduate school. **Table 12.1** illustrates a CV for a graduate school–bound student. The formatting guidelines are similar to those for a résumé (e.g., white or off-white paper, 12-point font; see Chapter 8). Use Table 12.1 as a guide for developing your own CV, which you might want to include in your graduate school application packets.

TABLE 12.1

A Sample Undergraduate Curriculum Vitae

Cavan A. Jeffries
Curriculum Vitae
1742 Roycroft Way
Gotha, FL 34734
555-777-8951
cavjef@gomail.org

EDUCATION
East Florida State University
BS in Psychology (expected May 2019)
GPA in major 3.85/overall 3.90

HONORS AND AWARDS
Dean's List, fall 2015–fall 2018
Wilson Humboldt Scholarship

RESEARCH AND TEACHING EXPERIENCE
September 2018–present Research assistant, Perception Lab, Department of Psychology, East Florida State University
Spring 2017 Teaching assistant, Dr. Susan Willamette, Introduction to Psychology (PS 101), East Florida State University
January 2016–May 2017 Tutor, Statistics and Methods I and II (PSY 221 & 222), East Florida State University

PUBLICATION
Jeffries, C. A. (2019). *A new view of the Müller-Lyer illusion.* Unpublished honors thesis, Department of Psychology, East Florida State University, Statesburg, FL. (Expected May 2019)

PRESENTATION
Jeffries, C. A. (2018, April). *New visual illusions and why they matter.* Presentation at East Florida State University's Annual Student Research Forum, Statesburg, FL.

PROFESSIONAL MEMBERSHIPS
Phi Beta Kappa
Psi Chi

REFERENCES
Available upon request

Putting It Together

As the application deadline draws near, if you have done your best and been organized, you will have a solid application package that you can submit to the graduate schools of your choice. Our advice is to allow yourself a cushion time of a week or so prior to any due date. That way, if you need it, you will still have time to complete any last-minute requirements for a given application — things almost always take longer than we expect. Falling victim to the *planning fallacy*, the failure to estimate the time needed to complete a task, will create very stressful conditions in which it becomes easy to make errors (e.g., leaving a critical piece out of the packet).

Table 12.2 lists the components that likely need to be included in a graduate admissions packet or, in the case of undergraduate transcripts and standardized test scores, need to be paid for in advance and sent independently. Keep in mind that some graduate programs require other materials (e.g., an additional standardized test, such as the Miller Analogies Test (MAT), an essay to go with your personal statement) that do not appear in this list. Always review each program's requirements one last time before submitting your application. Good luck!

If a Graduate School Interview Is in Your Future…

Some graduate programs, particularly those in clinical or counseling psychology, invite finalists to campus to meet and interview with the faculty. Following these campus visits, the faculty will convene and use observations from the interview to decide whom to admit to the program. If you are invited for an interview, always go if you can. If you can't attend an interview in person, inquire about the possibility of connecting with the interviewers online (for example, via Skype or Facetime), but recognize that this is not equivalent to an on-the-ground experience with the program faculty and your potential peers.

TABLE 12.2

Typical Materials Required for Graduate School Applications

Undergraduate transcript: Official copies must be sent to graduate programs from your undergraduate school's registrar.

GRE and GRE Psychology Subject Test scores: Official copies must be sent to graduate programs from ETS; any other required test scores must also be submitted.

Completed application form: Includes a list of major courses completed, in process, or to be completed in the future.

Your personal statement: The content may vary depending upon what a program asks you to discuss in the essay.

Letters of recommendation: Usually three; some letters must be sent directly by your recommender and you send others to the program in sealed envelopes signed by each recommender.

Optional: A copy of your curriculum vitae or résumé.

Besides being an opportunity for the program to get to know you, your visit represents a chance for you to get to know the faculty and the location, and to figure out whether you might want to attend that particular program. Keep in mind that being invited to an interview does not mean you have been admitted (unless you have been told that explicitly), thus how you present yourself in person matters a great deal. We suggest you review the section on interview skills in Chapter 10 and follow the recommendations outlined there (see pages 177–181). Instead of interviewing for a job, you are interviewing for graduate school, but the importance of being friendly, interested, open, attentive, curious (having good questions to ask), and so on is the same in both cases.

If at First You Don't Succeed

What if you apply to several programs and you aren't admitted to any of them? What then? As we've tried to convey, getting in to graduate school in psychology is often challenging. It can be easy to get discouraged if things don't work out as planned.

Still, we believe there are things you can do to strengthen your chances next time. First, take a hard look at your credentials: Did you apply to programs where the standards were too high? Second, review your standardized test scores. Would taking a prep class help you to improve your GRE scores? Third, should you try to get more research experience? If you still live near a university, can you apply for any research openings or even volunteer to help a faculty member with research? Fourth, did you apply to both doctoral and master's programs? If only the former, then you may want to try applying to both types of programs the next year. Fifth, ask your faculty advisor to review your credentials with a critical eye — is there anything missing? What can be improved upon for next time?

Remember, the path to graduate school is a long one, and it requires tenacity. If you sincerely want to become a professional in psychology, then we encourage you to keep trying. Persistence can pay off in the end.

Thought Questions

1. What specific reasons do you have for attending graduate school in psychology?

2. Will you pursue doctoral- or master's-level training? Why?

3. Is there a specific area of psychology that interests you? Within that area, are there particular topics you might like to study as a graduate student?

4. Have you had any research experience? If you have, what did you like and not like about doing research? If you haven't, do you plan to obtain some research experience? How?

5. If you were to write a personal statement right now to explain your motivation to study psychology at the graduate level, what would you say? Why?

6. What strategies might you use to persuade a researcher that you could enhance the research team's productivity?

7. What would you do to cope with the disappointment of not getting accepted? In other words, what is your plan B?

CHAPTER

13

Keeping Connected to Psychology

Look up at the stars and not down at your feet.
Try to make sense of what you see, and wonder about
what makes the universe exist.

~Stephen Hawking, physicist

W e relish hearing from our past students so that we can learn how their lives have unfolded after graduation. We love to hear about the successes they have made, and we are even more intrigued when they can pinpoint something that they learned in college from their major that has made a difference in their lives. What kinds of things do we hear?

- *Thanks for making me do public speaking in your class. I used to be petrified at the prospect but now I'm fearless.*

- *I just got a promotion that the boss linked to my ability to make teams succeed. Those ordeals in social psychology really paid off.*

- *I'm still not perfect in managing time (who is?), but I can usually manage to get everything done with time left over to enjoy life.*

- *I learned what I really wanted to do when you made me a develop a career plan. (By the way, none of those plans came to pass, but it was empowering to set those kinds of goals!)*

- *I have been surprised by how much I use the statistics knowledge I suffered through as an undergraduate. Who knew that I would have to deal with data almost every day!*

■ ■ ■

Regardless of the path you choose after graduation, by the time you complete an undergraduate degree in psychology, the imprint of psychology on you should be indelible. Chances are good you will have adopted a psychological worldview that will have an enduring impact on how you relate to the world and its many inhabitants, even if you don't pursue a job that would be identified as explicitly psychology oriented.

In this final chapter, we strive to strengthen the connection between you and your chosen discipline. First, we describe the specifics of the psychological worldview. Beyond demonstrating the characteristics or attributes of psychological thinkers, there are other ways students can keep strong connections to the discipline. We will discuss formal organizations as well as Internet and media resources that can help to keep your psychology interests alive and keep your curiosity about behavior vigorous and self-sustaining. First, let's examine the distinctive features of the psychological worldview.

What It Means to Be a Psychological Thinker

Specializing in a major also should have a distinctive and profound influence on a student's way of thinking about the world (Association of American Colleges & Universities, 2013). Education in psychology supports a specific set of values that can't help but change how the student sees the world.

We are going to use some quotations to try to capture the differences in temperament and perspective that tend to be fostered by an undergraduate major in psychology. Sometimes a psychology program formally commits to developing these characteristics in the official student-learning outcomes they incorporate into their courses; however, for the most part, the list refers to *metacognitive* (i.e., thinking about thinking) attributes that collectively set psychology majors apart from others in liberal education that we discussed in Chapter 4.

> "You see, but you do not observe."
> —*Sherlock Holmes (Sir Arthur Conan Doyle)*

Students regularly experience the necessity of being a careful observer when they are trying to make sense of behavior. They learn that effective observation is derived from careful definitions of behavior that make it easy to measure the behavior. Measurement is an essential feature of psychology that ensures observers are all observing the same thing and can track changes in behavior over time. Observers also learn to distinguish between merely describing behavior and attributing motives to behavior. Nearly all courses emphasize the importance of objective observation in making sense of behavior. **Psychological thinkers are observant**.

"In God we trust. All others, bring data."   —W. Edwards Deming

Psychologists advocate making decisions based on empirical evidence. They tend to disavow personal testimony as a flawed source for cause–effect conclusions. When confronted with a claim about behavior, psychology majors learn to ask, "What's the evidence?" If the conclusions don't derive from well-controlled empirical research ("Was there a control group?"), the psychologist is likely to decline to get on board. Psychologists prefer to take the stance of being amiable skeptics; that is, they have a generally questioning attitude toward the conclusions that most other people take for granted. **Psychological thinkers are empirically oriented**.

"Research is formalized curiosity. It is poking and prying with a purpose."
—Zora Neale Hurston

Many of our students describe a common phenomenon when they return home from college. At some point during their family reunions, someone is likely to ask, "Why do you have to *analyze* everything?" A good background in psychology provides a great foundation upon which curiosity can thrive. Psychologists deploy their curiosity in scientific investigation. They pry with an eye toward thoroughly understanding behavior. **Psychological thinkers are curious**.

"Everything should be made as simple as possible, but not simpler."
—Attributed to Albert Einstein

Before being educated in the ways of psychological thinking, people tend to be satisfied with simplistic explanations. For example, consider why new kindergartner Kimmie is so shy. A simplistic approach might suggest her shyness is genetic, that she inherited the condition from her very shy mother. However, a seasoned psychological thinker knows that such a simple answer is not adequate in explaining the complex origins of shyness. Psychological thinkers make the assumption that most behaviors usually have more than one cause ("What is Kimmie's home environment like?" "Do you see her only in situations that bring out her shyness, such as public gatherings?"). They challenge themselves to look for additional factors when others would be satisfied with a simple, shallow answer. **Psychological thinkers expect complexity**.

"Neurosis is the inability to tolerate ambiguity."   —Sigmund Freud

One of the cardinal characteristics of the psychological thinker is the capacity to tolerate ambiguity. No matter how sincere the curiosity, some phenomena will not yield to a satisfying explanation even under the best investigations. Psychologists strive to reduce ambiguity by developing well-controlled research designs but recognize that not all relevant factors may be controllable. Rather than feeling frustrated by an absence of answers, psychological thinkers tend to enjoy pondering how much remains unknown and are excited to identify plausible causal factors. **Psychological thinkers tolerate ambiguity**.

"Concision in style, precision in thought, decision in life."
—*Victor Hugo*

The discipline of psychology is at its core a quantitative enterprise. Psychologists believe that a true exploration of behavior requires precision in description that lends itself to measurement that, in turn, lends itself to statistical analysis. Psychology majors, especially those who enjoy the research aspects of psychology, learn that there is nothing more thrilling than being able to verify your conclusions with a statistically significant result. Precision also characterizes high-quality psychology writing. **Psychological thinkers strive for precision.**

"The analysis of character is the highest human entertainment."
—*Isaac Bashevis Singer*

As long as there is behavior to observe, a psychological thinker is unlikely to be bored. For example, a grocery line becomes a great laboratory to see principles of reinforcement in action. A sales negotiation demonstrates principles of persuasion. The goods offered in a kitchen store manifest human creativity and problem solving. On the other hand, we think the opportunity for psychological thinkers to entertain themselves by careful observation has been diminished to some degree by the omnipresence of smartphones. Being drawn into the small screen substantially reduces the time that can be spent merely watching, analyzing, and appreciating the human condition. **Psychological thinkers are easily entertained.**

"When people talk, listen completely. Most people never listen."
—*Ernest Hemingway*

Psychological thinkers develop a deep appreciation for the richness of communication. They recognize why undivided attention is so hard for humans to sustain but grasp how empowering it can be. They know that meaning lies not just in what is said but in what goes unspoken. They pay attention to subtleties and nuances of speech and body language. **Psychological thinkers are intentional in their communication strategies.**

"Empathy is about finding echoes of another person in yourself."
—*Mohsin Hamid*

Many experiences in the undergraduate psychology major help to develop empathy. Certain aspects of the formal curriculum (e.g., group projects, interviewing exercises) provide opportunities to see conditions from the perspective of another person. Basic counseling techniques (e.g., paraphrasing, questioning) give students the language and strategies with which to be empathic. Increased empathy reduces the human tendency to judge and to dismiss others' points of view. **Psychological**

thinkers are empathic and nonjudgmental. For a meaningful example of someone whose writing career reflects the principle of finding commonalities with others, see *A Major Success Story: Transcending Tragedy*.

A **Major** Success Story ⟨⟨⟨

Barbara Delinsky
BA, Novelist

FIGURE 13.1 Barbara Delinsky has had a successful career as a novelist after completing her bachelor's degree in psychology.

Joanne Rathe/The Boston Globe via Getty Images

Transcending Tragedy

Barbara Delinsky, who holds a BA in psychology, is no stranger to tragedy. At age 8, she lost her mother to breast cancer. She courageously faced her own midlife breast cancer diagnosis and survived surgery and treatment to write a nonfiction account of her experience. *Uplift: Secrets from the Sisterhood of Breast Cancer Survivors* summarizes practical ideas and stories of resilience from survivors and their support networks. All of the profit from her work goes into a fund to support a research fellowship at Massachusetts General Hospital. In addition to *Uplift*, she has published more than 20 novels under her own name and under various pseudonyms. Her books have appeared on the *New York Times* bestseller list more than a dozen times.

Barbara didn't start out with any inkling that she would be not just a popular but an award-winning writer. In her blog, she recounts the story of being kicked out of honors English in high school for failing to meet her writing deadlines. She says that she became inspired to write by reading about three famous women writers and simply set her mind to emulating their success. After 3 months of effort, she sold her first book. She established success in the romance genre, then her writing deepened into more complex treatments of marriage, parenthood, and friendship, capturing the emotional crises in our lives. She says, "Readers identify with my characters. They know them. They *are* them. I'm an everyday woman writing about everyday people facing not-so-everyday challenges." She attributes her success to her work ethic, typically putting in an 11-hour workday in the office over her garage.

As part of her adventure in psychological thinking, Barbara served as a researcher with the Massachusetts Society for the Prevention of Cruelty to Children and as a photographer and reporter for the *Belmont Herald*. How might her major have helped with her career?

Best Advice (for aspiring writers)? "Read. Read. Read. Find the kinds of books you most love. Read them once, twice, even three times. Study their structure by outlining them. The other thing you need to do if you want to be a writer is to start. That's it. Start. Sit down, set goals for yourself—even small ones, like writing a page or two each day—and do it!"

Information from: http://barbaradelinsky.com/biography/biography and https://www.goodreads.com/questions/458914-what-s-your-advice-for-aspiring-writers

"It is time for parents to teach young people early on that in diversity there is beauty and there is strength."

—*Maya Angelou*

One way that the discipline of psychology has dramatically changed is in its capacity to acknowledge and encourage the value of diversity. When the discipline began, it was clearly the enterprise of privileged white men. Things slowly started to change, beginning with the ascension of Mary Whiton Calkins, a brilliant female student denied entrance to Harvard in 1890 because of the school's policy of excluding women from enrolling. Although Calkins was not able to be a registered student at Harvard, she was allowed to study there under William James and soon became his favorite student (Furumoto, 1980). Calkins not only survived her Harvard snubbing but went on to become president of both the American Psychological Association (APA) and the American Philosophical Association (APS).

The field has changed with regard to race as well. In *Even the Rat Was White* (2003), a compelling look at the history of the field of psychology, Robert Guthrie identified the struggles that African American psychologists went through in the early years of the discipline. Over time, psychologists recognized the narrowness of their traditions and developed formal mechanisms to broaden and deepen their views, expanding the range of what is studied in the discipline. **Psychological thinkers are enthusiastic about diversity**.

"Service to others is the rent you pay for your room here on earth."

—*Muhammad Ali*

One of the main purposes of psychology has always been to solve problems, whether they be the intense intra- and interpersonal difficulties that are in the realm of clinical psychology or the practical puzzles that involve research psychology. Researchers address all manner of issues, from combating obesity to increasing awareness about the environment to reducing bullying on the playground. At its core, psychology is a helping profession. **Psychological thinkers are service oriented**.

"Life is a long lesson in humility."

—*James M. Barrie*

When Jane took her introductory psychology course, she experienced a critical moment when the lecturer described defense mechanisms. It was startling to recognize that humans actively distort their thinking to protect themselves. It was even more startling to recognize that she herself also engaged in such distortions. The idea of defense mechanisms explained a great deal, particularly how two people can be in the same space but not share the same reality. As cognitive research has flourished, we have a better understanding of how human judgment and decision making can produce the wrong conclusions. If we genuinely grasp the variety of ways that humans (including ourselves!) can make missteps, then it follows that we should exercise greater caution when in conflict and resist the impulse to need to be right. This humility should allow psychological thinkers to be open about other possibilities. **Psychological thinkers are tentative in their conclusions**.

The list of attributes we have explored in connection with learning to think like a psychologist is not exhaustive, but it includes some of the key differences that tend to set psychological thinkers apart from others. We recognize this discussion presents the psychological thinker in this series of quotations as an idealized form. Those trained in a psychological perspective lose their tempers, say things they regret, jump to conclusions, and demonstrate the myriad other human characteristics that complicate matters. But psychological thinkers have less fettered access to the tools that can help them build a peaceful, constructive, and creative life. See *Measuring Up: How Am I Doing So Far?* to determine your own progress in developing a psychological worldview.

 **Measuring Up**

How Am I Doing So Far?

Throughout the text we have identified the ways that people who have been trained to think like psychologists differ from those who have not. Time to take an inventory of those characteristics to see how far you've come and how far you have to go. See if you can describe a personal example that demonstrates each of the attributes discussed in this chapter.

Attribute	Personal Example
Observant	
Empirically oriented	
Curious	
Expecting complexity	
Tolerant of ambiguity	
Precise	
Intentional in communication	
Easily entertained	
Empathic	
Nonjudgmental	
Enthusiastic about diversity	
Service oriented	

Keeping Psychology Alive

Undergraduates who make a successful transition into a psychology graduate program will be immersed in the discipline in ways that they might not have been able to anticipate. In contrast, undergraduates who terminate their education after they receive a bachelor's or associate's degree may find themselves pining for the excitement of studying psychology. In this section, we explore some strategies for staying connected to the psychological community after graduation.

Psi Chi and Psi Beta

As described in Chapter 6, the international honor society Psi Chi provides a way to maintain intellectual ties to psychology. Psi Chi's mission is to help keep people engaged in and committed to psychology. By performing well as an undergraduate, you can be nominated by your faculty for induction into Psi Chi. Being part of Psi Chi has some career advantages, as its members are those who have shown great potential within the discipline. All members, whether they go on to graduate school or not, can stay abreast of national trends and interesting ideas through the communications Psi Chi sends out, and many people remain part of Psi Chi for the rest of their lives.

A similar honor society exists for the community college level called Psi Beta, which recognizes exemplary academic performance and encourages psychology-related service to the community.

Professional Organizations

You don't have to be a member of psychology's most prominent professional organizations to take advantage of the stimulation they offer. Both the APA and the APS have public portals on their websites where they share important new findings and developments in the professional psychology community.

Part of the APA's website is specifically designed for students (https://www.apa.org/about/students). The pages feature specific advice on applying to graduate school, securing funding for research, and writing and doing research. Student members receive copies of the organization's journal (*American Psychologist*) and magazine (*The Monitor on Psychology*). Undergraduates can join the American Psychology Association of Graduate Students (APAGS) for a nominal fee. Student affiliates also have access to the events the APA holds at its national convention that are specifically tailored to students.

The APS, which tends to focus primarily on the psychological research community, also maintains a division to strengthen students' interest (https://www.psychologicalscience.org/members/apssc/welcome-to-the-apssc). The APS Student Caucus manages student research competitions, has mentoring programs that match undergraduate students with graduate mentors, encourages leadership development through the campus representative program, and offers opportunities to publish work in the "Student Notebook" column of the APS *Observer* magazine and in the online publication *Undergraduate Update*.

Specialized professional psychology groups offer incentives to students to become and stay involved in their organizations. By being welcoming to students, the organizations are able to recruit them to be members and leaders in the future, which helps keep the groups vibrant and full. For example, both Jane and Dana are partial to the organization called the Society for the Teaching of Psychology (STP; teachpsych .org/) because its work has the most direct bearing on the way they both earn a living in psychology. Graduate students can join a formal subdivision called the Graduate Student Teaching Association (GSTA) of STP. Membership is especially useful for new graduate students who are about to begin to teach. Undergraduates can also join to take advantage of the teaching-related resources STP offers.

Cinema

Whitbourne (2012) has argued that the Academy Awards tend to be heavily biased toward subject matter that depicts psychological themes. She says, "Audiences are fascinated by heartless murderers, tragic heroes or heroines wrestling with psychological demons, couples who tear each other apart, and families that make their home life a constant nightmare" and concludes that Hollywood's preoccupation with psychological dynamics keeps the audience "glued to the screen" (p. 1).

To promote the connection between psychology and cinema, we provide a list in **Table 13.1** of our favorite psychology-oriented movies that are guaranteed to spark lively conversation. We offer one caveat: Not all Hollywood movies accurately portray what we know from psychological science about human behavior. For example, the compelling film *A Beautiful Mind* misrepresents the mathematician John Nash's schizophrenia; people with schizophrenia tend to have auditory hallucinations rather than the visual hallucinations portrayed in the film. An even bigger offender is the recent movie *Split*, which presents a melodramatic treatment of dissociative identity disorder that most clinical psychologists would dispute. Creative license makes for a compelling story, if not an accurate depiction, of the symptoms of schizophrenia or DID. Psychological thinkers simply include the conceptual errors in the psychological content of films to the list of elements they analyze when they watch movies. (For further suggestions of psychology-focused films, see Niemiec & Wedding, 2014; Wedding & Niemiec, 2010.)

Books

Books with psychological themes are too numerous to list in this short volume. However, we do have some pointers for your search. Recognize that psychologists would not approve of many of the books featured in psychology sections in bookstores. They are likely to be contaminated with self-help and pseudoscience volumes. Be sure to check out the science and education sections as well as the psychology section. In ***Reality Check: What's on Your Nightstand?***, you have the opportunity to review what kinds of books should go on your permanent future reading list.

TABLE 13.1

Recommended Films for Sparking Psychological Conversations

A Beautiful Mind (2001): A flawed but engaging treatment of a troubled mathematician.

BlacKkKlansman (2018): A black undercover cop must provide security for white nationalist David Duke.

A Clockwork Orange (1971): A futuristic tale of aversion therapy.

As Good As It Gets (1997): A film about friendship and compulsive disorder.

Awakenings (1990): Encephalitis sufferers get sudden but temporary relief from a new drug.

Black Swan (2010): A ballet dancer breaks down during her role in *Swan Lake.*

Born on the Fourth of July (1989): Ron Kovic becomes a political activist after being disabled in the Vietnam War.

Brokeback Mountain (2005): Critically acclaimed story of two cowboys who discover a deep relationship and feel its impact on their families and them.

David and Lisa (1962): Sweet romance between two people with mental impairments.

Dunkirk (2017): A volunteer rescue effort saves British soldiers from annihilation in World War II.

Eighth Grade (2018): The ups and downs of a 13-year-old on the cusp of graduation from middle school.

The Deer Hunter (1978): Vietnam veterans try to adjust to postwar life in a small town in Pennsylvania.

Fearless (1993): Personality change in the aftermath of a major airline crash.

Get Out (2017): A mixed-race couple runs into some challenge when a white woman takes her black boyfriend home to meet her parents.

Girl, Interrupted (1999): A young woman spends 18 months in a 1960s mental hospital.

Good Will Hunting (1997): A math genius seeks help from a psychologist.

The King's Speech (2010): Stuttering troubles the ascent of a British monarch to the throne.

Hidden Figures (2016): Black female mathematicians do their part to help the United States in the race for space.

Kinky Boots (2005): Drag queens, business practices, and friendship intertwine in this story about British boot manufacturing.

Lady Bird (2017): The strained relation between an independent young woman and a mother striving to keep her from being independent.

Little Miss Sunshine (2006): A funky family reveals wild dynamics as they help the youngest achieve her dream of competing in a beauty pageant.

The Lost Weekend (1945): A chronic alcoholic engages in a 4-day drinking binge.

Lucky (2017): An aging cowboy deals with the meaning of life and death.

The Manhunter (1986): An FBI specialist tracks a serial killer.

Marjorie Prime (2017): A demented woman spends her final days in conversation with a holographic representation of her husband.

Manchester by the Sea (2016): Fatherhood is suddenly thrust upon a middle-aged man with no interest in having a family.

Memento (2000): Short-term memory loss troubles a man trying to solve a murder.

Moonlight (2016): A young gay black man's story of grappling with identity in a coming-of-age-story.

Continued

My Left Foot (1989): A man with cerebral palsy learns to paint with his left foot.

One Flew Over the Cuckoo's Nest (1975): A con man tries to exploit the mental health system and runs into surprising obstacles, including an oppressive nurse.

Ordinary People (1980): Robert Redford's film about a family's attempt to cope with the death of a teenager in the family.

The Perks of Being a Wallflower (2012): An exploration about the challenge of adolescent self-acceptance.

Platoon (1986): The Vietnam War produces violence and moral crisis.

Rain Man (1988): Two brothers connect despite autism and narcissism.

Requiem for a Dream (2000): Profiles of four New Yorkers struggling with addiction.

The Sessions (2012): Interactions between a sex therapist and her client, a man in an iron lung.

The Silence of the Lambs (1992): A young FBI cadet collaborates with an incarcerated, manipulative killer to catch another serial killer.

Silver Linings Playbook (2012): Two troubled people connect through dancing.

The Snake Pit (1948): A mid-twentieth-century portrayal of inpatient mental health care.

Split (2016). A young man with dissociative identity disorder wreaks havoc in the lives of three women and a female therapist.

Taxi Driver (1976): A mentally unstable taxi-driving Vietnam veteran attempts to save a preadolescent prostitute.

The Theory of Everything (2014): The life story of Stephen Hawking, the brilliant physicist who has the neurodegenerative disease ALS.

Three Faces of Eve (1957): An abusive childhood fractures a young woman's personality.

Twelve Angry Men (1957): A definitive look at small-group dynamics in the context of a court case.

Vertigo (1958): A Hitchcock film about obsession and acrophobia.

What About Bob? (1991): A wildly disturbed patient upends his therapist's family dynamics.

A Woman Under the Influence (1974): John Cassavetes showcases the story of the impact of schizophrenia on family dynamics.

 Reality Check

What's on Your Nightstand?

Most psychologically oriented thinkers tend to gravitate toward books that explore themes of interests about human behavior. Here we share our current recent favorites on our own nightstands in the interest of building your custom reading list.

Jane likes the uplifting conclusions drawn by Steven Pinker in *Enlightenment Now: The Case for Reason, Science, Humanism, and Progress* (Viking, 2018).

Dana's choice is Sarah Williams Goldhagen's *Welcome to Your World: How the Built Environment Shapes Our Lives* (HarperCollins, 2017).

Now it's your turn. What books would you recommend as a must for the psychological thinker? What books would your classmates suggest would be beneficial to your future?

Web Crawling

So many treasures exist in cyberspace that it is relatively easy to get lost in the exploration of good psychology resources. You are likely to find an array of interesting choices to explore when you pose any question to a search engine. Some of our recent favorites include the following:

- Conferences are for students, too.
  https://www.psychologytoday.com/us/blog/head-the-class/201803
  /psychology-conferences-are-students-too

- Why do so few men major in psychology?
  https://www.apa.org/gradpsych/2011/01/cover-men.aspx

- What are the highest-paying jobs a person can get with a degree in psychology?
  https://www.bls.gov/ooh/life-physical-and-social-science/psychologists
  .htm#tab-5

- What is a psychology degree worth?
  https://www.psychologytoday.com/us/blog/head-the-class/201403
  /question-what-s-psychology-degree-worth-anyway

Several organizations continually update their websites with interesting information. For example, *Psychology Today* includes new writings daily from a number of experts in its list of blogs and blog topics (http://www.psychologytoday.com/). Dana is the author of entries on the blog *Head of the Class* on the *Psychology Today* website. The website has topic streams (e.g., obesity, creativity, resilience) that are drawn from its archives and can serve as stimuli for thinking about potential research topics. (Remember that most professors don't consider references from *Psychology Today* to be good primary sources; however, the readability of the magazine can help unlock creativity about potential new directions that could emerge from the research it reports on.)

Another helpful site, the Social Psychology Network, operated by Scott Plous of Wesleyan University, includes links to more than 150 blogs, podcasts, and RSS feeds that feature some of the most important psychologists conducting research today (https://www.socialpsychology.org/blogs.htm). The site is organized to highlight resources in general psychology and neuroscience; politics and public policy; judgment and decision making; happiness, fulfillment, and life meaning; interpersonal relationships; and teaching and education, among others.

TED (Technology, Entertainment, and Design) Talks have also done a great job of making psychology more accessible to the public. Included among the psychology superstars of the TED talks are the following. Search for them by their name at www.ted.com/talks.

- Philip Zimbardo: "The Psychology of Evil"
- Barry Schwartz: "The Paradox of Choice"

- Alison Gopnik: "What Do Babies Think?"
- Steven Pinker: "Human Nature and the Blank Slate"
- Mihaly Csikszentmihalyi: "Flow, the Secret to Happiness"
- Elizabeth Loftus: "The Fiction of Memory"
- Regan A.R. Gurung: "Get Psyched: Think Stronger, Live Longer"
- Jill Bolte Taylor: "My Stroke of Insight"
- Susan Cain: "The Power of Introverts"
- Robert Waldinger: "What Makes a Good Life? Lessons from the Longest Study on Happiness"
- Dan Gilbert: "The Surprising Science of Happiness"
- Kelly McGonigal: "How to Make Stress Your Friend"
- Keith Barry: "Brain Magic"
- Kang Lee: "Can You Really Tell if a Kid Is Lying?"
- Carol Dweck: "The Power of Believing You Can Improve"
- Adam Grant: "The Surprising Habits of Original Thinkers"
- Meg Jay: "Why 30 is Not the New 20"
- Esther Perel: "The Secret to Desire in a Long-Term Relationship"
- Shawn Anchor: "The Happy Secret to Better Work"
- Elizabeth Dunn: "Helping Others Makes Us Happier — But It Matters How We Do It"

A comprehensive list of psychology TED talks can be found at https://www.ted.com /topics/psychology.

Kindred Spirits

Jane likes to claim that good psychology majors can often finish each other's sentences. So, it is great fun to meet new people who have studied psychology because the shared interest in human behavior accelerates bonding. With a conservative estimate of 1 million students taking psychology courses every year (Munsey, 2008), the potential for finding common ground with new college-educated acquaintances is pretty high.

Although only a few psychologists have reached a level of public recognition that they could be considered famous, many famous people have majored in psychology. See **Table 13.2** for a list of recognizable names of people who share your interest in behavior and either started or completed an undergraduate degree in psychology (based on Halonen, 2011). Some of the names on this list may surprise you. How do you think psychology helped them in their careers? You can see that the range of careers is vast!

TABLE 13.2

Notable People Who Either Started or Finished a Bachelor's Degree in Psychology

Actors

Katherine Hepburn (*Lion in Winter, The Philadelphia Story*)

Natalie Portman (*Black Swan, Star Wars*)

Brooke Shields (*Suddenly Susan, Pretty Baby*)

Selma Blair (*Hellboy, Legally Blonde*)

Barbara Bach (*The Spy Who Loved Me*)

Marcia Cross (*Desperate Housewives*)

Harry Hamlin (*L.A. Law, Madmen*)

John Ritter (*Three's Company*)

Jonathan Frakes (*Star Trek: The Next Generation*)

Claire Danes (*Stardust, Homeland*)

Lisa Kudrow (*Friends, Web Therapy*)

Ben Browder (*Farscape, Stargate*)

Colin Firth (*The King's Speech, Bridget Jones's Diary*)

Eric Winter (*The Mentalist*)

Entertainers and Media Producers

Ted Allen, playwright and wine specialist (*Queer Eye for the Straight Guy, Chopped*)

Dana Bourne, science programmer at WGBH

Jerry Bruckheimer, producer (*Pirates of the Caribbean*)

Wes Craven, writer and director (*Nightmare on Elm Street*)

Gloria Estefan, performer and songwriter

Penney Finkelman Cox, producer (*Snakes on a Plane, Terms of Endearment*)

Jordan Mechner, video game designer (*Prince of Persia*)

Doug Henning and the Amazing Kreskin, magicians

Al Jarreau, jazz singer

Lil Wayne, hip-hop artist

Phil McGraw, media psychologist

Jon Stewart, producer and late-night satirist

J. Michael Straczynski, producer and creator (*Babylon 5*)

Yanni Chryssomallis, New Age musician

Artists

Annie Truitt, minimalist artist

Elyn Zimmerman, landscape artist and sculptor

Athletes

Herb Brooks, Olympic hockey coach

Gina Carana, mixed martial artist

Natalie Coughlin, Olympic swimmer

Tim Duncan, NBA player

Mia Hamm, soccer star

Wendy Norris, NASCAR pit reporter

Tori Murden, first woman to row across the Atlantic

Doctor

Ben Carson, pediatric neurosurgeon and presidential candidate

Educators

Norman B. Anderson, CEO, American Psychological Association

Sissela Bok, ethicist

Alan Leshner, CEO, American Association for the Advancement of Science

Judith Rodin, director, Rockefeller Foundation, and president, University of Pennsylvania

Peter Salovey, president, Yale University

Beverly Daniel Tatum, president, Spelman College

Politicians/Government

Ken Blackwell, diplomat

Tipper Gore, Second Lady

Marlene Jenning, Canadian politician

Princess Kate of Great Britain

Ted Strickland, former governor of Ohio

Hendrik Frensch Verwoerd, prime minister of South Africa

Continued

Entrepreneurs

Gary Bridge, senior vice president, CISCO Systems

Peter Butterfield, president and CEO, KIA Motors America

Richard Chaifetz, founder and CEO, Compsych Corp Employee Assistance Programs

Tom Dillon, manager of rail operations, Ringling Bros. and Barnum & Bailey

Jamie Dimon, CEO, JPMorgan Chase

Hugh Hefner, *Playboy* founder and publisher

Mark Zuckerberg, Facebook creator and founder

Guy Kawasaki, Apple promoter

Jim McCann, founder, 1-800-Flowers

Irene Rosenfeld, Kraft Foods executive

Lisa M. Weber, MetLife CEO

Vaira Vike-Freiberga, president of Latvia

Jeff T. H. Pon, Director of Office Personnel Management (federal human resources)

Pilot

Chesley "Sully" Sullenberger

Writers

Barbara Delinksy, mystery writer

Abbie Hoffman, political activist (*Steal This Book*)

Jonathan Kellerman, mystery writer

Henry K. Lee, novelist (*The Missing Wife*)

John Most, poet

Carol Tavris, pseudoscience debunker

Robert Anton Wilson, novelist

Chip Reid, CBS national news correspondent

Although not all of the following people were psychology majors, each carved out a special place in history by winning the Nobel Prize for their work on psychological phenomena.

- Ivan Pavlov (1904): Nobel Prize in Physiology or Medicine for his pioneering work in understanding the physiology of digestion

- Herbert A. Simon (1978): Nobel Prize in Economic Sciences for applying economic principles to the decision processes that affect the dynamics of organizations

- Roger Sperry (1981): Nobel Prize in Physiology or Medicine for his work in establishing the functional specializations of different parts of the brain

- Daniel Kahneman (2002): Nobel Prize in Economic Sciences for carefully differentiating rational and irrational processes that influence decision making

- John O'Keefe, May-Britt Moser, and Edvard I. Moser (2014): Nobel Prize in Physiology or Medicine for discovering cells that provide positioning feedback in the brain

Psychology also has many National Medal of Science laureates. These include the following psychologists along with the major areas of their contributions:

- Neal Elgar Miller (1964) for learning and motivation

- Harry Harlow (1967) for comparative and experimental psychology

- B. F. Skinner (1968) for broad impact on understanding human behavior
- Herbert Simon (1986) for decision making and problem solving
- Anne Anastasi (1987) for individual differences and testing
- George A. Miller (1991) for language and cognition
- Eleanor J. Gibson (1992) for perceptual development in childhood
- Roger N. Shepard (1995) for visual spatial perception
- William K. Estes (1997) for learning and memory
- Duncan Luce (2003) for mathematical behavioral models
- Gordon H. Bower (2005) for cognitive psychology
- Michael I. Posner (2008) for neuroscience and brain function
- Mortimer Mishkin (2009) for memory and perceptual processes
- Anne Treisman (2011) for perception and attention
- Albert Bandura (2015) for social cognitive theory

The Alumni Opportunity

Just because you graduate, it doesn't mean that your connection to your undergraduate major is over. Most psychology departments welcome attention from their graduates, and faculty particularly like to know what directions their students' lives have taken. Many departments sponsor an active psychology alumni network. These organizations serve multiple functions because alumni can do the following:

- be outstanding mentors to undergraduate students. Some departments recognize that external mentors can provide additional support for students who are trying to find their way.
- make great career night speakers. When students don't have much notion about what the future holds, it helps to hear someone talk about finding a meaningful psychology-related focus.
- provide introductions to other professionals working in areas that undergraduates think might be their calling.
- designate the psychology department to be the beneficiary of their donations. Most universities allow donors to stipulate how their contributions can be used. Creating an endowment for the best student poster or contributing to student travel funds are great ways to pay back on the investment the department made in you.
- galvanize activity across classes for special events, such as celebrating the retirement of a particularly beloved faculty member.

Staying a Fan of Psychology

Falling in love with psychology was one of the most satisfying experiences of our lives. We were lucky that the course of our lives facilitated this choice. If we had to do it over, we'd do it again with big smiles. We envy those who are just starting out on the adventure and hope that the *Companion* has provided some insight and guidance that will allow you to fall and stay in love with psychology, too. In the words of Dr. Seuss,

"Will you succeed? Yes you will indeed!

(98 and 3/4 percent guaranteed.)"

We hope that is true.

Thought Questions

1. What kinds of attributes tend to characterize the psychological thinker?
2. How can professional organizations support a life long interest in psychology?
3. What are your favorite movies with psychological themes?
4. How can you use the Internet to stay current with trends in psychology?
5. Who are some famous psychology majors?
6. In what ways can you continue to support your undergraduate program after you graduate?

APPENDIX A

This appendix contains a sample APA-style student paper. We have included it to illustrate the general characteristics of a solid experimental first effort by a student.

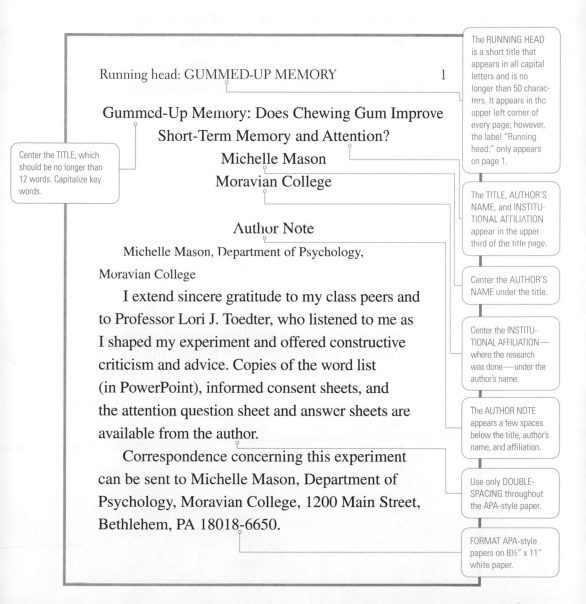

Running head: GUMMED-UP MEMORY   1

Gummed-Up Memory: Does Chewing Gum Improve
Short-Term Memory and Attention?

Michelle Mason

Moravian College

Author Note

Michelle Mason, Department of Psychology,

Moravian College

I extend sincere gratitude to my class peers and to Professor Lori J. Toedter, who listened to me as I shaped my experiment and offered constructive criticism and advice. Copies of the word list (in PowerPoint), informed consent sheets, and the attention question sheet and answer sheets are available from the author.

Correspondence concerning this experiment can be sent to Michelle Mason, Department of Psychology, Moravian College, 1200 Main Street, Bethlehem, PA 18018-6650.

The RUNNING HEAD is a short title that appears in all capital letters and is no longer than 50 characters. It appears in the upper left corner of every page; however, the label "Running head:" only appears on page 1.

Center the TITLE, which should be no longer than 12 words. Capitalize key words.

The TITLE, AUTHOR'S NAME, and INSTITUTIONAL AFFILIATION appear in the upper third of the title page.

Center the AUTHOR'S NAME under the title.

Center the INSTITUTIONAL AFFILIATION—where the research was done—under the author's name.

The AUTHOR NOTE appears a few spaces below the title, author's name, and affiliation.

Use only DOUBLE-SPACING throughout the APA-style paper.

FORMAT APA-style papers on 8½" x 11" white paper.

Abstract

Experiments regarding chewing gum's ability to aid or hinder cognitive function have yielded inconsistent results. I hypothesized that flavored chewing gum would assist memory recall and attention due to its sugar content and not because of the motion of chewing. There were 47 participants, ages 18–24, all of whom attended a liberal arts college. Participants were randomly assigned to one of four groups—regular gum, regular mints, sugar-free candy, or sugar-free mints—and were shown a list of 20 nouns and an attention video. The two dependent measures were counterbalanced and the scores recorded. Analyses revealed no significant results for any of the main variables, suggesting that chewing gum does not bolster memory recall or attention scores, nor does the gum's sugar content influence memory recall and attention.

Keywords: attention, short-term memory, gum chewing, glucose, cognitive functioning

The ABSTRACT always appears on page 2. It is labeled with a centered heading.

The ABSTRACT PARA-GRAPH is not indented and, for an empirical study, is no more than 120 words in length.

The MARGINS on all sides of all pages are no more than 1 inch wide.

Use LEFT-JUSTIFICATION throughout the paper.

Center KEYWORDS under the Abstract paragraph.

Gummed-Up Memory: Does Chewing Gum Improve Short-Term Memory and Attention?

Chewing gum was the first human-made candy— prehistoric men and women chewed on tree resins and saps. Every succeeding civilization has shown evidence of gum chewing. The average American citizen chews 182 pieces of gum per year and the United States produces 1,000 different varieties of gum (International Chewing Gum Association, 2005), making gum production a $3.3 billion industry in America (Euromonitor International, 2011). Chewing gum's popularity may be attributed to its increasing association with benefits such as tooth whitening, breath freshening, being a source of vitamins, and as a smoking-cessation or weight-loss aid (International Chewing Gum Association, 2005). Recent debate focuses on chewing gum's potential cognitive health benefits.

The topic of chewing gum's effect on cognitive ability has been highly controversial. Research has shown inconsistent results; some studies find beneficial effects while others find adverse effects (Tucha & Koerts, 2012). Studies that found that gum chewing improved cognitive function also concluded that it impaired attention (Tucha, Mecklinger, Maeir, Hammerl, & Lange, 2004). Other studies contest these claims, perhaps because they use different operational definitions of attention and diverse scales of measurement, making the findings extremely difficult to compare.

The INTRODUCTION appears on page 3.

Repeat and center the MANUSCRIPT'S TITLE above the opening paragraph of the introduction. Capitalize the title's main or key words. Do not set the title bold.

PARENTHETICAL CITATIONS use an ampersand (&) instead of "and" but citations appearing outside parentheses use "and" between author names.

GUMMED-UP MEMORY   4

Studies that find that chewing gum has a positive effect on cognitive function disagree about whether initial learning affects cognitive functions. Baker, Bezance, Zellaby, and Aggleton (2004) concluded that gum chewing has context-dependent effects on memory. If a person chews gum when initially learning a concept, then they test better if they are also chewing gum when asked to recall information. If they are learning a concept when they are not chewing gum, however, their recall is disrupted by gum chewing. In contrast, Miles and Johnson (2007) concluded that no such context-dependent relationship exists.

> CITE ALL AUTHORS (up to six) the first time their work is used.

Baker et al. (2004) used a sample of 83 undergraduates, ages 18 to 46. Participants were given a written list and 2 minutes to study the list. They were later tested after a 2-minute and a 24-hour delay. Participants either had gum or no gum during both recall and learning, or gum-no gum and no gum-gum for learning and recall. The authors of the study concluded that chewing gum had a context-dependent component, due to differing recall scores, and improved cognitive function.

> After the first citation, CITE THREE OR MORE AUTHORS using "et al."

Subsequently, Miles and Johnson (2007) tried to replicate the experiment. However, they used a smaller sample of only 24 undergraduates, ages 18 to 21. They did not give out the word list but displayed it visually at 5-second intervals. They also ensured that people in the gum-gum conditions

replaced their gum to ensure that the context of chewing gum (consistency, texture, and flavor) was the same. Their experiment showed that there were no context-dependent effects nor was gum chewing responsible for better cognitive function. The main difference in the studies concerned sample size, and in larger samples, even relatively small differences can be found to reach statistical significance.
A second difference was that Baker et al. presented an actual written list of words, thereby allowing participants to choose which words they wanted to study and recall. Miles and Johnson used an evenly paced, single exposure to each word.

  Stephens and Tunncy (2004) tested whether glucose availability causes beneficial cognitive effects. However, their procedure had some confounding variables. They used regular drinking water and compared it to glucose-enriched (25 g) water as two independent variables for glucose consumption. From these two variables, they concluded that glucose increased cognitive function, such as memory recall and spatial skills. However, their gum-chewing component was confounded. They used a sugar-free gum and a sugared candy to compare the cognitive effects of chewing gum; this confounds the impact on cognition both of sugar content and of chewing versus a sucking motion. Effectively, they proposed a reasonable theory but failed to properly test it.

GUMMED-UP MEMORY   6

APA style supports writing in the first person (ACTIVE VOICE) instead of third person (PASSIVE VOICE). "I designed" is better than "A study was designed."

Present the HYPOTHESIS clearly prior to the Method section.

In an attempt to disambiguate chewing gum's effect on memory, I designed a study with an independent variable comprised of four potential mental facilitators: Stride spearmint chewing gum, Stride sugar-free spearmint gum, generic mint Life Savers, and sugar-free mint Life Savers. These conditions account for the effect of sugar content on cognitive functioning as well as the unique properties of chewing gum (i.e., the chewing motion). There were two dependent variables. The first tested memory, defined as the number of words correctly recalled from a 20-item list; and the second tested attention, which was defined as the number of questions correctly answered concerning the content of a YouTube video.

Based upon Stephens and Tunney's theory (2004) that glucose availability causes beneficial cognitive effects, I hypothesized that both the regular Stride chewing gum and the regular mint Life Savers would improve cognitive function due to their sugar content, meaning memory recall and attention improvement are not unique properties of chewing gum and the chewing motion. Participants in the regular mint Life Saver condition may show more improved cognitive function than those in the regular Stride spearmint gum condition due to the elevated sugar content.

GUMMED-UP MEMORY   7

Method

Participants

Forty-seven (20 men, 27 women) Moravian College students, aged 18 to 24 (M = 19.85), participated and most received extra credit in one of their psychology courses. Recruitment was done through the use of flyers in the psychology building. All participants were volunteers who signed up to participate in the experiment. Informed consent was a prerequisite for participation. Participants were assigned to four different groups: the regular Stride spearmint gum group (n = 12), the sugar-free Stride spearmint gum group (n = 14), the regular mint Life Savers group (n = 10) and the sugar-free mint Life Savers group (n = 11). All were treated in accordance with the American Psychological Association's Ethical Principles of Psychologists and Code of Conduct.

Materials

The same word list of 20 nouns was presented via PowerPoint to all experimental groups. Each participant was later given a pen and paper to write down recalled items. Each participant received either regular Stride spearmint gum (2 g sugar), sugar-free Stride spearmint gum (0 g sugar), generic mint Life Saver candy (3 g sugar), or sugar-free mint Life Saver candy (0 g sugar). The Rémi Gaillard football video (2007; 3 min 22 sec in length) can

FIRST-LEVEL HEADINGS appear in boldface.

Write the METHOD SECTION in the past tense.

SECOND-LEVEL HEADINGS appear at the left margin and in boldface.

Italicize STATISTICAL SYMBOLS.

PARTICIPANT INFORMATION includes number, gender, race, age, selection procedure, and any reason for participation.

Use Arabic numerals to represent NUMBERS OF 10 OR MORE.

The MATERIAL SUBSECTION describes the nature and purpose of the materials used in the study.

Abbreviate STANDARD UNITS OF MEASUREMENT.

be found on YouTube at http://www.youtube.com /watch?v=SFsHPFhtEYQ. The question-and-answer sheets for the Rémi Gaillard video, which functions as the measure of attention, were also used.

Procedure

Participants were immediately given informed consent paperwork and reminded that anyone with diabetes, extensive dental work (e.g., crowns, braces), or an allergy to gum or mint could not participate. Participants were then randomly assigned to one of the four experimental conditions. All papers and surveys used during the experiment were placed in the coded envelope and returned at the end of the experiment.

Participants were instructed to chew their gum or suck their candy. A list of 20 nouns was presented via PowerPoint at 5-second intervals. Each noun appeared on a separate slide. After watching the complete presentation, participants were instructed to write down all the words that they could recall within a 2-minute time frame. Papers of recalled words were collected for scoring. Each word accurately recalled scored 1 point. Any forgotten or falsely recollected word received no score (and no penalty).

After being instructed to use a new candy/ piece of gun, participants then watched the Rémi Gaillard video, which functioned as the attention component of the study. Participants were given

12 multiple-choice questions regarding the video they watched and the papers were scored in the same manner as the word recall list. To control for any ordering effects, word-recall testing and attention testing was counterbalanced during different sessions of experimentation. The experiment lasted approximately 30 minutes. Participants were debriefed as soon as the data were collected.

Results

Did the sugar in the gum or candy influence recall and attention scores? A 2 (chewing gum vs. sucking a mint) x 2 (sugar vs. sugar-free candy) analysis of variance (ANOVA) revealed no significant difference between gum chewing and candy sucking (F [1, 46] = .250) and no significant differences were detected between the sugar-free and sugared candy (F [1, 46] = 2.755) conditions for memory recall (see Figure 1) and attention to detail (see Figure 2). No interaction was found between the two variables (F [1, 46] = .173), either. One of the factors, mints versus gum, approached a marginal level of significance (p = .104).

In an exploratory analysis of falsely recalled words, the factor of gum versus candy was significant, with gum groups experiencing more false recall (M = .88) than mint groups (M = .33; see Figure 3). However, post hoc testing yielded an

Sections of the APA-style paper appear with NO PAGE BREAKS in between.

Write the RESULTS section in the past tense.

Define ABBREVIA-TIONS the first time they appear.

Accompany STATISTI-CAL RESULTS with a verbal description of the findings.

eta-squared of .119, indicating that only 12% of false recall was accounted for by use of gum versus mint candies. The number of correct words recalled and falsely recalled words was negatively correlated at −.429 ($p < .01$), meaning fewer false recalls occurred when more correct recalls were made. Self-reported memory ratings had a .244 correlation, a trend at the .10 level. However, no significant correlations were observed between self-reported memory ratings and false recall. Gender, age, and familiarity with the sport in the video had no significant effect on word recall or attention scores.

Discussion

> Write the DISCUS-SION section largely in the present tense.

The results fail to support my hypothesis that consumption of regular chewing gum and regular candy during memory tasks improves memory because of the persistent availability of sugar to the brain, contradicting the findings of Stephens and Tunney (2004). Due to the nonsignificant results on memory recall and attention to detail, it appears that chewing gum neither hinders nor abets memory recall or attention, and any differences in score do not result from chewing versus sucking movements, which had been unaccounted for by Stephens and Tunney.

> DISCUSSION SEC-TIONS highlight what the findings do and do not reveal.

A possible confound was that five participants forgot to wear glasses, rendering their scores on both dependent measures suspect. Of the five participants,

> Note an EXPERIMENT'S LIMITATIONS in the Discussion.

GUMMED-UP MEMORY   11

three were in the experimental regular sugared
gum group. In the case of the gum versus candy
comparison, which was close to marginal significance,
it could be argued that a larger sample size could
have led to significant results. Thus, replication of
this experiment may yield more conclusive results
regarding the main effect. However, gum versus mint
candy influences the amount of false recalls that
occur (with candy groups having fewer false recalls).
This could indicate that the chewing versus sucking
mechanism may negatively impact attention and the
motivation to correctly recall words.

In order to address the issue of falsely recalled
words in future studies, I would add a confidence
interval to the word recall list. A possible explanation
for falsely recalled words is illustrated by the
negative correlation between word recall and falsely
recalled words. Subjects who recalled more words
were less likely to falsely recall words. Therefore,
it is possible that subjects who could not remember
words were willing to just make up words to write
down. Motivation may be a confounding factor
concerning whether words are remembered correctly
and future studies may need to address the motivation
of the participants to actually perform well on the
experimental tasks.

> Present directions for possible future research in the DISCUSSION.

References

Baker, J. R., Bezance, J. B., Zellaby, E., & Aggleton, J. P. (2004). Chewing gum can produce context-dependent effects upon memory. *Appetite, 43*, 207–210.

Euromonitor International. (2011). *Gum in the US* [Data file]. Retrieved from http://www .euromonitor.com/gum-in-the-us/report

International Chewing Gum Association. (2005). *Fun facts about gum* [Data file]. Retrieved from http://www.gumassociation.org/default .aspx?Cat=4

Miles, C., & Johnson, A. J. (2007). Chewing gum and context-dependent memory effects: A re-examination. *Appetite, 48*, 154.

Stephens, R., & Tunney, R. (2004). Role of glucose in chewing gum-related facilitation of cognitive function. *Appetite, 43*, 211–213.

Tucha, L., & Koerts, J. (2012). Gum chewing and cognition: An overview. *Neuroscience and Medicine, 3*, 243–250.

Tucha, O., Mecklinger, L., Maeir, K., Hammerl, M., & Lange, K. (2004). Chewing gum differentially affects aspects of attention in healthy subjects. *Appetite, 42*, 327–329

Begin the REFERENCE SECTION on a new page.

Use a hanging indent format and double-space APA-STYLE REFERENCES.

APA-STYLE REFERENCES appear in alphabetical order.

Capitalize only the first word in title and subtitle sections of journal articles and books, as well as any proper nouns.

Italicize journal names, book titles, and volume numbers.

Capitalize each word in JOURNAL TITLES with the exception of articles (e.g., the, and) and prepositions (e.g., of) that are shorter than four letters.

Use an ampersand (&) in lieu of "and" for MULTIPLE-AUTHORS REFERENCES.

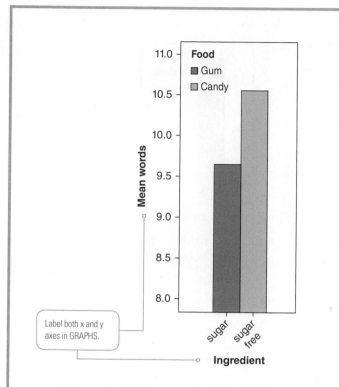

Label both x and y axes in GRAPHS.

Ingredient

Figure 1. Mean number of words recalled in the memory task.

FIGURE NUMBERS AND TITLES are flush left, with the figure number in italics, followed by a period, and the figure title not in italics.

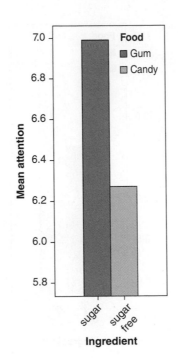

Figure 2. Mean scores on the attention test.

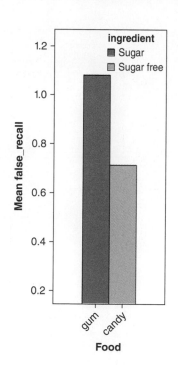

Figure 3. Mean false recall and condition of gum
or candy.

Paper courtesy of Michelle Mason

GLOSSARY

academic dishonesty Acts that violate student and professional ethics in academic situations (e.g., cheating, misrepresentation)

ambiguity Conditions of uncertainty

American Psychological Association See *APA*

amiable skepticism An attitude that promotes the good-natured challenge of conclusions in the absence of research-based evidence

anti-science major Psychology students who dislike or resist the science elements of the major

APA The American Psychological Association, a national professional psychology organization that addresses practice, policy, research, and educational issues

APA format Writing conventions that psychologists agree to follow to disseminate their work (e.g., active voice, 1-inch margins, section headings)

APA *Guidelines for the Undergraduate Psychology Major, Version 2.0* The best-practice recommendations sponsored by the American Psychological Association for high-quality undergraduate curricula in psychology

APA style American Psychological Association style, the writing style required for publishing in the majority of research journals in psychology that emphasizes precision, clarity, and an objective (rather than subjective) point of view

APS The Association for Psychological Science, a professional psychology organization that focuses on research and educational concerns

archival research Research that involves using existing records to identify patterns among variables

associate of arts (AA) degree A type of degree emphasizing liberal arts conferred upon the conclusion of a 2-year program in a community college setting and sometimes made available after the completion of the first 2 years of coursework in a bachelor of arts degree

associate of science (AS) degree A type of degree emphasizing science and technology conferred upon the conclusion of a 2-year program in a community college setting and sometimes made available after the completion of the first 2 years of coursework in a 4-year program

Association for Psychological Science See *APS*

bachelor of arts (BA) degree An undergraduate degree conferred upon the completion of a 4-year program that emphasizes a background in the liberal arts

bachelor of science (BS) degree An undergraduate degree conferred upon the completion of a 4-year program that emphasizes a background in science or technology

behaviorism The orientation or school of thought in psychology that emphasizes observable behaviors as the focus of scientific exploration

binge method An ineffective study strategy that involves studying intensively in limited sessions rather than spreading study over time

blocked classes A set of classes that a group of students takes together, designed to promote a sense of being in a cohort or learning community

boldface Typeface that is bolded for emphasis

brainstorming Generating ideas by writing down as many thoughts that come to mind about a particular topic without judging their worth until a sufficient list is created

capstone course A course taken near the end of the major that facilitates an integration of learning across courses in the major

career An occupation that tends to provide opportunities for long-term satisfaction and promotion

case notes Written notes documenting interactions with clients (e.g., objective observations, confidential treatment) that must be written to clinical standards

case study research Qualitative research that relies on a detailed, in-depth examination of a person and usually includes a narrative description of the person's behavior or life experience

clinical-or-bust majors Students who are committed to the major as the clinical major they think it is rather than to the major it actually is

cognitive psychology The branch of psychology that emphasizes both covert (e.g., dreaming and thinking) and overt activity (e.g., observable behavior) as the focus of scientific exploration

coherent argument Positions that hold together in a clear and logical argument

committed learner William Perry's term for advanced students who can make decisions and plans despite complex conditions and ambiguity

content-centered approach Teaching strategies that emphasize as the primary focus of education transmitting the ideas of the discipline, typically through lecturing

contextual cues Stimulus triggers in the environment that facilitate retrieval of information from memory storage

control, or comparison, group Participants in an experiment who receive no manipulation or treatment; they provide a controlled comparison with participants who do receive a treatment or manipulation

controlled conditions Research design strategies that ensure that participants in all conditions of an experiment are treated equivalently with the exception of the independent variable; this assures being able to judge whether the experimental treatment produces the desired effect

correlational study Research that assesses whether there are positive, negative, or zero associations among variables; correlational studies identify associations among variables, but such associations should not be assumed to be causal-effect connections

cover letter The letter of introduction that accompanies a résumé

curriculum vitae (CV) A résumé that emphasizes range and quality of performance in academic settings

cyberidentity Personal details available through the Internet

debt load The amount of money owed upon the completion of a degree

dependent variable The measurement of participants' responses in an experiment; this variable is not under the control of the experimenter

Discussion The fourth section of an APA-style report or article; discusses the meaning and implications of a project's results, often identifying questions for further investigation

doctor of education See *EdD*

doctor of philosophy See *Phd*

doctor of psychology See *PsyD*

driftwood major Students who aimlessly float through a major without paying much attention to what will happen in the future

drive-by reading A shallow reading strategy in which the student reads materials too quickly to absorb the most critical information

dualistic learner A concept developed by William Perry to describe a beginning student in the stage of learning in which students tend to see issues in black-and-white terms

Dunning–Kruger effect The tendency to overestimate the quality of one's own performances; sometimes called the *overconfidence effect*

EdD An education-focused doctoral degree that prepares clinicians to work in mental health settings, typically with people who have mild to moderate dysfunction

Educational Testing Service (ETS) A corporation that creates, administers, and interprets the results of a variety of standardized tests, including the Graduate Record Exam (GRE)

empirical Derived from observation and experience rather than logic and theory

empiricism Developing evidence based on observation and experimentation

exam wrappers Questions aimed at getting students to review their test performance

experiential learning See *service learning*

experiment Research that involves controlled conditions and manipulating variables

experimental group Participants in an experiment who experience a manipulated condition or treatment

functionalism The orientation or school of thought in psychology that emphasizes the motives behind, and the purposes of, behavior

grade point average (GPA) A cumulative, numerical indicator of a student's academic performance that is measured on a scale from 0 to 4.0

Graduate Record Exam (GRE) A high-stakes standardized examination that tests math and verbal skills as well as discipline-specific content; used to make decisions about admission for graduate school

Graduate Study in Psychology **(GSIP)** An annual publication from the American Psychological Association that lists graduate programs in psychology in the United States and Canada as well as admissions data and related information

grant Funds allocated by an organization to address a specific problem

grant proposal A detailed request for funding to carry out research aimed at addressing a specific problem

growth mindset The mindset that involves believing that learning skills, intelligence, and academic abilities can be improved through practice and effort

guide on the side Teachers who prefer to use a mix of strategies in teaching that emphasize active-learning approaches rather than lectures

high-impact practice (HIP) An activity that facilitates a deeper relationship between the student and his or her chosen discipline, faculty, institution, or community, such as service learning or participating on a professor's research team

hindsight bias Claim that you could have predicted how things would turn out *after* the outcome became known to you

Holland code A three-letter code that designates which general occupational areas correspond most strongly to an individual's personal preferences

honors program A selective program for students with strong academic potential that offers more intellectual challenge, increased access to high-impact activities, and enhanced social opportunity when compared to a standard curriculum

hypothesis An empirically testable question

independent study A formal opportunity a student arranges to complete work in an area of personal interest, usually under the supervision of one faculty member

independent variable The variable, controlled by the experimenter, that has at least two levels, one representing the treatment of interest and the other the control group

instructional scaffolding A design feature of an academic curriculum that intentionally sequences experiences (e.g., requiring courses in a specific order) to support learning as cognitive challenges become more difficult

interlibrary loan The process by which people can acquire from other libraries books and journals that aren't available in their home school

internship A volunteer placement in a work setting that allows a student to learn about a particular career and try out professional life in a specific work setting

Introduction The first section of an APA-style report or article; provides an overview and literature review of a research topic

job An activity that produces a source of income

job shadowing Following a professional during his or her typical workday to learn about a particular career

journal entries Personal written reflections that tend to focus on the emotional impact of learning experiences, readings, and class discussions

learning-centered approach Teaching strategies that focus on helping students successfully learn course content through active learning experiences rather than through lectures

learning community A group of students who gather out of a shared interest (e.g., international students, athletes, psychology majors) and who have access to high-impact learning experiences designed to address those interests

liberal arts Areas in higher education that provide students with general knowledge rather than specific technical knowledge

Library of Congress Subject Headings (LCSH) A six-volume alphabetized guide of subject headings (search terms), often found in a library's reference department, that is useful for conducting searches

literature review Research that summarizes what is known about a particular topic

Materials A subsection of the Method section of an APA-style report or article; describes any equipment, surveys, questionnaires, and the like that were used

meaning A sense of direction in life

memorandum A business memo than can be either a stand-alone document or the body of an email message

mentor An experienced person who provides guidance for those who are new to a profession or activity

meta-analyses Analyses that synthesize trends across related studies to determine where the weight of evidence actually explains some behavior

Method The second section of an APA-style report or article; provides a detailed, step-by-step explanation about what was done during the course of an experiment or other research investigation

multiple retrieval cues Memory cues that enhance the capacity for recall of ideas

naturalistic research Research that involves making careful records of behavior in nonexperimental contexts

nota bene Latin for *note well*; an alert to the reader to pay special attention to the point being made

novice A beginner

objectivity Maintenance of an unbiased perspective in interpreting behavior

Occupational Information Network (O*NET) An online center dedicated to providing information about a wide variety of occupations

operational definitions Descriptions of behaviors in terms of the procedures required to produce the behavior

Participants A subsection of the Method section of an APA-style research or lab report; describes the people who took part in the research

peer review The formal process of evaluating the ideas and argument in a manuscript or other work by other professionals working in the same field

personal statement A written description of an applicant's interest in and plans for attending graduate school; this statement is a standard part of a graduate school application

PhD A doctor of philosophy degree. This degree is scholarly or research focused. Having a PhD indicates that a person knows how to understand and conduct original research within a given discipline.

placebo A substance that presumably has no direct therapeutic effect on behavior that is used in an experiment's control groups

plagiarism The act of taking the ideas of others and presenting them as one's own

portfolio A collection of evidence of a person's achievements and skills

positive psychology The branch of psychology that focuses on the science of human virtue and happiness

poster A brief, graphic summary of a research project that follows the main sections of APA-style papers (i.e., Introduction, Method, Results, Discussion), highlighting main findings using tables and figures; the researcher stands with his or her poster and explains the nature of the work to interested conference participants

prerequisite In college, a course that must be completed prior to taking another course

principal investigator (PI) The lead author on a grant proposal

Procedure A subsection of the Method section of an APA-style report or article; provides a chronology of what took place, who said and did what, and when they did so during the course of a study

pseudoscience Explanations that seem scientific but have no scientific evidence to support them

Psi Beta The honor society for students who study psychology at 2-year or community colleges

Psi Chi The international honor society for undergraduate psychology majors who maintain high grades (top 35% overall and a minimum of a 3.0 GPA in the major)

PsycARTICLES A database that provides users access to the complete text of electronic articles that were originally published in APA journals

psychological advantage The beneficial effects that completing a psychology major has on effective performance in the workplace (e.g., demonstrating appropriate skepticism in the absence of evidence regarding claims about behavior)

psychological literacy Knowing the content and demonstrating the skills that characterize the thinking of people trained in psychology; also, the adaptive and intentional application of psychology to meet personal, professional, and societal needs

psychologist A person with an academic background in the scientific study of human behavior; also, the designation for clinicians with a doctoral degree

psychology The scientific study of mind and behavior in human and nonhuman animals

psychophysics The branch of psychology that deals with sensation and perception

PsycINFO A reference database maintained and continuously updated by the APA

PsyD A doctor of psychology degree, oriented more toward clinical practice (in contrast to the PhD, which involves training to work in research and academic settings)

Publication Manual of the American Psychological Association The guide to writing and publishing using APA style

quasi-experimental research Research that uses the general format of experimental research without random assignment of participants to either a treatment or a control group

random assignment The process that ensures that all volunteers in an experiment have an equal opportunity to serve in either the control or treatment condition

References The section of an APA-style report or article that contains detailed citations for all the research sources used therein

relativistic learner According to William Perry, a person who recognizes and accepts that there are few hard and fast truths

replication The process of repeating an experiment to confirm the original results

research assistant (RA) Someone, often a student, who volunteers to help a faculty member conduct his or her research; some RAs receive course credit while others are paid or simply help out in the lab or other setting for the educational experience

Results The third section of an APA-style report or article; describes the specific findings observed following an experiment or other research investigation

résumé A brief summary that outlines a job applicant's personal, educational, and professional qualifications

running head An abbreviated title of the paper that appears in the upper left corner of every page of an APA-style research paper

sage on the stage Teachers who prefer to lecture over using other teaching methods

scientific method An approach characterized by hypothesis testing, careful observation and experimentation, manipulation and measurement of variables, rigorous analysis, and replication

search terms Keywords that are used to find relevant literature in a search

self-assessment The process by which we estimate the quality of our own performance

self-regulation The capacity to manage personal and professional demands

service learning A means of having students apply what they are learning in the classroom to practical problems in the larger world through hands-on volunteer work in the community or other settings; also called *experiential learning*

sleep deficit Getting an insufficient amount of sleep, which interferes with the recovery and replenishing of the brain and body

spaced learning Learning distributed over time rather than in one major study or cram session

SPSS® A powerful statistical program designed to identify relationships among sets of variables

SQ4R method A traditional study strategy that entails five steps: survey, question, read, recite, and review

structuralism The orientation in psychology dedicated to mapping the capacity of the senses

structured interview questions A company's standard set of questions that all prospective employees are asked during an interview

survey research Research that entails having a sample of people from a larger population answer a set of standardized questions in order to infer what most people in the larger population feel or think about a given topic or issue

technical report A report that outlines the process, progress, or results of a technical or scientific research problem

terminal degree The level of education typically recognized as the highest degree available (doctoral or master's degree) in an academic or professional track; for some professions, obtaining the terminal degree may be required to enter the field

trait model An explanatory framework used to explain enduring personality characteristics

unstructured interview questions Informal questions asked by untrained interviewers during an employment interview

variable An element or feature in a research design that can be changed

verbatim The content of a communication (e.g., lecture, message) that is duplicated word for word

vocation A professional calling

wishful thinking Hoping for the best and sometimes not actively working to achieve that outcome

REFERENCES

American Psychological Association. (2010). *Publication manual of the American Psychological Association* (6th ed.). Washington, DC: Author.

American Psychological Association. (2013, August). *APA Guidelines for the Undergraduate Psychology Major: Version 2.0*. Washington, DC: Author. Retrieved from http://www.apa.org/ed/precollege/about/psymajor-guidelines.pdf

American Psychological Association. (2014). Careers in psychology. Washington, DC: Author. Retrieved from http://www.apa.org/careers/resources/guides/careers.aspx?item=4

American Psychological Association. (2015). Divisions. Retrieved from http://www.apa.org/about/division/

American Psychological Association. (2016). By the numbers: How do undergraduate psychology majors fare? *Monitor on Psychology, 47*(2), 11.

American Psychological Association. (2016). *Graduate study in psychology 2016*. Washington, DC: Author.

American Psychological Association. (2018). Degree pathways in psychology. [Interactive data tool]. Retrieved from https://www.apa.org/workforce/data-tools/degrees-pathways

APA Center for Workforce Studies. (2015). How many psychology bachelor's-degree holders work in STEM occupations? *Monitor on Psychology, 46*(5), 17.

Appleby, D. (2000). Job skills valued by employers who interview psychology majors. *Eye on Psi Chi, 4*(3), 17.

Appleby, D. C. (2011, August). Academic integrity and the student-athlete. Lecture presented during IUPUI Student-Athlete Orientation Program. Indianapolis, IN.

Arkowitz, H., & Lilienfeld, S. O. (2009, January 27). Lunacy and the full moon: Does a full moon really trigger strange behavior? *Scientific American*. Retrieved from http://www.scientificamerican.com/article/lunacy-and-the-full-moon/?page=2

Arum, R., & Roksa, J. (2011). *Academically adrift: Limited learning on college campuses*. Chicago, IL: University of Chicago Press.

Association of American Colleges & Universities. (2013). What is a 21st century liberal education? Retrieved from http://www.aacu.org/leap/What_is_liberal_education.cfm

Association for Psychological Science. (2019). Retrieved from https://www.psychologicalscience.org/about

Astin, A. (1999, September/October). Student involvement: A developmental theory for higher education. *Journal of College Student Development, 40*, 518–529.

Barr, R. B., & Tagg, J. (1995, November/December). From teaching to learning: A new paradigm for undergraduate education. *Change*, 13–25.

Benjamin, L. T., Jr., Cavell, T. A., & Shallenberger, W. R., III. (1984). Staying with initial answers on objective tests: Is it a myth? *Teaching of Psychology, 11*, 133–141.

Boneau, C. A. (1990). Psychological literacy: A first approximation. *American Psychologist, 45*, 891–900.

Bringle, R., & Hatcher, J. (1995). A service-learning curriculum for faculty. *Michigan Journal of Community Service Learning, 2*, 112–122.

Bubb, R. R., Sailors, J.,Wilbanks, S., Vollenweider, M., Cumbie, E., & Ferry, H. (October 1, 2018). Professional development through reflective student ePortfolios. Retrieved from https://teachpsych.org/E-xcellence-in-Teaching-Blog/6701297

Buehler, R., Griffin, D., & Ross, M. (1994). Exploring the "planning fallacy": Why people underestimate their task completion times. *Journal of Personality and Social Psychology, 67*(3), 366–381.

Bureau of Labor Statistics, U.S. Department of Labor, *Occupational Outlook Handbook,* Psychologists, retrieved from: https://www.bls.gov/ooh/life-physical-and-social-science /psychologists.htm (visited *May 10, 2019*).

Bureau of Labor Statistics. (2013). Occupational employment statistics. Washington, DC: U.S. Department of Labor. Retrieved from http://www.bls.gov/oes/2013/may/oes_nat.htm#19-0000

Bureau of Labor Statistics. (2014). Occupational outlook handbook: Psychology. Retrieved from http://www.bls.gov/ooh/life-physical-and-social-science/psychologists.htm

Celebrity Net Worth. (2018). Dr. Phil McGraw net worth. Retrieved from https://www.celebrity networth.com/richest-celebrities/actors/dr-phil-net-worth/

Cherry, K. (2014). 10 ways psychology can improve your life: Practical ways to apply psychology in everyday life. About.com. Retrieved from http://psychology.about.com/od/psychology101/tp /applying-psychology.htm

Cherry, K. (2014). What is a hindsight bias? Retrieved from http://psychology.about.com/od/hindex /g/hindsight-bias.htm

Cherry, K. (2019). PsyD doctorate psychology degree. Verywell Mind. Retrieved from https://www .verywellmind.com/what-is-a-psyd-2795135

Clay, R. A. (2012, March). What's behind the internship match crisis? *gradPSYCH Magazine.* Washington, DC: American Psychological Association. Retrieved from http://www.apa .org/gradpsych/2012/03/cover-match-crisis.aspx

Clay, R. A. (November 2017). Trends report: Psychology is more popular than ever. *Monitor on Psychology, 48*(10), 44. Retrieved from http://www.apa.org/monitor/2017/11/trends-popular.aspx

Council of Graduate Schools Ph.D. Completion Project. (2008). *Program completion and attrition data.* Retrieved from http://cgsnet.org/phd-completion-project

Cranney, J., & Dunn, D. S. (Eds.). (2011a). *The psychologically literate citizen: Foundations and global perspectives.* New York, NY: Oxford University Press.

Cranney, J., & Dunn, D. S. (2011b). Psychological literacy and the psychologically literate citizen: New frontiers for a global discipline. In J. Cranney & D. S. Dunn (Eds.), *The psychologically literate citizen: Foundations and global perspectives* (pp. 3–12). New York, NY: Oxford University Press.

Cranney, J., Morris, S., & Botwood, L. (2014). *Psychological literacy in undergraduate psychology education.* New York, NY: Oxford University Press.

Curry, M. (2008, August 25). The war on college cafeteria trays. *Time.* Retrieved from http:// content.time.com/time/nation/article/0,8599,1834403,00.html

Darley, J. M. & Latané, B. (1964). Bystander intervention in emergencies: Diffusion of responsibility. *Journal of Personality and Social Psychology, 8,* 377–383.

Dement, W. E., & Vaughn, C. (2000). *The promise of sleep.* New York, NY: Dell.

Diener, E., & Biswas-Diener, R. (2008). *Happiness: Unlocking the mysteries of psychological wealth.* Malden, MA: Blackwell.

Doran, J. M., Kraha, A., Marks, L. R., Ameen, E. J., & El-Ghoroury, N. H. (2016). Graduate debt in psychology: A quantitative analysis. *Training and Education in Professional Psychology, 10,* 3–13. http://dx.doi.org/10.1037/tep0000112

Dunlosky, J., Rawson, K. A., Marsh, E. J., Nathan, M. J., & Willingham, D. T. (2013). Improving students' learning with effective learning techniques: Promising directions from cognitive and educational psychology. *Psychological Science in the Public Interest, 14,* 4–58.

Dunlosky, J., Rawson, K. A., Marsh, E. J., Nathan, M. J., & Willingham, D. T. (2013). What works, what doesn't. *Scientific American Mind, 24*(4), 46–53.

Dunn, D. S. (2011). *A short guide to writing about psychology* (3rd ed.). New York, NY: Pearson-Longman.

Dunn, D. S. (2013a). *The practical researcher: A student guide to conducting psychological research* (3rd ed.). Hoboken, NJ: Wiley.

Dunn, D. S. (2013b). *Research methods for social psychology* (2nd ed.). Hoboken, NJ: Wiley.

Dunn, D. S., Brewer, C. L., Cautin, R. L., Gurung, R. A., Keith, K. D., McGregor, L. N., … Voight, M. J. (2010). The undergraduate psychology curriculum: Call for a core. In D. F. Halpern (Ed.), *Undergraduate Education in Psychology: A Blueprint for the Future of the Discipline* (pp. 47–61). Washington, DC: American Psychological Association.

Dunn, D. S., & McCarthy, M. (2010). The capstone course in psychology as liberal education opportunity. In D. S. Dunn, B. Beins, M. McCarthy, & G. Hill (Eds.), *Best practices for teaching beginnings and endings in the psychology major: Research, cases, and recommendations* (pp. 155–170). New York, NY: Oxford University Press.

Dunn, D. S., Saville, B. K., Baker, S. C., & Marek, P. (2013). Evidence-based teaching: Tools and techniques that promote learning in the psychology classroom. *Australian Journal of Psychology, 65,* 5–13.

Dweck, C. S. (2016). *Mindset: The new psychology of success.* New York: Ballantine Books.

Eagan, K., Stolzenberg, E. B., Ramirez, J. J., Aragon, M. C., Suchard, M. R., & Hurtado, S. (2016). *The American freshman: National norms fall 2014.* Los Angeles, CA: Higher Education Research Institute, UCLA.

Eagan, M. K., Stolzenberg, E. B., Zimmerman, H. B., Aragon, M. C., Whang Sayson, H., & Rios-Aguilar, C. (2017). *The American freshman: National norms fall 2016.* Los Angeles: Higher Education Research Institute, UCLA.

Fischer, P., Krueger, J. I., Greitemeyer, T., Vogrincic, C., Kastenmüller, A., Frey, D., & … Kainbacher, M. (2011). The bystander-effect: A meta-analytic review on bystander intervention in dangerous and non-dangerous emergencies. *Psychological Bulletin, 137*(4), 517–537. doi:10.1037/a0023304

Furumoto, L. (1980). Mary Whiton Calkins (1863–1930). *Psychology of Women Quarterly, 5,* 55–68.

Gardner, P. (2007). *Moving up or moving out of the company? Factors that influence the promoting or firing of new college hires.* Collegiate Research Brief 1-2007. East Lansing, MI: Michigan State University.

Gurung, R. A. R. (2013). Introduction. In S. Afful, J. J. Good, J. Keeley, S. Leder, & J. J. Stiegler-Balfour (Eds.), *Introductory psychology teaching primer: A guide for new teachers of PSYCH 101* (pp. 3–5). Retrieved from http://teachpsych.org/ebooks/intro2013/index.php

Guthrie, R. V. (2003). *Even the rat was white: A historical view of psychology* (2nd ed.). New York, NY: Allyn & Bacon.

Halonen, J. S. (2002, Winter). Love on the boundary: When the personal and professional collide. St. Petersburg, FL: National Institute for the Teaching of Psychology.

Halonen, J. S. (2011). Are there too many psychology majors? [White paper.] Invitation issued by the Board of Governors of the State University System of Florida. Retrieved from http://www.cogdop.org/page_attachments/0000/0200/FLA_White_Paper_for_cogop_posting.pdf

Halonen, J. S. (2012). Are there too many psychology majors? [White paper.] Invitation issued by the Board of Governors of the State University System of Florida. Retrieved from http://www.cogdop.org/page_attachments/0000/0200/FLA_White_Paper_for_cogop_posting.pdf

Halonen, J. S. (2014). A makeover for APA's *Guidelines for Undergraduate Psychology. Psychology Teacher Network.* Washington, DC: American Psychological Association. Retrieved from http://www.apa.org/ed/precollege/ptn/2014/02/undergraduate-guidelines.aspx

Halonen, J. S. (2014, January). Why would you want to major in *that?* Desmystifying your psychology major. *Psychology Student Network, 2*(1). Retrieved from http://www.apa.org/ed /precollege/psn/2014/01/why-major.aspx

Halonen, J. S., Bosack, B., Clay, S., McCarthy, M., Dunn, D. S., Hill, G. W., IV., ... Whitlock, K. (2003). A rubric for learning, teaching, and assessing scientific inquiry in psychology. *Teaching of Psychology, 30,* 197–208.

Halpern, D. (Ed.). (2010). *Undergraduate education in psychology: A blueprint for the future of the discipline.* Washington, DC: American Psychological Association.

Hansen, R. S., & Hansen, K. (2014). What do employers really want? Top skills and values employers seek from job seekers. QuintCareers.com. Retrieved from http://www.quintcareers .com/job_skills_values.html

Henriques, G. (2014, January 18). Psychology's fragmentation trap. In Theory of Knowledge [Blog]. *Psychology Today.* Retrieved from http://www.psychologytoday.com/blog/theory -knowledge/201401/psychologys-fragmentation-trap

Hettich, P. (2004, April). *From college to corporate culture: You're a freshman again.* Paper presented at the Annual Meeting of the Midwest Psychological Association, Chicago, IL.

Higher Education Research Institute (HERI). (2013, January). Your First College Year Survey 2012. *HERI Research Brief.* Retrieved from http://www.heri.ucla.edu/briefs/YFCY2012-Brief.pdf

Higher Education Research Institute (HERI). (2015, October). Findings from the 2015 Your First College Year Survey. *HERI Research Brief.* Retrieved from http://www.heri.ucla.edu /briefs/YFCY/YFCY-2015-Brief.pdf

Holland, J. (1996). Exploring careers with a typology: What we have learned and some new directions. *American Psychologist, 51,* 397–406.

Holland, J. (1997). *Making vocational choices* (3rd ed.). Odessa, FL: Psychological Assessment Resources.

Hunt, M. (1961). *The story of psychology.* New York, NY: Random House.

James, W. (1961). *Psychology: Briefer course.* New York, NY: Harper & Row (Original work published 1892).

Kahneman, D. (2011). *Thinking fast and slow.* New York, NY: Farrar, Straus, & Giroux.

Kahneman, D., & Deaton, A. (2010). High income improves evaluations of life but not emotional well-being. *Proceedings of the National Academy of Sciences of the United States of America, 107*(38), 16489–16493. doi:10.1073/pnas.1011492107

Kahneman, D., Krueger, A. B., Schkade, D., Schwarz, N., & Stone, A. A. (2006). Would you be happier if you were richer? A focusing illusion. *Science, 312,* 1908–1910.

Kalwarski, T., Mosher, D., Paskin, J., & Rosato, D. (2014). *Money* magazine's best jobs in America. Retrieved from http://people.uncw.edu/guinnc/MoneyMag.html

Keith-Spiegel, P., & Weiderman, M. W. (2000). *The complete guide to graduate school admissions: Psychology and related fields.* Hillsdale, NJ: Erlbaum.

Kimble, G. A. (1984). Psychology's two cultures. *American Psychologist, 39,* 833–839.

King, A. (1993, Winter). From sage on the stage to guide on the side. *College Teaching, 41,* 30–35.

Konnikova, M. (2014, June 2). What's lost as handwriting fades. *New York Times.* Retrieved from http://www.nytimes.com/2014/06/03/science/whats-lost-as-handwriting-fades.html

Korkki, P. (2010, September 11). Job satisfaction vs. a big paycheck. *New York Times,* BU10.

Kruger, J., & Dunning, D. (1999). Unskilled and unaware of it: How difficulties in recognizing one's own incompetence lead to inflated self-assessments. *Journal of Personality and Social Psychology, 77*(6), 1121–1134. doi: 10.1037/0022-3514.77.6.1121

Kuh, G. (2008). *High-impact practices: What they are, who has access to them, and why they matter.* Washington, DC: Association of American Colleges and Universities.

Kuh, G. D., Kinzie, J., Schuh, J., & Whitt, E. J. (2010). *Student success in college: Creating conditions that matter.* San Francisco, CA: Jossey-Bass.

Kuther, T. L. (2014). You missed class: What do you do? About.com. Retrieved from http://gradschool.about.com/od/survivinggraduateschool/a/missedclass.htm

Landrum, R. E. (2001). I'm getting my bachelor's degree in psychology—What can I do with it? *Eye on Psi Chi, 6*(1), 20–22.

Landrum, R. E. (2002, Winter). Maximizing undergraduate opportunities: The value of research and other experiences. *Eye on Psi Chi, 6*(2), 15–18.

Landrum, R. E., Beins, B. C., Bhalla, M., Brakke, K., Briihl, D. S., Curl-Langager, R. M., … Van Kirk, J. J. (2010). Desired outcomes of an undergraduate education in psychology from departmental, student, and societal perspectives. In D. F. Halpern (Ed.), *Undergraduate education in psychology: A blueprint for the future of the discipline* (pp. 145–160). Washington, DC: American Psychological Association.

Landrum, R. E., & Davis, S. (2014). *The psychology major: Career options and strategies for success* (5th ed.). New York: Pearson.

Landrum, R. E., & Harrold, R. (2003). What employers want from psychology graduates. *Teaching of Psychology, 30,* 131–133.

Langley, T. (October 29, 2015). #Thispsychmajor answers candidate's claim we work fast food. Retrieved from https://www.psychologytoday.com/us/blog/beyond-heroes-and-villains/201510/thispsychmajor-answers-candidates-claim-we-work-fast-food

Lederman, D. (December 9, 2017). Who changes majors: Not who you think. *Inside Higher Ed.* Retrieved from https://www.insidehighered.com/news/2017/12/08/nearly-third-students-change-major-within-three-years-math-majors-most

Leonhardt, D. (2014, May 27). Is college worth it? Clearly, new data say. *New York Times.* Retrieved from http://www.nytimes.com/2014/05/27/upshot/is-college-worth-it-clearly-new-data-say.html?_r=0

Library of Congress. (2012). *Library of Congress subject headings* (34th ed., 6 vols.). Washington, DC: Author.

Light, J. (2010, October 11). Psych majors aren't happy with options. *Wall Street Journal.* Retrieved from http://online.wsj.com/news/articles/SB10001424052748704011904575538561813341020

Lilienfeld, S. O. (2004). Teaching psychology students to distinguish science from pseudoscience: Pitfalls and rewards. Retrieved from http://www.lscp.net/persons/dupoux/teaching/JOURNEE_AUTOMNE_CogMaster_2011-12/docs/Lilienfeld_2004_Teaching_PseudoScience.pdf

Lilienfeld, S. O., Lynn, S. J., Ruscio, J., & Beyerstein, B. L. (2010). *50 great myths of popular psychology: Shattering widespread misconceptions about human behavior.* New York, NY: John Wiley & Sons.

Lin, L., Green, C., Stamm, K., & Christidis, P. (2017, February). How long does it take to earn a research doctorate in psychology? News from APA's Center for Workforce Studies. *Monitor on Psychology, 48*(2), 15. Retrieved from https://www.apa.org/monitor/2017/02/datapoint

Lin, L., Stamm, K., & Christidis, P. (2018, May). What jobs do psychology degree holders have? News on occupations for psychology degree holders. *Monitor on Psychology, 49*(5), 19. Retrieved from https://www.apa.org/monitor/2018/05/datapoint

Lopatto, D. (2010, Spring). Undergraduate research as a high-impact student experience. *Peer Review,* 27–30. Washington, DC: American Association of Colleges and Universities.

Lovett, M. B. (2013). Using exam wrappers to promote metacognition. In M. Kaplan, N. Silver, D. LaVaque-Manty, D. Meizlish, & J. Rhem (Eds.), *Using reflection and metacognition to improve student learning: Across the disciplines, across the academy* (pp. 18–52). Sterling, VA: Stylus.

Luo, S., & Klohnen, E. C. (2005). Assortative mating and marital quality in newlyweds: A couple-centered approach. *Journal of Personality and Social Psychology, 88*(2), 304–326. doi:10.1037/0022-3514.88.2.304

Maas, J. B., & Robbins, R. S. (2011). *Sleep for success: Everything you must know about sleep but are too tired to ask.* Bloomington, IN: AuthorHouse.

Martin, D. W. (2007). *Doing psychology experiments.* Belmont, CA: Thompson/Wadsworth.

Mayfield, L., & Mayfield, J. (2012, February 21). How and why to get an on-campus job. US News and World Report. Retrieved from https://www.usnews.com/education/blogs/twice-the-college-advice/2012/02/21/how-and-why-to-get-an-on-campus-job

McClendon, J. III (August 9, 2018). In Challenge accepted: Articulation and redesign of the two-tiered undergraduate psychology major. American Psychological Convention, San Francisco.

McCrae, R. R., & Costa, P. T., Jr. (2003). *Personality in adulthood: A five-factor theory perspective.* New York, NY: Guilford.

McGovern, T. V., Corey, L., Cranney, J., Dixon, W. E., Jr., Homes, J. D., Kuebli, J. E., ... Walker, S. J. (2010). Psychologically literate citizens. In D. F. Halpern (Ed.), *Undergraduate education in psychology: A blueprint for the future of the discipline* (pp. 9–27). Washington, DC: American Psychological Association.

Michalski, D., Kohout, J., Wicherski, M., & Hart, B. (2011). *2009 Doctorate Employment Survey.* Washington, DC: American Psychological Association.

Miller, G. A. (1956). The magical number seven, plus or minus two: Some limits on our capacity for processing information. *Psychological Review, 63,* 81–97.

Mills, C. (October 24, 2015). Jeb Bush: Psych majors work at Chik-fil-A. *Washington Examiner.* Retrieved from https://www.washingtonexaminer.com/jeb-bush-psych-majors-work-at-chick-fil-a

Mitchell, J. (2016, May 2). Student debt is about to set another record, but the picture isn't all bad: This spring's college seniors will see a good return: Higher starting salaries. *Wall Street Journal.* Retrieved from https://blogs.wsj.com/economics/2016/05/02/student-debt-is-about-to-set-another-record-but-the-picture-isnt-all-bad/?mod=e2tw#:Xhy9NQQoFnzvDA

Mueller, P., & Oppenheimer, D. (2014). The pen is mightier than the keyboard: Advantages of longhand over laptop note taking. *Psychological Science, 25,* 1159–1168.

Munsey, C. (2008, September). Charting the future of undergraduate psychology. *Monitor on Psychology, 39*(8), 54.

Murray, B. (2000, January). The degree that almost wasn't: The PsyD comes of age. *Monitor on Psychology, 31*(1), 52. Retrieved from http://www.apa.org/monitor/jan00/ed1.aspx

National Association of Colleges and Employers (NACE). (2014). Class of 2014: Top-paid liberal arts majors. Retrieved from http://www.naceweb.org/s05142014/top-paid-liberal-arts-grad.aspx

National Bureau of Labor Statistics. (2013). May 2013 national occupational and wage estimates United States. Retrieved from http://www.bls.gov/oes/current/oes_nat.htm#19-0000

National Center for Education Statistics. (2015). *2014 digest of education statistics.* Retrieved from http://nces.ed.gov/programs/digest/d14/tables/dt14_325.80.asp

National Center for Education Statistics. (2016). College student employment. In *The condition of education 2016.* Retrieved from https://nces.ed.gov/programs/coe/pdf/Indicator_SSA/coe_ssa_2015_11.pdf

National Center for Education Statistics. (2018). Postsecondary education. In *Digest of education statistics: 2016* (NCES 2017-094).

National Center for Education Statistics. (2018). Postsecondary education. In *Digest of education statistics: 2017.* Retrieved from https://nces.ed.gov/programs/digest/d17/ch_3.asp

National Sleep Foundation. (2015). Napping. Retrieved from http://sleepfoundation.org/sleep-topics/napping?page=0%2C0

Nelson, E., & Fonzi, G. (1995). An effective peer advising program in a large psychology department. *NACADA Journal: The Global Community for Academic Advising, 15*(2), 41–43.

Niemiec, R. M., & Wedding, D. (2014). *Positive psychology at the movies: Using films to build character strength and well-being*. Boston, MA: Hogrefe.

Norcross, J. C. & Castle, P. H. (2002). Appreciating the PsyD: The facts. *Eye on Psi Chi*. Retrieved from https://cms.bsu.edu/-/media/WWW/DepartmentalContent/Psychology/Docs/PsyD.pdf

Norcross, J. D. (2015, August 7). Undergraduate study in psychology: What APA's national survey tells and warns. American Psychological Association convention, Toronto, Canada.

O'Brien, K. (July 4, 2010). What happened to studying? Boston.com. Retrieved from http://www.boston.com/bostonglobe/ideas/articles/2010/07/04/what_happened_to_studying/?page=1

Otto, J., Sandford, D. A., & Ross, D. N. (2008). Does ratemyprofessor.com really rate my professor? *Assessment and Evaluation in Higher Education*, 33(4), 355–368.

Pascarella, E.T., & Terenzini, P.T. (2005). *How college affects students: A third decade of research* (Vol. 2). San Francisco, CA: Jossey-Bass.

Pena, L. W. (2010, August). Understanding the working college student. *Academe*. Washington, DC: American Association of University Professors. Retrieved from http://www.aaup.org/article/understanding-working-college-student#.U7xsFiitbb8

Perry, W. G., Jr. (1970). Forms of intellectual and ethical development in the college years: A scheme. New York, NY: Holt, Rinehart, & Winston.

Plous, S. (1996). Attitudes toward the use of animals in psychological research and education: Results from a national survey of psychologists. *American Psychologist*, 51, 1167–1180.

Plous, S. (1998). *Advice on letters of recommendation*. Retrieved from https://www.socialpsychology.org/rectips.htm

Psi Chi. (2019). About Psi Chi. Retrieved from https://www.psichi.org/page/about#.XJ1LcOtKg_U

Psychology Career Center. (2014, July 14). Psychologist professor among top jobs in United States. Retrieved from http://www.psychologycareercenter.org/psychology-professor-jobs.html

Psychology Career Center. (2015). Psychologist salary and benefits information. Retrieved from http://www.psychologycareercenter.org/salaries.html

Psychology Graduate School. (n.d.). Debt and income. Retrieved from http://psychologygradschool.weebly.com/debt-and-income.html

Robinson, F. P. (1970). *Effective study* (4th ed.). New York, NY: Harper & Row.

Roese, N. J., & Vohs, K. D. (2012). Hindsight bias. *Perspectives on Psychological Science*, 7, 411–426.

Ronan, G. B. (2005, November 29). College freshmen face major dilemma. Personal finance on NBCNews.com. Retrieved from http://www.nbcnews.com/id/10154383/ns/business-personal_finance/t/college-freshmen-face-major-dilemma/#.U8Ahoiitbb8

Salley, A. K. (2014, June–July). Meet Julian MacQueen of Pensacola. *850 Magazine*. Retrieved from http://www.850businessmagazine.com/June-July-2014/Meet-Julian-MacQueen-of-Pensacola/

Shin, L. (2014, September 30). Is grad school worth it? 7 steps to calculating the ROI. *Forbes*. Retrieved from http://www.forbes.com/sites/laurashin/2014/09/30/is-grad-school-worth-it-7-steps-to-calculating-the-roi/#4edacd2587ae

Smith, S. M., Glenberg, A., & Bjork, R. A. (1978). Environmental context and human memory. *Memory & Cognition*, 6, 342–353.

Staff. (July 16, 2018). Class of 2017's overall starting salary shows little gain. National Association of Colleges and Employers. Retrieved from https://www.naceweb.org/job-market/compensation/class-of-2017s-overall-starting-salary-shows-little-gain/

Stamm, K., Michalski, D., Cope, C., Fowler, G., Christidis, P., & Lin, L. (2016, February). What are the acceptance rates for graduate psychology programs? *Monitor on Psychology*, 47(2), 16.

Stanny, C. J., & Halonen, J. S. (2011). Accreditation, accountability, and assessment: Faculty development's role in addressing multiple agendas. In L. Stefani (Ed.), *Evaluating the effectiveness of academic development practice: A professional guide*. New York, NY: Routledge.

Stanovich, K. E. (2019). *How to think straight about psychology* (11th ed). Boston, MA: Allyn & Bacon.

Steuer, F. B., & Ham, K. W., II. (2008). Psychology textbooks: Examining their accuracy. *Teaching of Psychology, 35*, 160–168.

Stewart, T. (2015). *Do unto animals. A friendly guide to how animals live, and how we can make their lives better.* New York: Artisan.

Stoloff, M., McCarthy, M., Keller, L., Varfolomeeva, V., Lynch, J., Makara, K., … Smiley, W. (2010). The undergraduate psychology major: An examination of structure and sequence. *Teaching of Psychology, 37*(1), 4–15. doi:10.1080/00986280903426274

Taylor, S. E., & Brown, J. D. (1994). Positive illusions and well-being revisited: Separating fact from fiction. *Psychological Bulletin, 116*(1), 21–27. doi.org/10.1037/0033-2909.116.1.21

Thaiss, C., & Sanford, J. F. (2000). *Writing for psychology.* Boston, MA: Allyn and Bacon.

Watson, J. B. (1913). Psychology as the behaviorist views it. *Psychological Review, 20*, 158–177.

Weaver, R., & Qi, J. (2005). Classroom organization and participation: College students' perceptions. *Journal of Higher Education, 76*(5), 570–601.

Wedding, D., & Niemiec, R. M. (2010). *Movies and mental illness: Using films to understand psychopathology* (3rd ed.). Boston, MA: Hogrefe.

Weimer, M. (2013, May 8). Helping students understand the benefits of study groups [Blog post]. Retrieved from http://www.facultyfocus.com/articles/teaching-professor-blog/helping-students-understand-the-benefits-of-study-groups/

Weir, R. (December 13, 2009). They don't read. *Inside Higher Ed.* Retrieved from https://www.insidehighered.com/advice/2009/11/13/they-dont-read

Whitbourne, S. K. (2012, January 14). Psychology's best movies: And the Oscar goes to…which psychological disorder? *Psychology Today.* Retrieved from http://www.psychologytoday.com/blog/fulfillment-any-age/201201/psychologys-best-movies

Wilson, J. H., & Schwartz, B. M. (2015). *An easy guide to research presentations.* Thousand Oaks, CA: Sage.

Wrzesniewski, A., McCauley, C., Rozin, P., & Schwartz, B. (1997). Jobs, careers, and callings: People's reactions to their work. *Journal of Research in Personality, 31*, 21–33.

Wrzesniewski, A., Rozin, P., & Bennett, G. (2003). Working, playing, and eating: Making the most of most moments. In C. L. M. Keyes & J. Haidt (Eds.), *Flourishing: Positive psychology and the life well-lived* (pp. 185–204). Washington, DC: American Psychological Association.

Zhao, C.-M., & Kuh, G. D. (2004). Adding value: Learning communities and student engagement. *Research in Higher Education, 45*(2), 115–139.

Zimmermann, J., & Neyer, F. J. (2013). Do we become a different person when hitting the road? Personality development of sojourners. *Journal of Personality and Social Psychology, 105*(3), 515–530. Retrieved from http://dx.doi.org/10.1037/a0033019

NAME INDEX

Note: Page numbers followed by f indicate figures; those followed by t indicate tables.

SUBJECT INDEX

Note: Page numbers followed by f indicate figures; those followed by t indicate tables; and those preceded by A indicate the Appendix.